TINY RICK

Titan
COMICS

[adult swim]

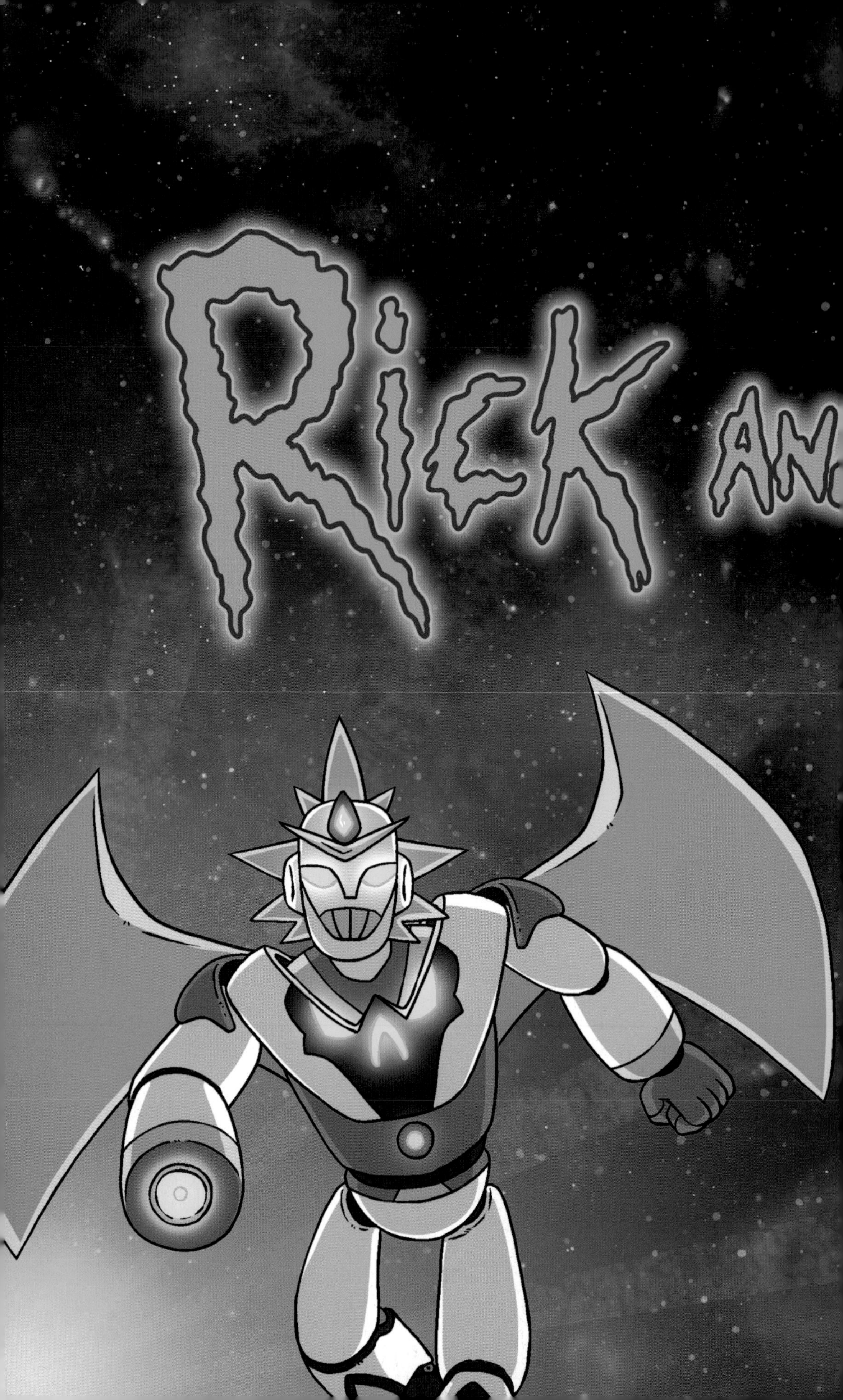
RICK AN

TINY RICK

RICK AND MORTY CREATED BY **DAN HARMON** AND **JUSTIN ROILAND**

COVER BY

CJ CANNON AND **KATY FARINA**

TITAN
COMICS

[adult swim]

TITAN
COMICS

[adult swim]™

RICK AND MORTY: VOLUME FIVE, TINY RICK, AUGUST 2017. PUBLISHED BY TITAN COMICS, A DIVISION
OF TITAN PUBLISHING GROUP LTD., 144 SOUTHWARK ST., LONDON, SE1 0UP. CONTAINS MATERIAL
ORIGINALLY PUBLISHED IN SINGLE COMIC FORM AS RICK AND MORTY NO 21-25. © CARTOON NETWORK
(S17) ALL RIGHTS RESERVED. RICK AND MORTY, CARTOON NETWORK, THE LOGOS, AND ALL RELATED
CHARACTERS AND ELEMENTS ARE TRADEMARKS OF AND © CARTOON NETWORK. ALL CHARACTERS,
EVENTS AND INSTITUTIONS DEPICTED HEREIN ARE FICTIONAL. ANY SIMILARITY BETWEEN ANY OF
THE NAMES, CHARACTERS, PERSONS, EVENTS AND/OR INSTITUTIONS IN THIS PUBLICATION TO
ACTUAL NAMES, CHARACTERS, AND PERSONS, WHETHER LIVING OR DEAD AND/OR INSTITUTIONS ARE
UNINTENDED AND PURELY COINCIDENTAL.

A CIP CATALOGUE RECORD FOR THIS TITLE IS AVAILABLE FROM THE BRITISH LIBRARY.

PRINTED IN SPAIN.

10 9 8 7 6 5 4 3 2

ISBN: 9781785864186
WWW.TITAN-COMICS.COM

SPECIAL THANKS TO JUSTIN ROILAND, DAN HARMON, MARISA MARIONAKIS, AND MIKE MENDEL.

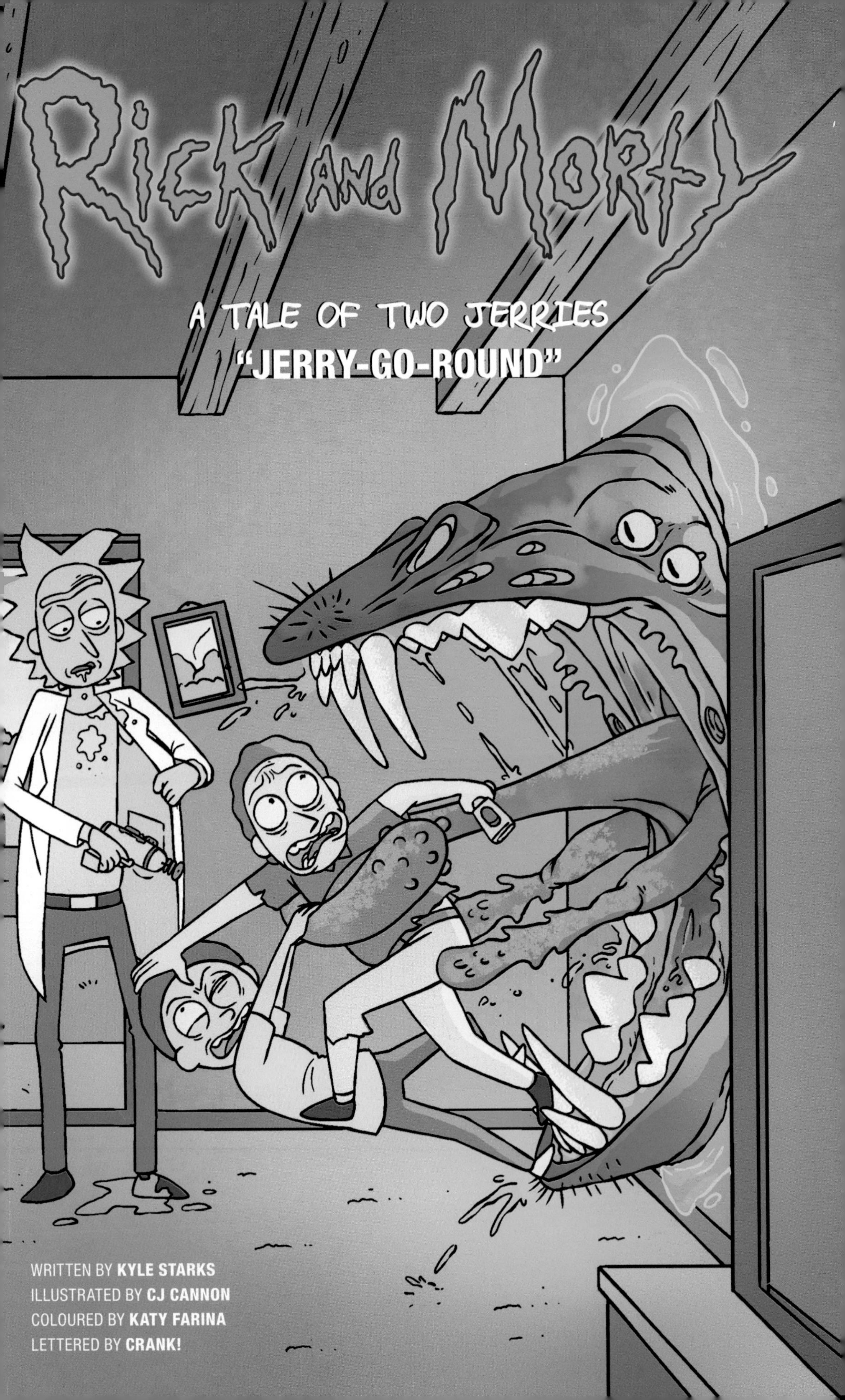
Rick and Morty™

A TALE OF TWO JERRIES

"JERRY-GO-ROUND"

WRITTEN BY **KYLE STARKS**
ILLUSTRATED BY **CJ CANNON**
COLOURED BY **KATY FARINA**
LETTERED BY **CRANK!**

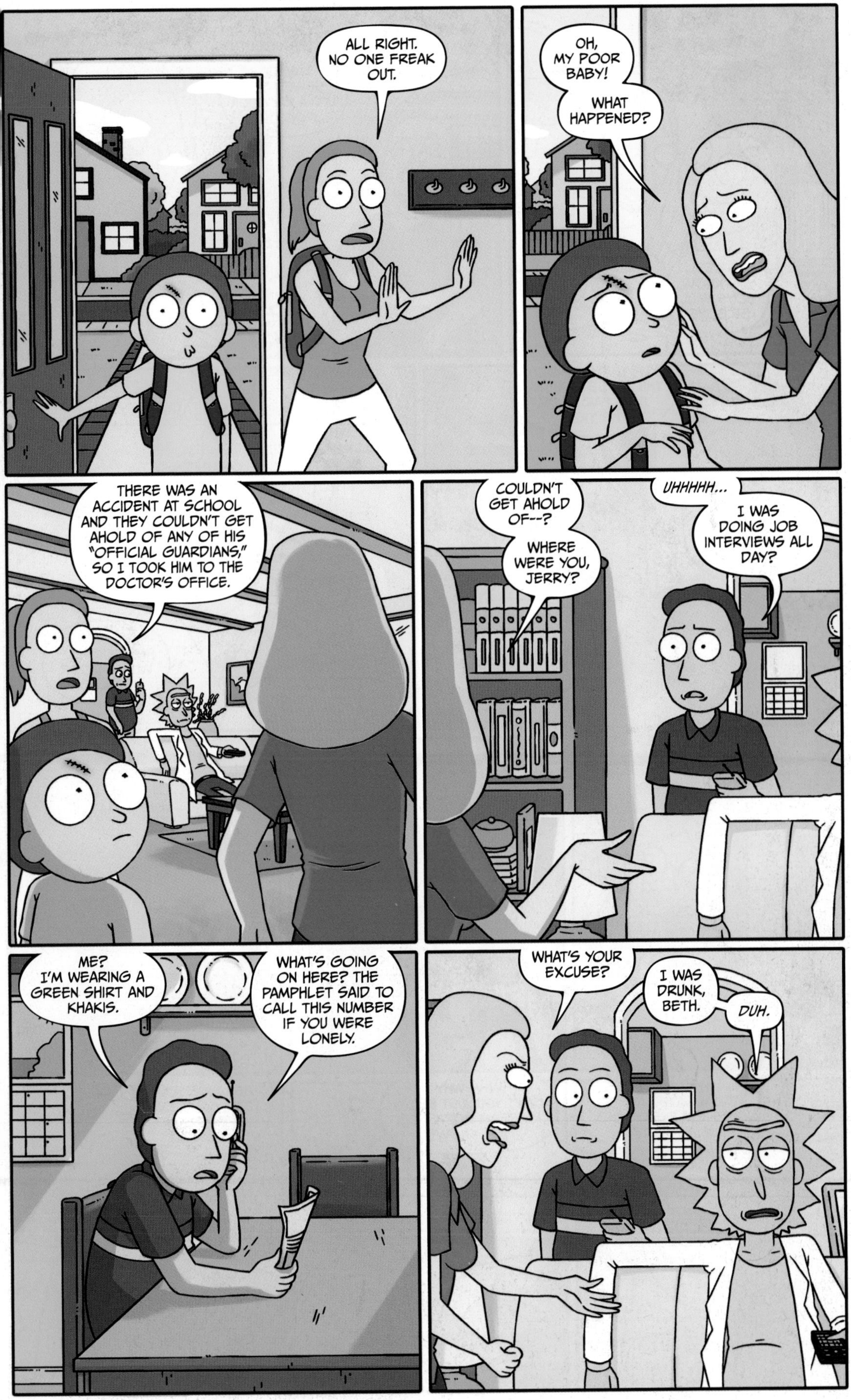
ALL RIGHT. NO ONE FREAK OUT.
OH, MY POOR BABY!
WHAT HAPPENED?
THERE WAS AN ACCIDENT AT SCHOOL AND THEY COULDN'T GET AHOLD OF ANY OF HIS "OFFICIAL GUARDIANS," SO I TOOK HIM TO THE DOCTOR'S OFFICE.
COULDN'T GET AHOLD OF--?
WHERE WERE YOU, JERRY?
UHHHHH...
I WAS DOING JOB INTERVIEWS ALL DAY?
ME? I'M WEARING A GREEN SHIRT AND KHAKIS.
WHAT'S GOING ON HERE? THE PAMPHLET SAID TO CALL THIS NUMBER IF YOU WERE LONELY.
WHAT'S YOUR EXCUSE?
I WAS DRUNK, BETH.
DUH.

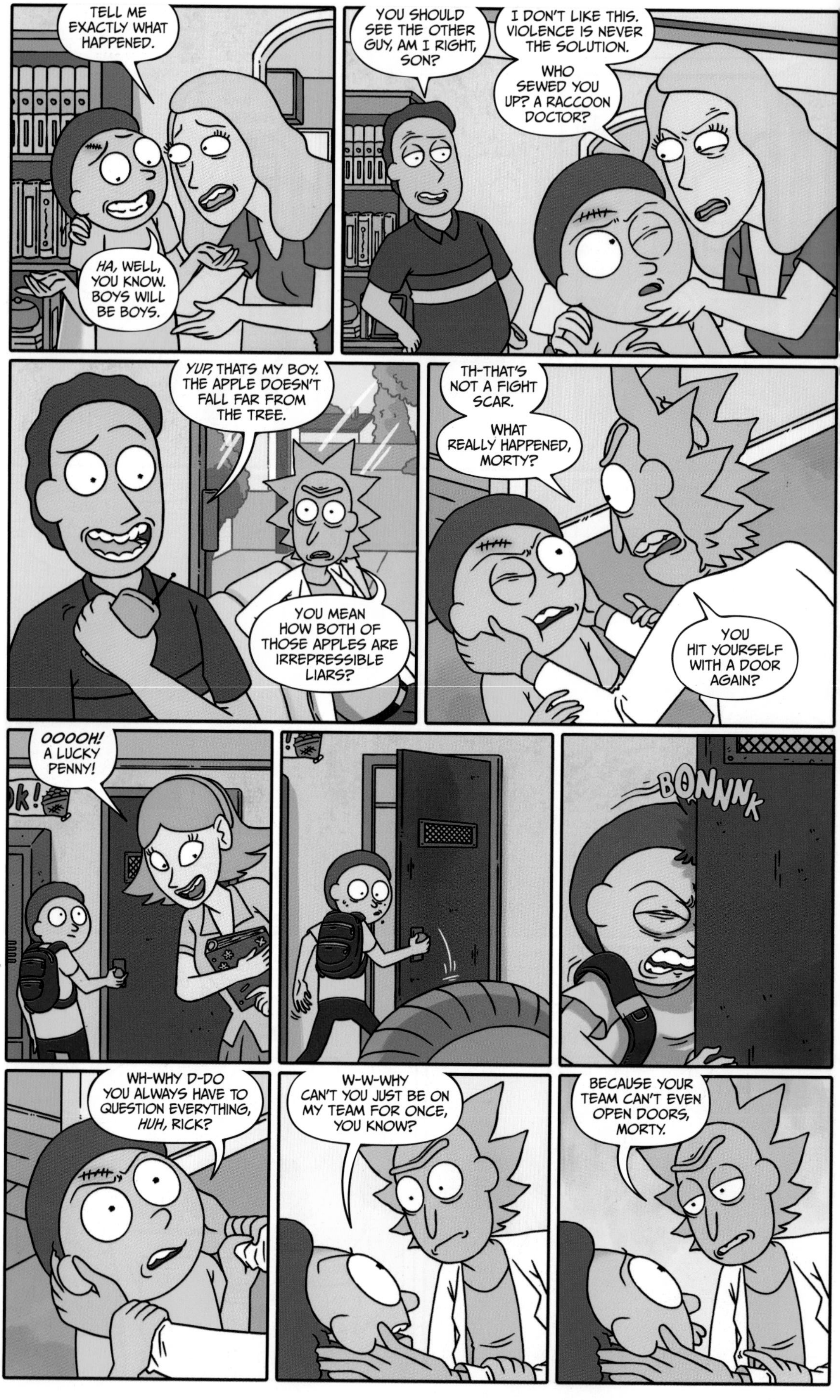
TELL ME EXACTLY WHAT HAPPENED.
HA, WELL, YOU KNOW. BOYS WILL BE BOYS.
YOU SHOULD SEE THE OTHER GUY, AM I RIGHT, SON?
I DON'T LIKE THIS. VIOLENCE IS NEVER THE SOLUTION.
WHO SEWED YOU UP? A RACCOON DOCTOR?
YUP, THATS MY BOY. THE APPLE DOESN'T FALL FAR FROM THE TREE.
YOU MEAN HOW BOTH OF THOSE APPLES ARE IRREPRESSIBLE LIARS?
TH-THAT'S NOT A FIGHT SCAR.
WHAT REALLY HAPPENED, MORTY?
YOU HIT YOURSELF WITH A DOOR AGAIN?
OOOOH! A LUCKY PENNY!
BONNNK
WH-WHY D-DO YOU ALWAYS HAVE TO QUESTION EVERYTHING, HUH, RICK?
W-W-WHY CAN'T YOU JUST BE ON MY TEAM FOR ONCE, YOU KNOW?
BECAUSE YOUR TEAM CAN'T EVEN OPEN DOORS, MORTY.

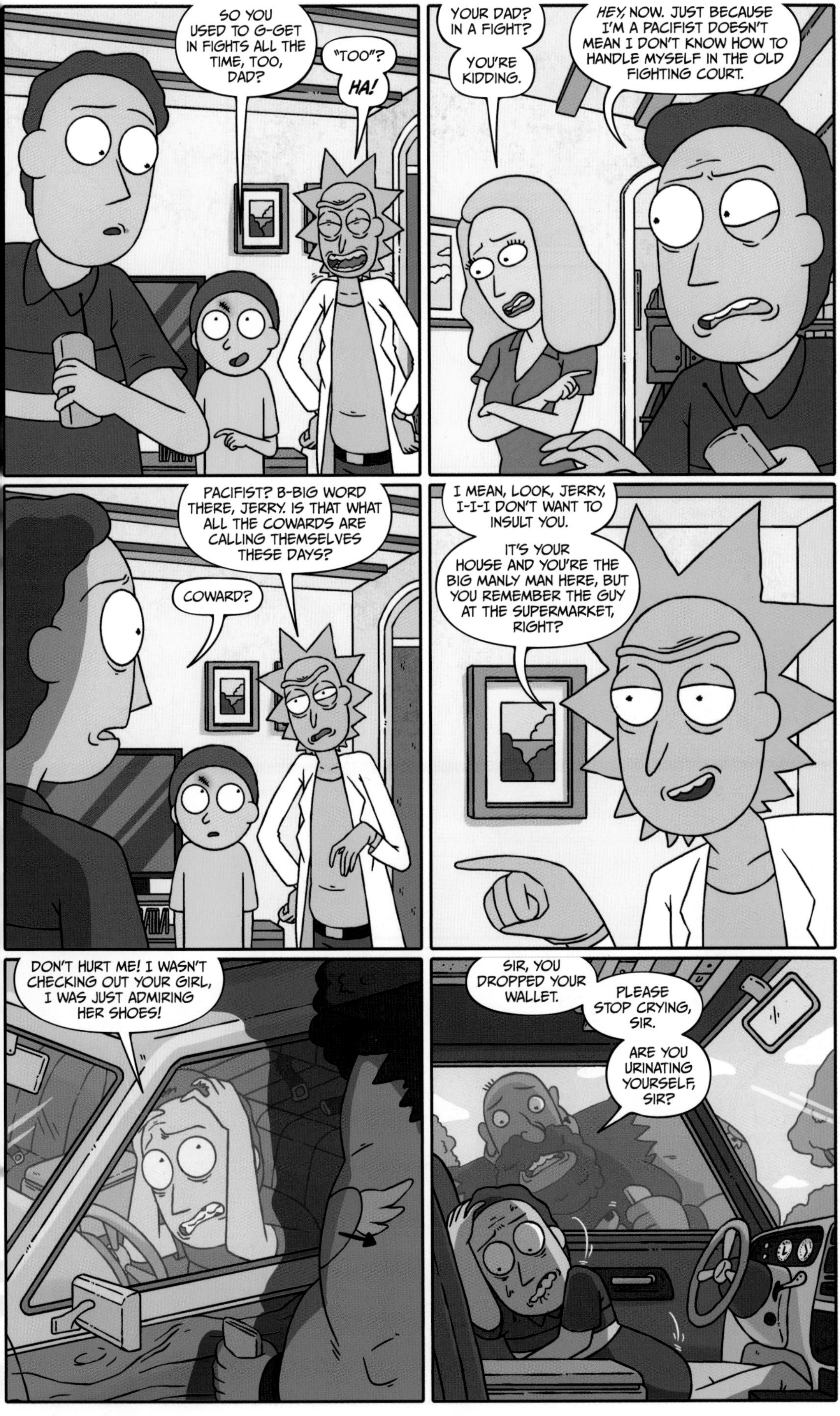
SO YOU USED TO G-GET IN FIGHTS ALL THE TIME, TOO, DAD?
"TOO"?
HA!
YOUR DAD? IN A FIGHT?
YOU'RE KIDDING.
HEY, NOW. JUST BECAUSE I'M A PACIFIST DOESN'T MEAN I DON'T KNOW HOW TO HANDLE MYSELF IN THE OLD FIGHTING COURT.
PACIFIST? B-BIG WORD THERE, JERRY. IS THAT WHAT ALL THE COWARDS ARE CALLING THEMSELVES THESE DAYS?
COWARD?
I MEAN, LOOK, JERRY, I-I-I DON'T WANT TO INSULT YOU.
IT'S YOUR HOUSE AND YOU'RE THE BIG MANLY MAN HERE, BUT YOU REMEMBER THE GUY AT THE SUPERMARKET, RIGHT?
DON'T HURT ME! I WASN'T CHECKING OUT YOUR GIRL, I WAS JUST ADMIRING HER SHOES!
SIR, YOU DROPPED YOUR WALLET.
PLEASE STOP CRYING, SIR.
ARE YOU URINATING YOURSELF, SIR?

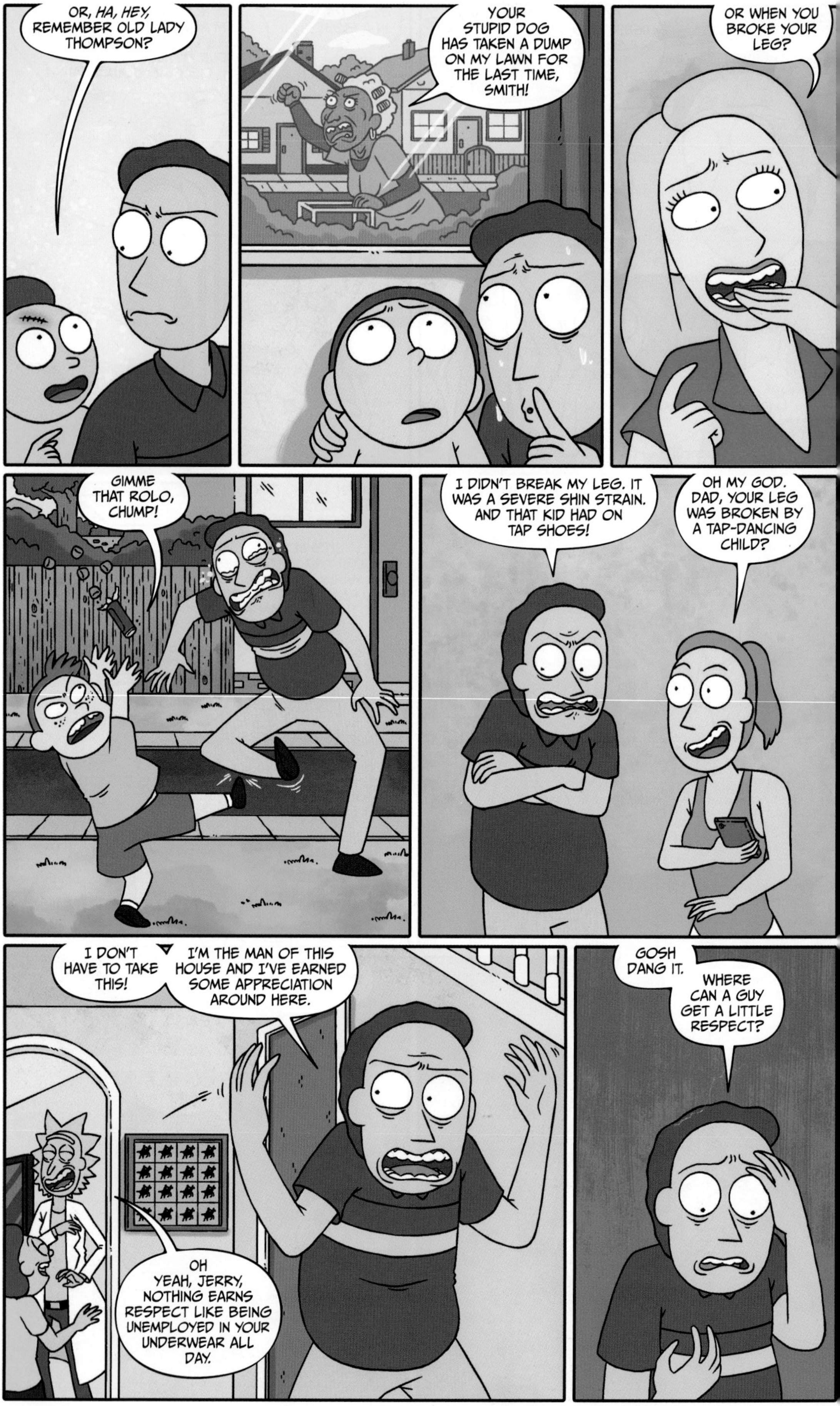
OR, HA, HEY, REMEMBER OLD LADY THOMPSON?
YOUR STUPID DOG HAS TAKEN A DUMP ON MY LAWN FOR THE LAST TIME, SMITH!
OR WHEN YOU BROKE YOUR LEG?
GIMME THAT ROLO, CHUMP!
I DIDN'T BREAK MY LEG. IT WAS A SEVERE SHIN STRAIN. AND THAT KID HAD ON TAP SHOES!
OH MY GOD. DAD, YOUR LEG WAS BROKEN BY A TAP-DANCING CHILD?
I DON'T HAVE TO TAKE THIS!
I'M THE MAN OF THIS HOUSE AND I'VE EARNED SOME APPRECIATION AROUND HERE.
OH YEAH, JERRY, NOTHING EARNS RESPECT LIKE BEING UNEMPLOYED IN YOUR UNDERWEAR ALL DAY.
GOSH DANG IT.
WHERE CAN A GUY GET A LITTLE RESPECT?

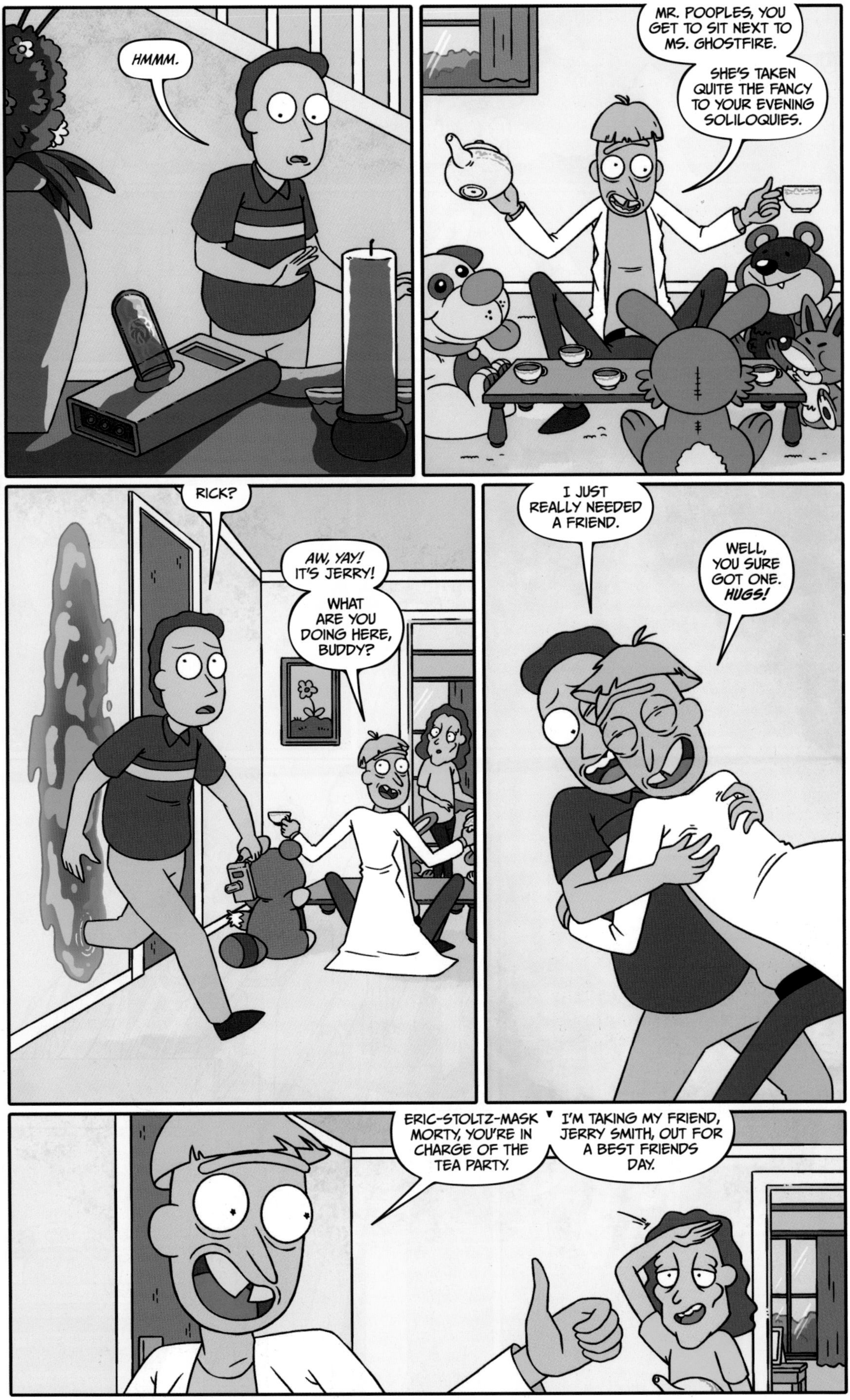
HMMM.
MR. POOPLES, YOU GET TO SIT NEXT TO MS. GHOSTFIRE.
SHE'S TAKEN QUITE THE FANCY TO YOUR EVENING SOLILOQUIES.
RICK?
AW, YAY! IT'S JERRY!
WHAT ARE YOU DOING HERE, BUDDY?
I JUST REALLY NEEDED A FRIEND.
WELL, YOU SURE GOT ONE. HUGS!
ERIC-STOLTZ-MASK MORTY, YOU'RE IN CHARGE OF THE TEA PARTY.
I'M TAKING MY FRIEND, JERRY SMITH, OUT FOR A BEST FRIENDS DAY.

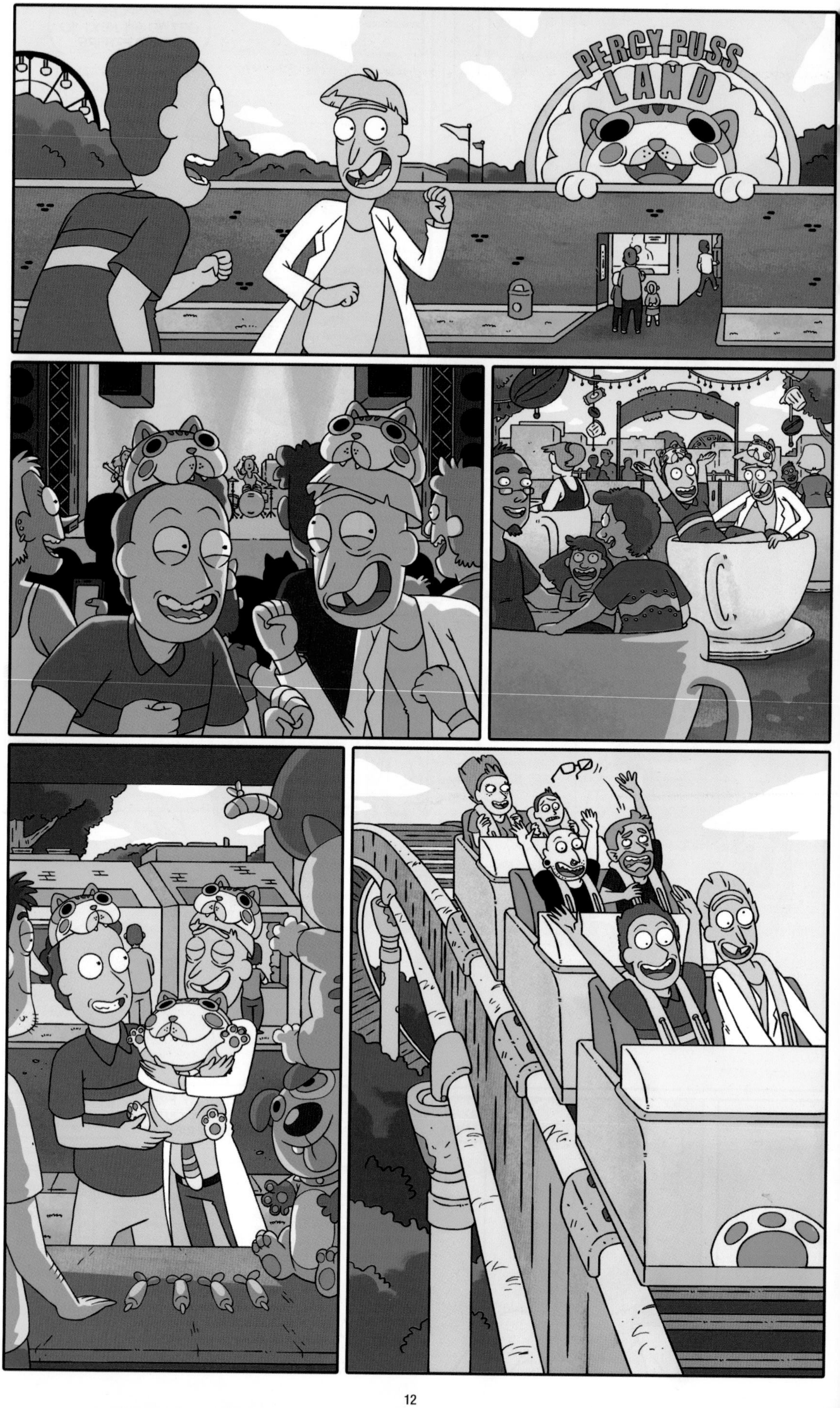
PERCY PUSS
LAND

SIR, THERE'S SOMETHING I THINK YOU NEED TO SEE ON THE SECURITY CAMERAS.

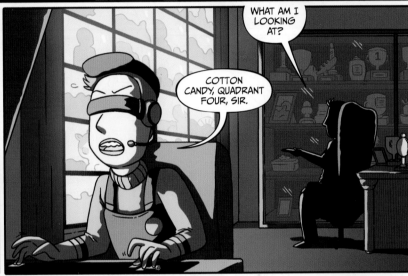

WHAT AM I LOOKING AT?

COTTON CANDY, QUADRANT FOUR, SIR.

WHAT AM I LOOKING AT? AN INBRED MUSHROOM?

NO, SIR, THE MAN WITH THE MUSHROOM.

WELL, ISN'T THIS INTERESTING.

BRING ME THAT MAN AT ONCE.

13

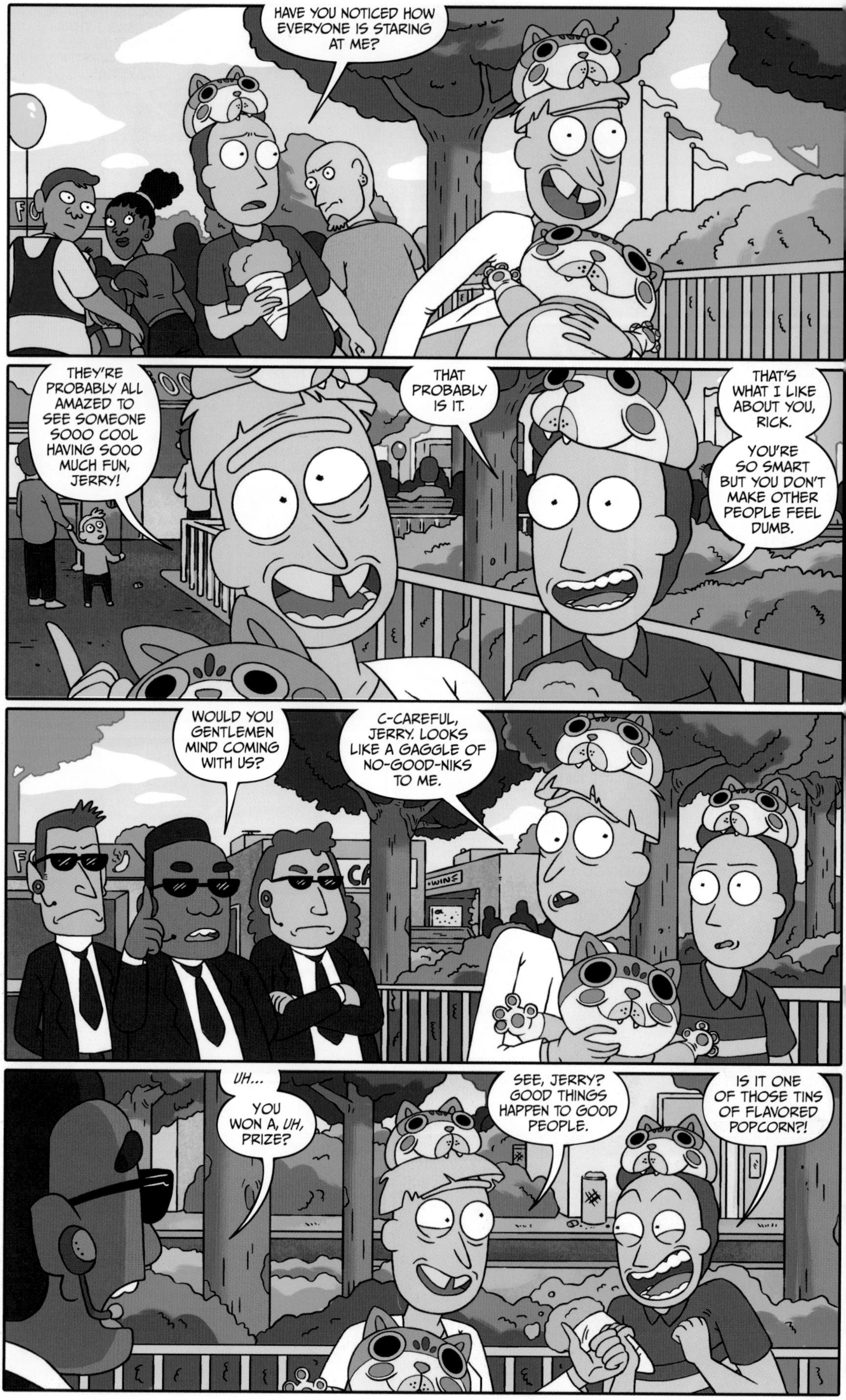
HAVE YOU NOTICED HOW EVERYONE IS STARING AT ME?
THEY'RE PROBABLY ALL AMAZED TO SEE SOMEONE SOOO COOL HAVING SOOO MUCH FUN, JERRY!
THAT PROBABLY IS IT.
THAT'S WHAT I LIKE ABOUT YOU, RICK.
YOU'RE SO SMART BUT YOU DON'T MAKE OTHER PEOPLE FEEL DUMB.
WOULD YOU GENTLEMEN MIND COMING WITH US?
C-CAREFUL, JERRY. LOOKS LIKE A GAGGLE OF NO-GOOD-NIKS TO ME.
UH...
YOU WON A, UH, PRIZE?
SEE, JERRY? GOOD THINGS HAPPEN TO GOOD PEOPLE.
IS IT ONE OF THOSE TINS OF FLAVORED POPCORN?!

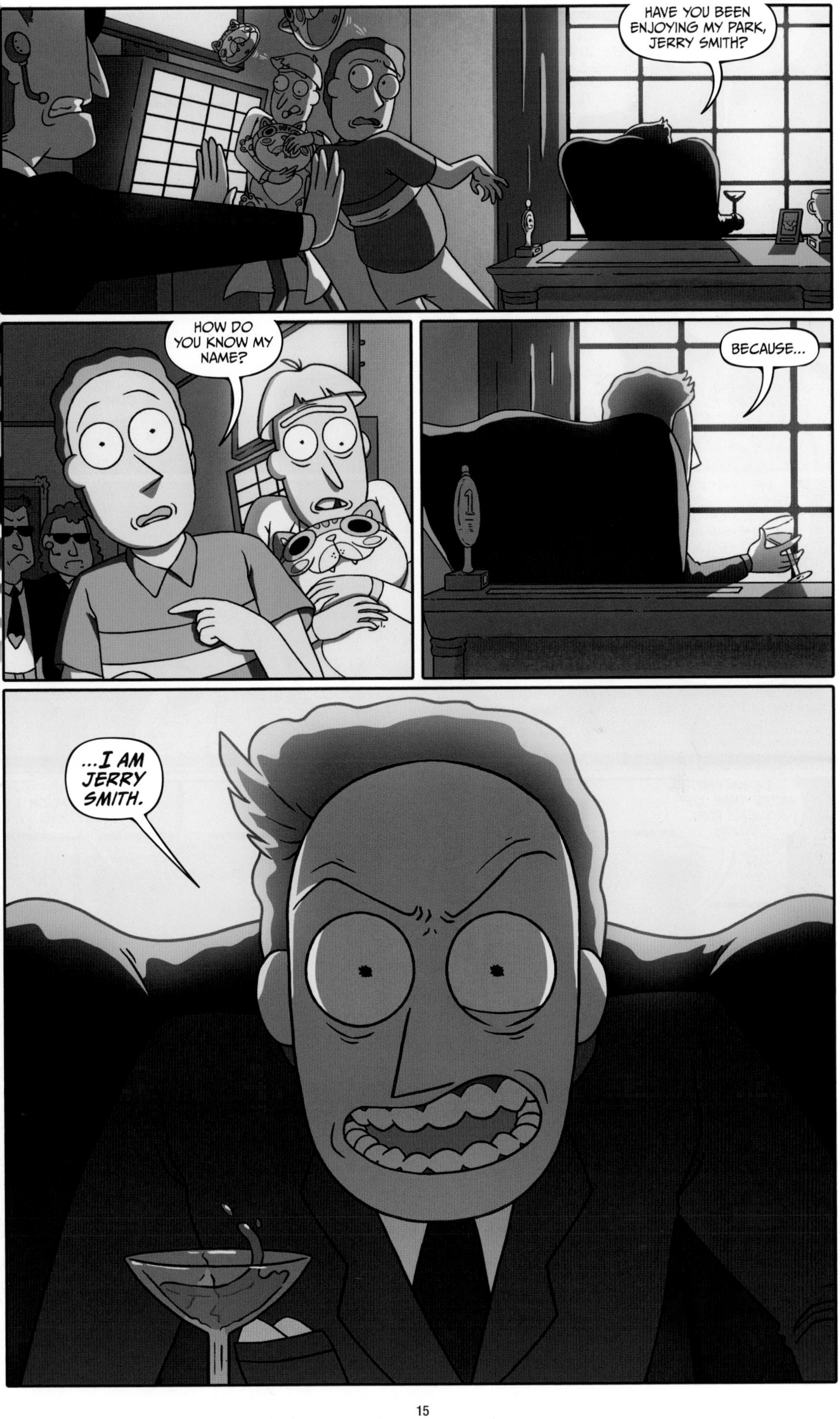
HAVE YOU BEEN ENJOYING MY PARK, JERRY SMITH?
HOW DO YOU KNOW MY NAME?
BECAUSE...
...I AM JERRY SMITH.

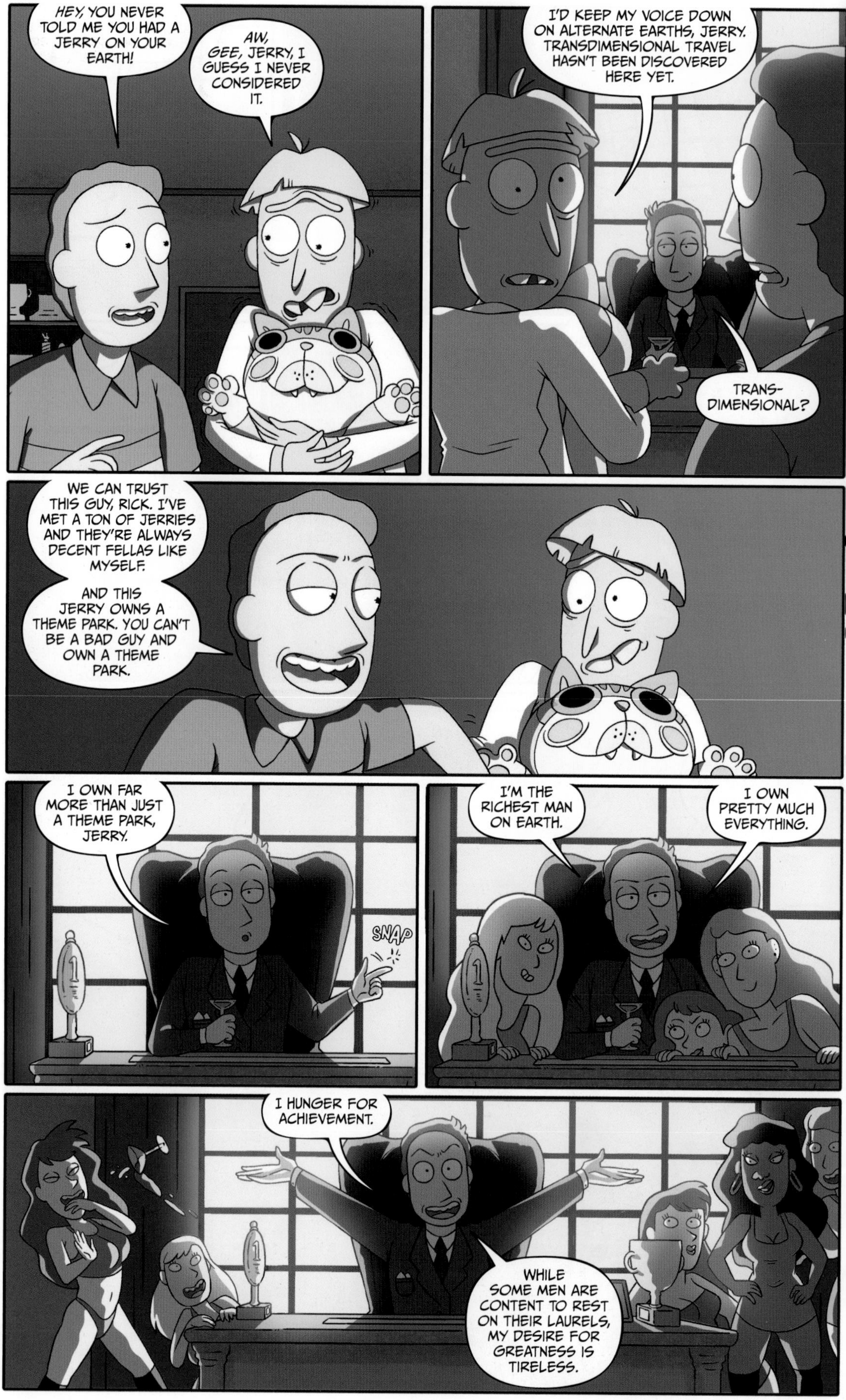
HEY, YOU NEVER TOLD ME YOU HAD A JERRY ON YOUR EARTH!
AW, GEE, JERRY, I GUESS I NEVER CONSIDERED IT.
I'D KEEP MY VOICE DOWN ON ALTERNATE EARTHS, JERRY. TRANSDIMENSIONAL TRAVEL HASN'T BEEN DISCOVERED HERE YET.
TRANS-DIMENSIONAL?
WE CAN TRUST THIS GUY, RICK. I'VE MET A TON OF JERRIES AND THEY'RE ALWAYS DECENT FELLAS LIKE MYSELF.
AND THIS JERRY OWNS A THEME PARK. YOU CAN'T BE A BAD GUY AND OWN A THEME PARK.
I OWN FAR MORE THAN JUST A THEME PARK, JERRY.
SNAP
I'M THE RICHEST MAN ON EARTH.
I OWN PRETTY MUCH EVERYTHING.
I HUNGER FOR ACHIEVEMENT.
WHILE SOME MEN ARE CONTENT TO REST ON THEIR LAURELS, MY DESIRE FOR GREATNESS IS TIRELESS.

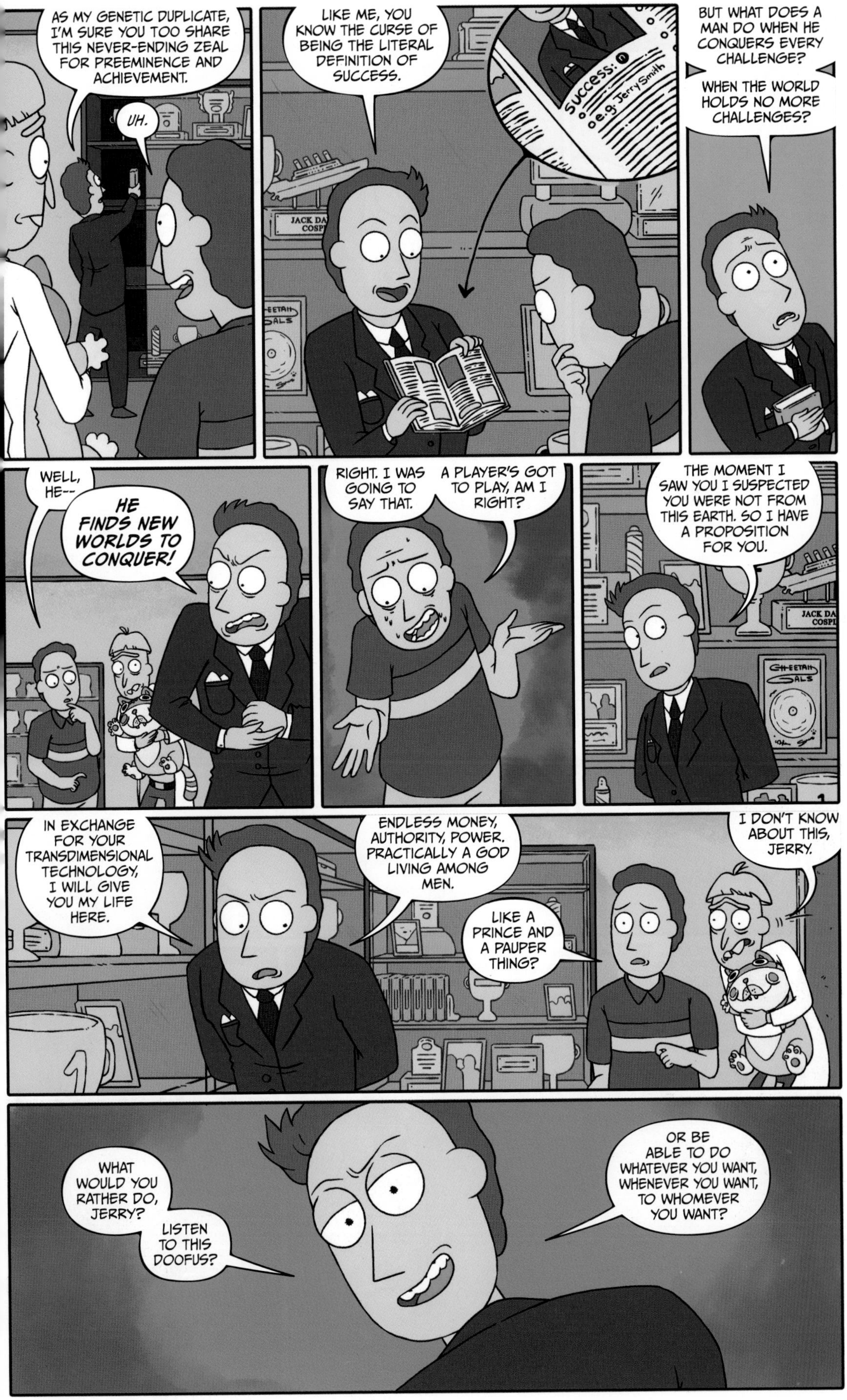
AS MY GENETIC DUPLICATE, I'M SURE YOU TOO SHARE THIS NEVER-ENDING ZEAL FOR PREEMINENCE AND ACHIEVEMENT.
UH.
LIKE ME, YOU KNOW THE CURSE OF BEING THE LITERAL DEFINITION OF SUCCESS.
SUCCESS:
e.g. Jerry Smith
BUT WHAT DOES A MAN DO WHEN HE CONQUERS EVERY CHALLENGE?
WHEN THE WORLD HOLDS NO MORE CHALLENGES?
WELL, HE--
HE FINDS NEW WORLDS TO CONQUER!
RIGHT. I WAS GOING TO SAY THAT.
A PLAYER'S GOT TO PLAY, AM I RIGHT?
THE MOMENT I SAW YOU I SUSPECTED YOU WERE NOT FROM THIS EARTH. SO I HAVE A PROPOSITION FOR YOU.
IN EXCHANGE FOR YOUR TRANSDIMENSIONAL TECHNOLOGY, I WILL GIVE YOU MY LIFE HERE.
ENDLESS MONEY, AUTHORITY, POWER. PRACTICALLY A GOD LIVING AMONG MEN.
LIKE A PRINCE AND A PAUPER THING?
I DON'T KNOW ABOUT THIS, JERRY.
WHAT WOULD YOU RATHER DO, JERRY?
LISTEN TO THIS DOOFUS?
OR BE ABLE TO DO WHATEVER YOU WANT, WHENEVER YOU WANT, TO WHOMEVER YOU WANT?

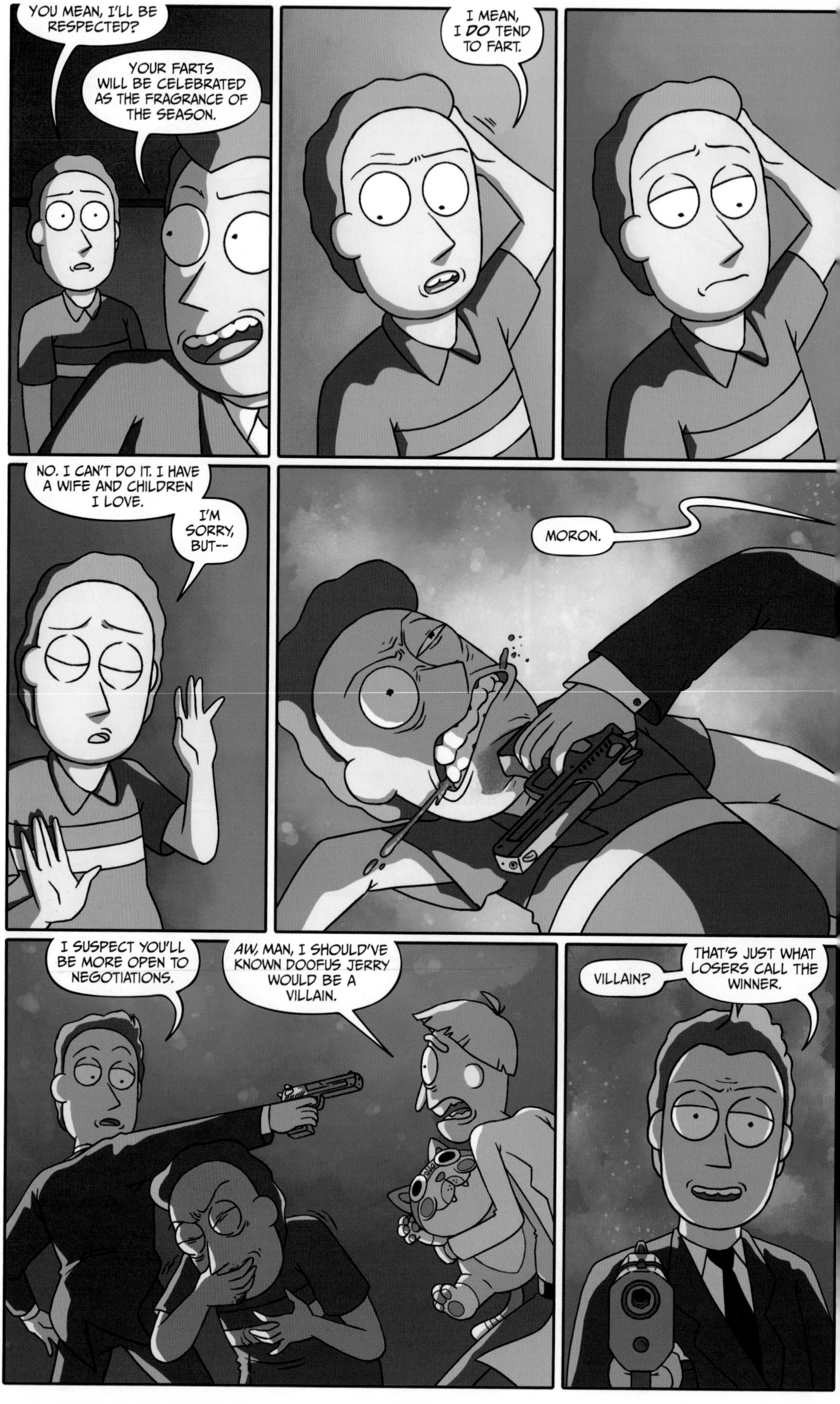

YOU MEAN, I'LL BE RESPECTED?
YOUR FARTS WILL BE CELEBRATED AS THE FRAGRANCE OF THE SEASON.
I MEAN, I DO TEND TO FART.
NO. I CAN'T DO IT. I HAVE A WIFE AND CHILDREN I LOVE.
I'M SORRY, BUT--
MORON.
I SUSPECT YOU'LL BE MORE OPEN TO NEGOTIATIONS.
AW, MAN, I SHOULD'VE KNOWN DOOFUS JERRY WOULD BE A VILLAIN.
VILLAIN?
THAT'S JUST WHAT LOSERS CALL THE WINNER.

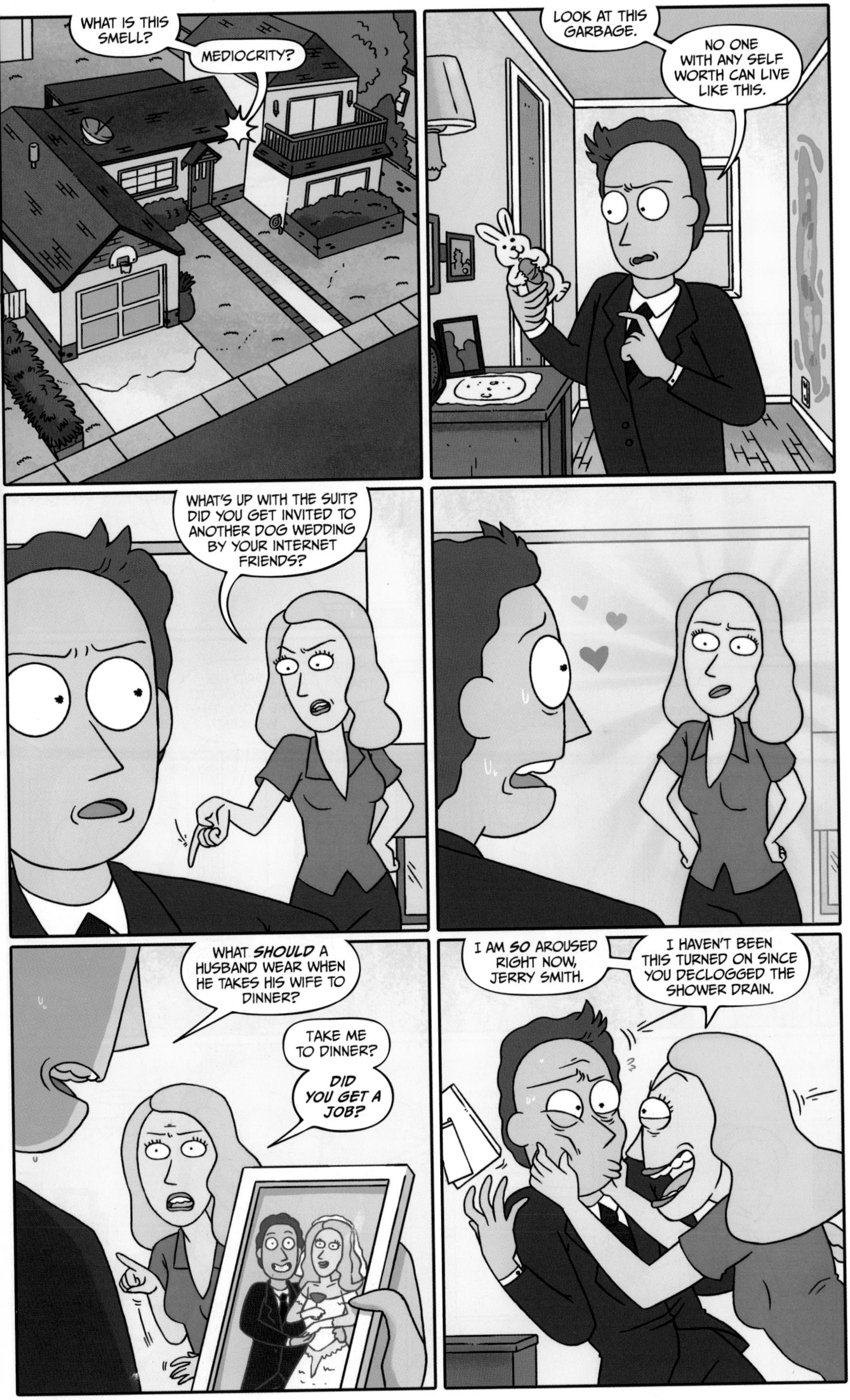
WHAT IS THIS SMELL?
MEDIOCRITY?
LOOK AT THIS GARBAGE.
NO ONE WITH ANY SELF WORTH CAN LIVE LIKE THIS.
WHAT'S UP WITH THE SUIT? DID YOU GET INVITED TO ANOTHER DOG WEDDING BY YOUR INTERNET FRIENDS?
WHAT *SHOULD* A HUSBAND WEAR WHEN HE TAKES HIS WIFE TO DINNER?
TAKE ME TO DINNER?
DID YOU GET A JOB?
I AM *SO* AROUSED RIGHT NOW, JERRY SMITH.
I HAVEN'T BEEN THIS TURNED ON SINCE YOU DECLOGGED THE SHOWER DRAIN.

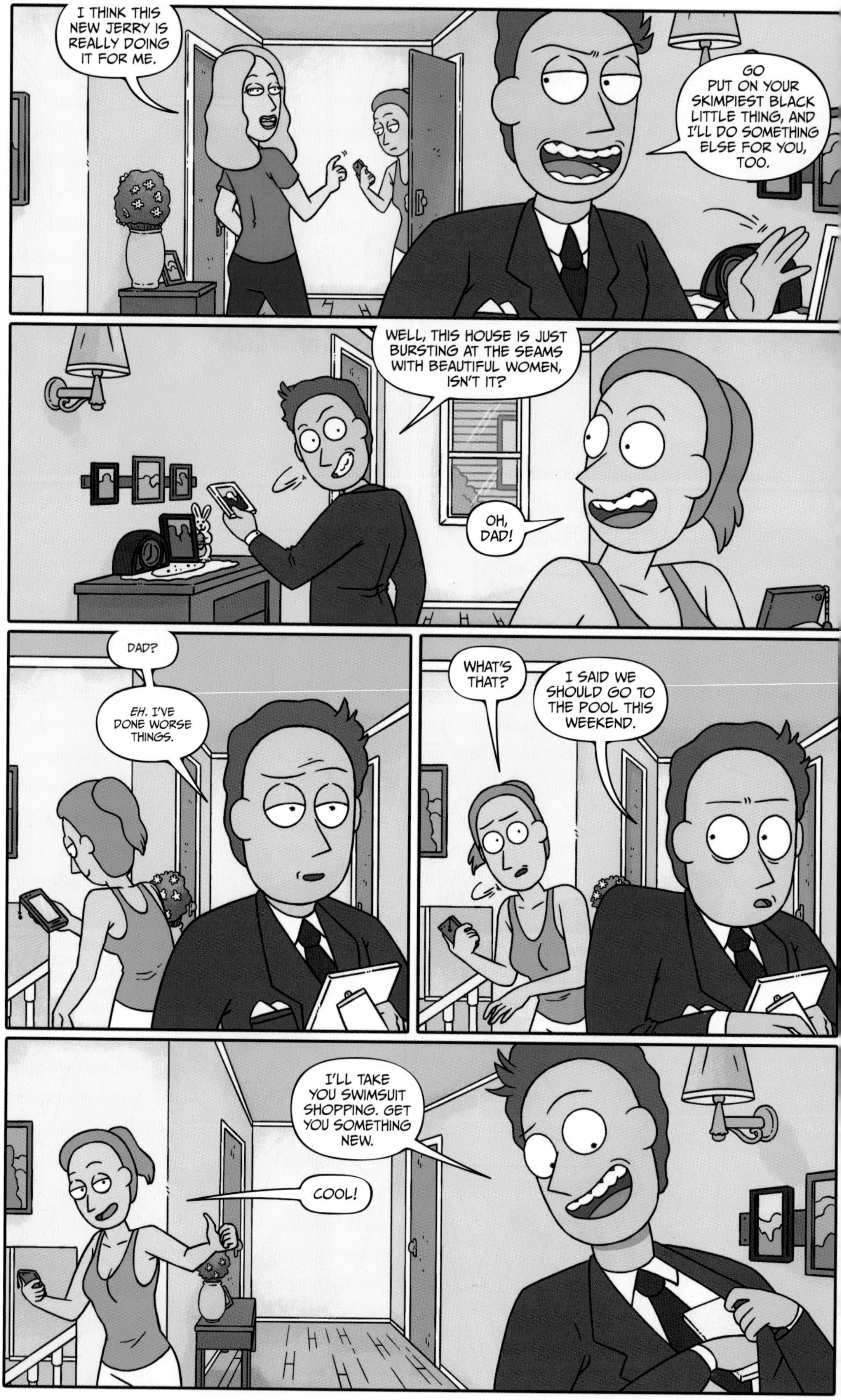
I THINK THIS NEW JERRY IS REALLY DOING IT FOR ME.
GO PUT ON YOUR SKIMPIEST BLACK LITTLE THING, AND I'LL DO SOMETHING ELSE FOR YOU, TOO.
WELL, THIS HOUSE IS JUST BURSTING AT THE SEAMS WITH BEAUTIFUL WOMEN, ISN'T IT?
OH, DAD!
DAD?
EH. I'VE DONE WORSE THINGS.
WHAT'S THAT?
I SAID WE SHOULD GO TO THE POOL THIS WEEKEND.
I'LL TAKE YOU SWIMSUIT SHOPPING. GET YOU SOMETHING NEW.
COOL!

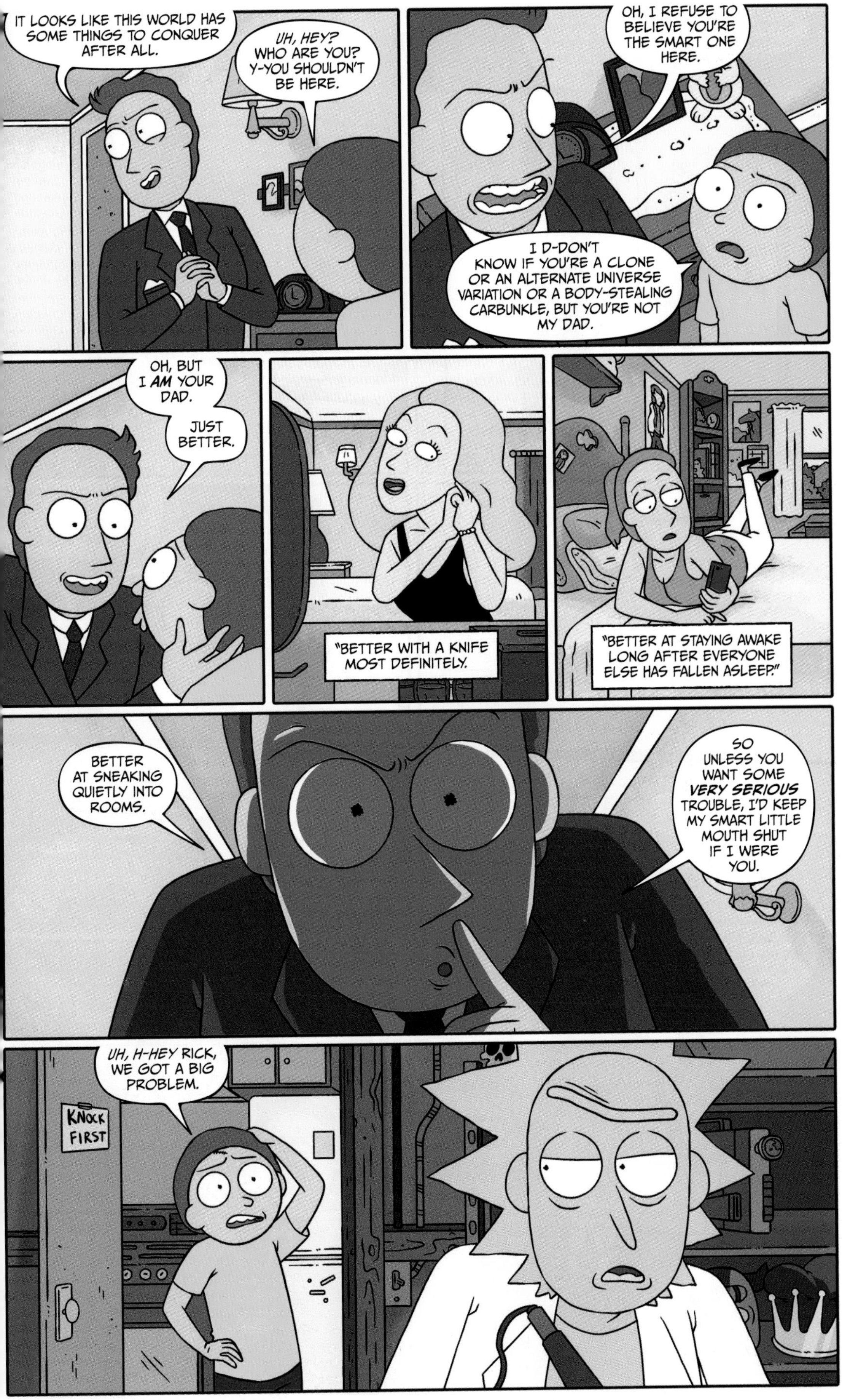
IT LOOKS LIKE THIS WORLD HAS SOME THINGS TO CONQUER AFTER ALL.
UH, HEY? WHO ARE YOU? Y-YOU SHOULDN'T BE HERE.
OH, I REFUSE TO BELIEVE YOU'RE THE SMART ONE HERE.
I D-DON'T KNOW IF YOU'RE A CLONE OR AN ALTERNATE UNIVERSE VARIATION OR A BODY-STEALING CARBUNKLE, BUT YOU'RE NOT MY DAD.
OH, BUT I AM YOUR DAD.
JUST BETTER.
"BETTER WITH A KNIFE MOST DEFINITELY.
"BETTER AT STAYING AWAKE LONG AFTER EVERYONE ELSE HAS FALLEN ASLEEP."
BETTER AT SNEAKING QUIETLY INTO ROOMS.
SO UNLESS YOU WANT SOME VERY SERIOUS TROUBLE, I'D KEEP MY SMART LITTLE MOUTH SHUT IF I WERE YOU.
UH, H-HEY RICK, WE GOT A BIG PROBLEM.
KNOCK FIRST

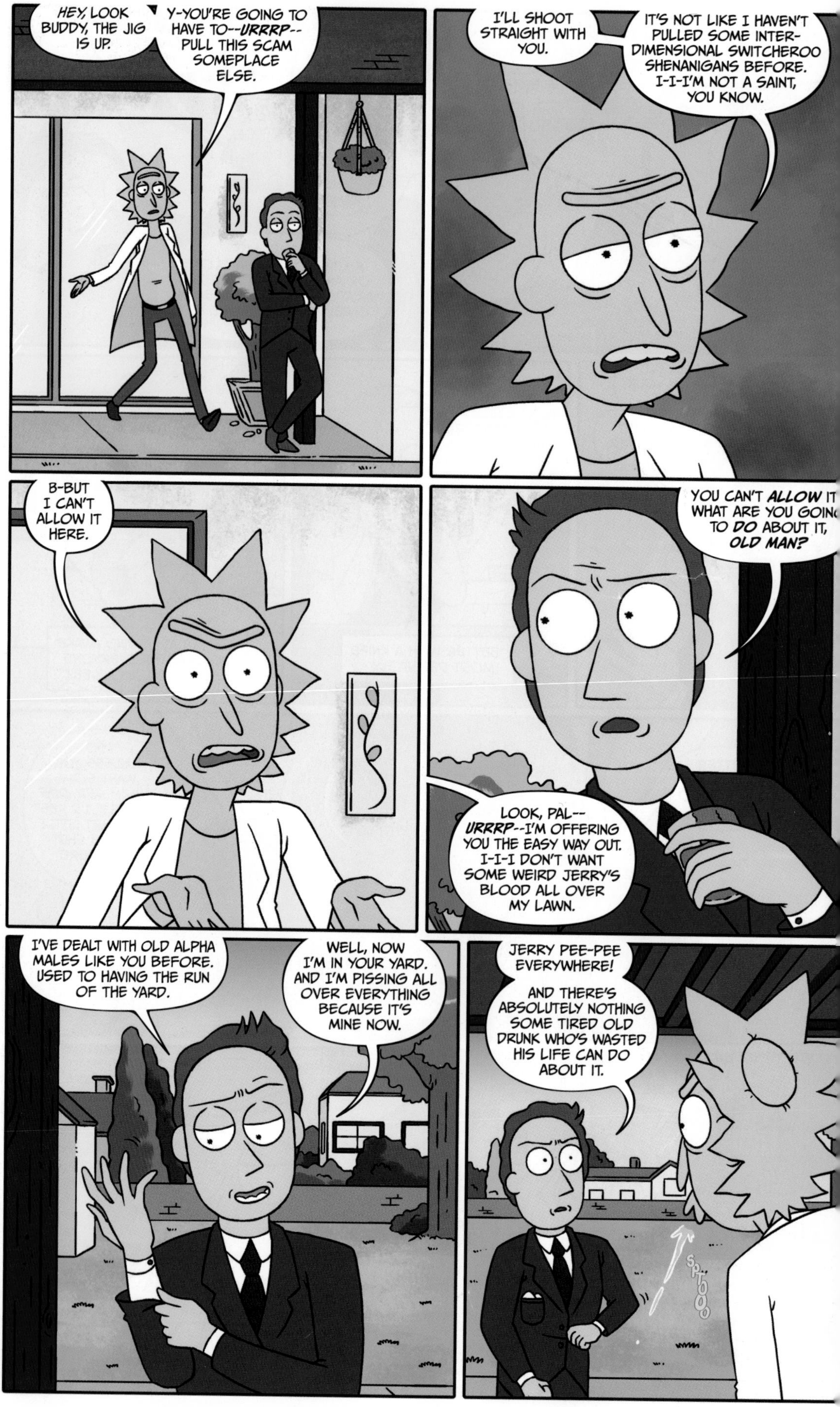
HEY, LOOK BUDDY, THE JIG IS UP.
Y-YOU'RE GOING TO HAVE TO--URRRP--PULL THIS SCAM SOMEPLACE ELSE.
I'LL SHOOT STRAIGHT WITH YOU.
IT'S NOT LIKE I HAVEN'T PULLED SOME INTER-DIMENSIONAL SWITCHEROO SHENANIGANS BEFORE. I-I-I'M NOT A SAINT, YOU KNOW.
B-BUT I CAN'T ALLOW IT HERE.
YOU CAN'T ALLOW IT
WHAT ARE YOU GOIN
TO DO ABOUT IT, OLD MAN?
LOOK, PAL--URRRP--I'M OFFERING YOU THE EASY WAY OUT. I-I-I DON'T WANT SOME WEIRD JERRY'S BLOOD ALL OVER MY LAWN.
I'VE DEALT WITH OLD ALPHA MALES LIKE YOU BEFORE. USED TO HAVING THE RUN OF THE YARD.
WELL, NOW I'M IN YOUR YARD. AND I'M PISSING ALL OVER EVERYTHING BECAUSE IT'S MINE NOW.
JERRY PEE-PEE EVERYWHERE!
AND THERE'S ABSOLUTELY NOTHING SOME TIRED OLD DRUNK WHO'S WASTED HIS LIFE CAN DO ABOUT IT.
SPTOOO

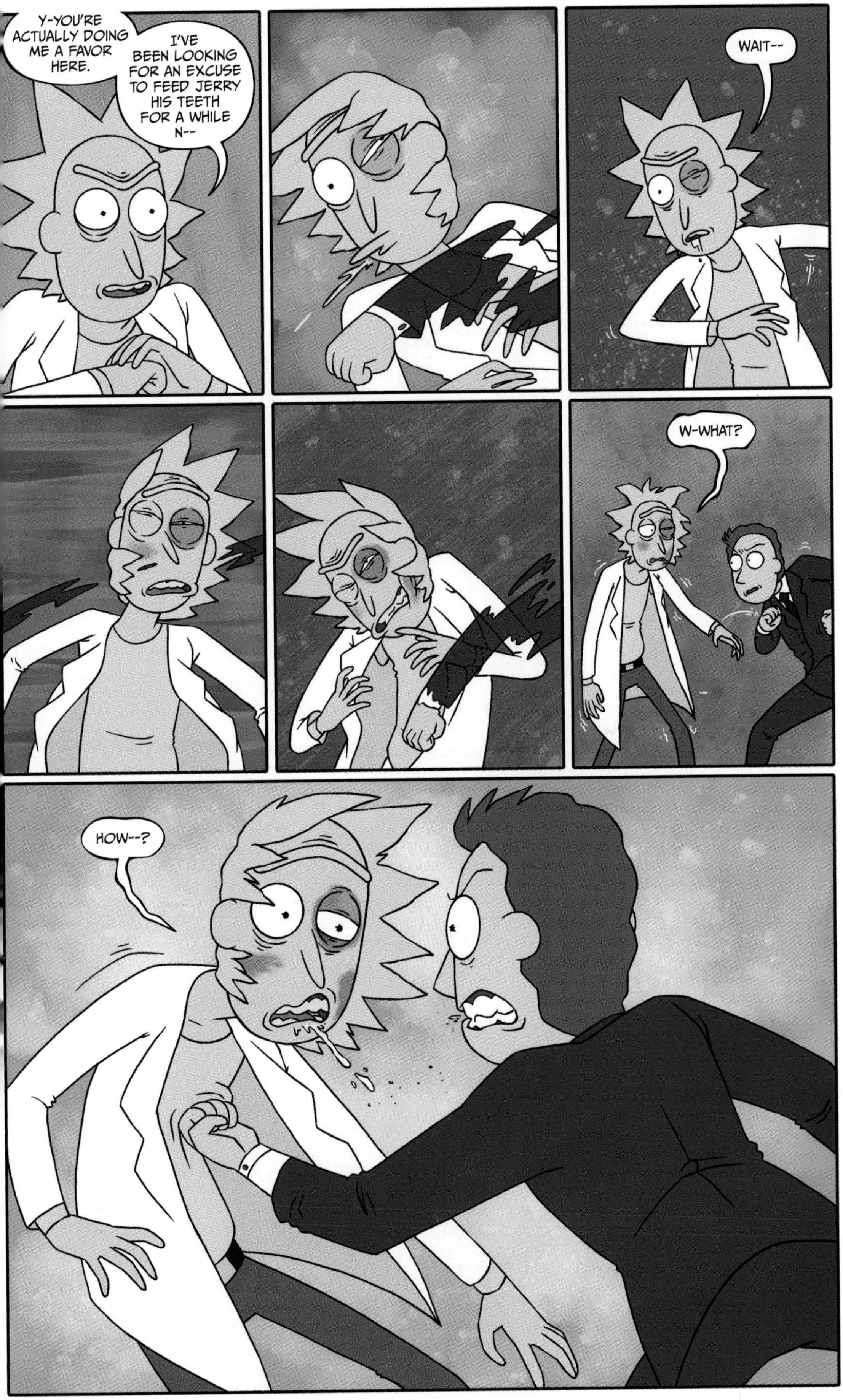
Y-YOU'RE ACTUALLY DOING ME A FAVOR HERE.
I'VE BEEN LOOKING FOR AN EXCUSE TO FEED JERRY HIS TEETH FOR A WHILE N--
WAIT--
W-WHAT?
HOW--?

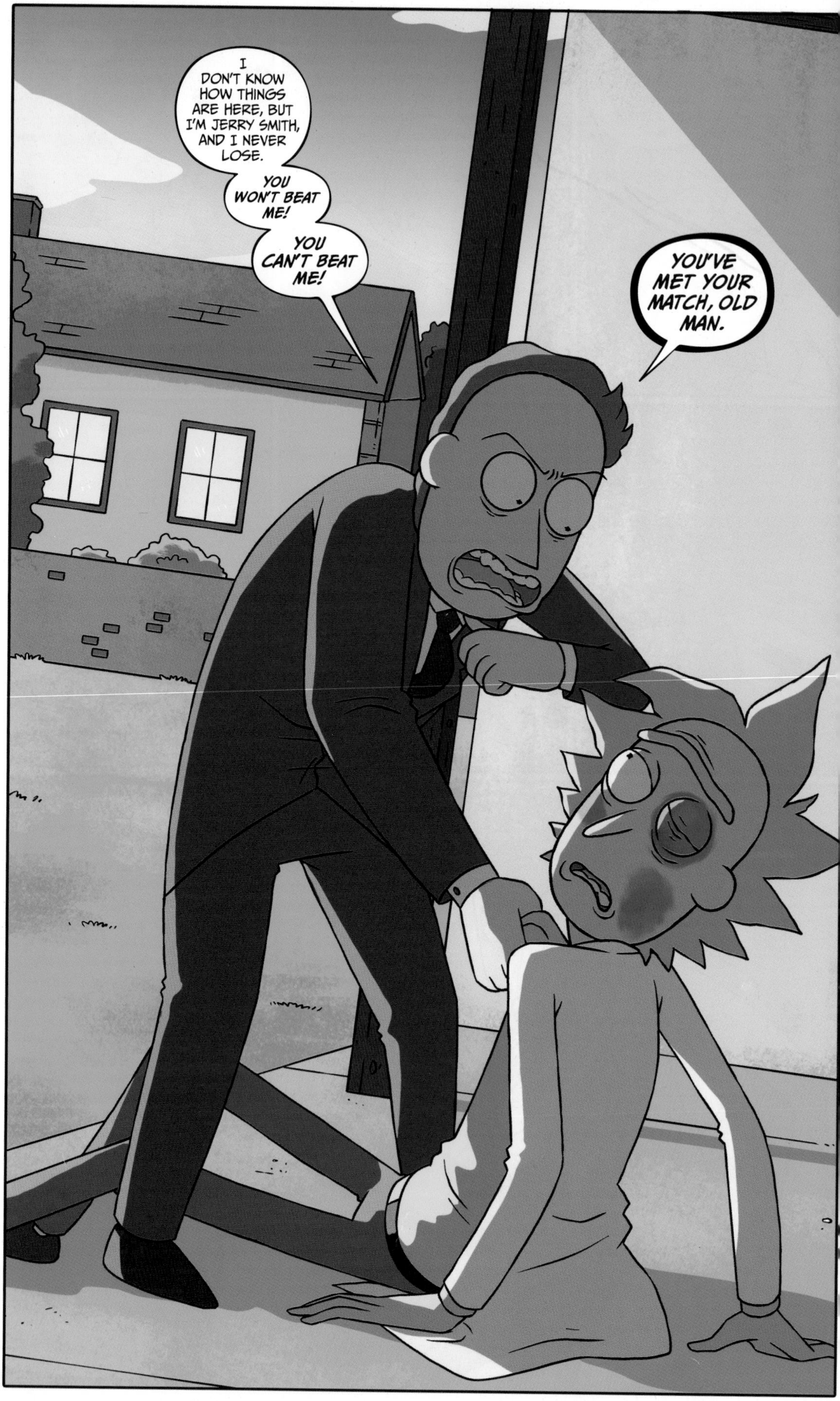
I DON'T KNOW HOW THINGS ARE HERE, BUT I'M JERRY SMITH, AND I NEVER LOSE.
YOU WON'T BEAT ME!
YOU CAN'T BEAT ME!
YOU'VE MET YOUR MATCH, OLD MAN.

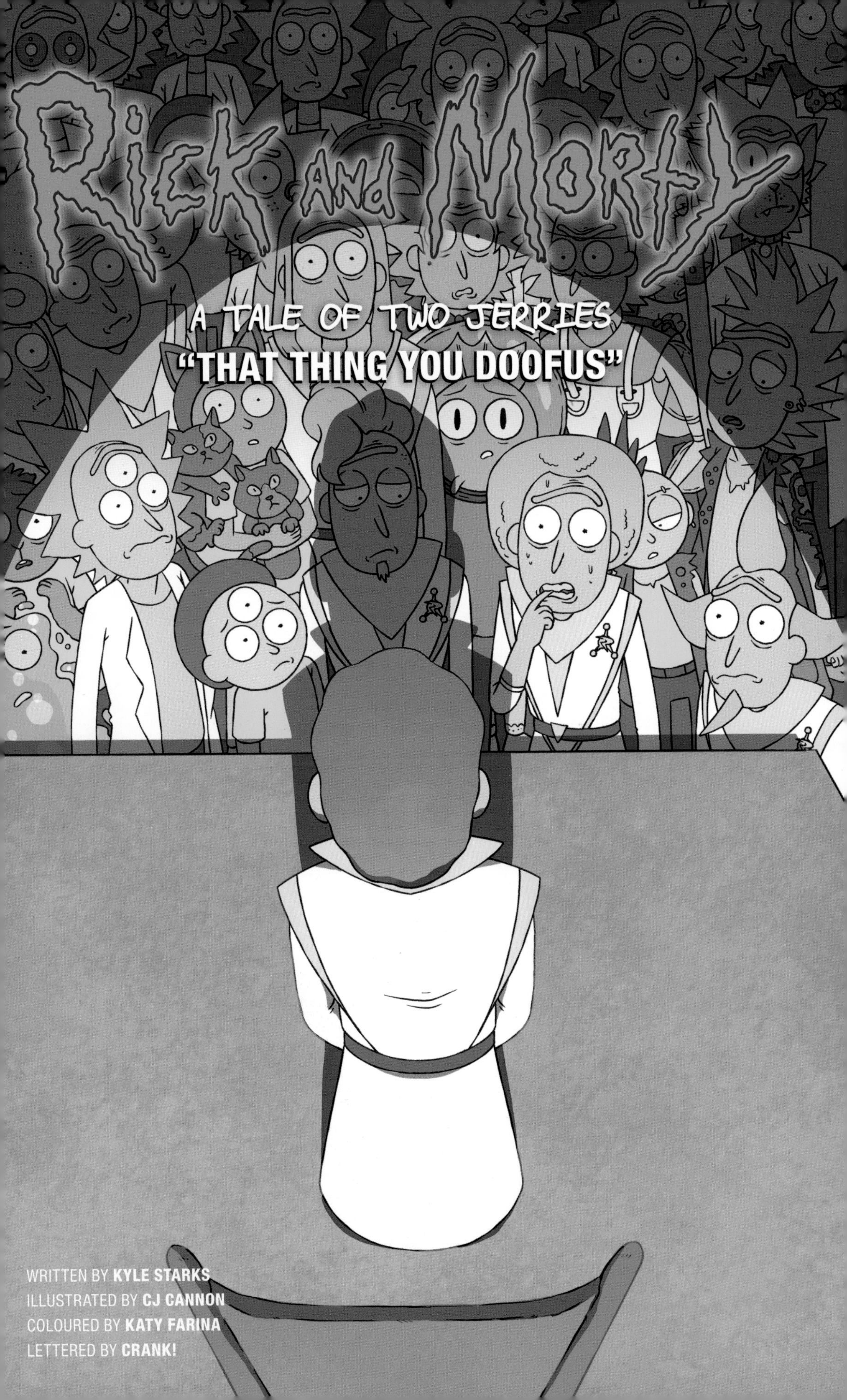
Rick and Morty
A TALE OF TWO JERRIES
"THAT THING YOU DOOFUS"
WRITTEN BY KYLE STARKS
ILLUSTRATED BY CJ CANNON
COLOURED BY KATY FARINA
LETTERED BY CRANK!

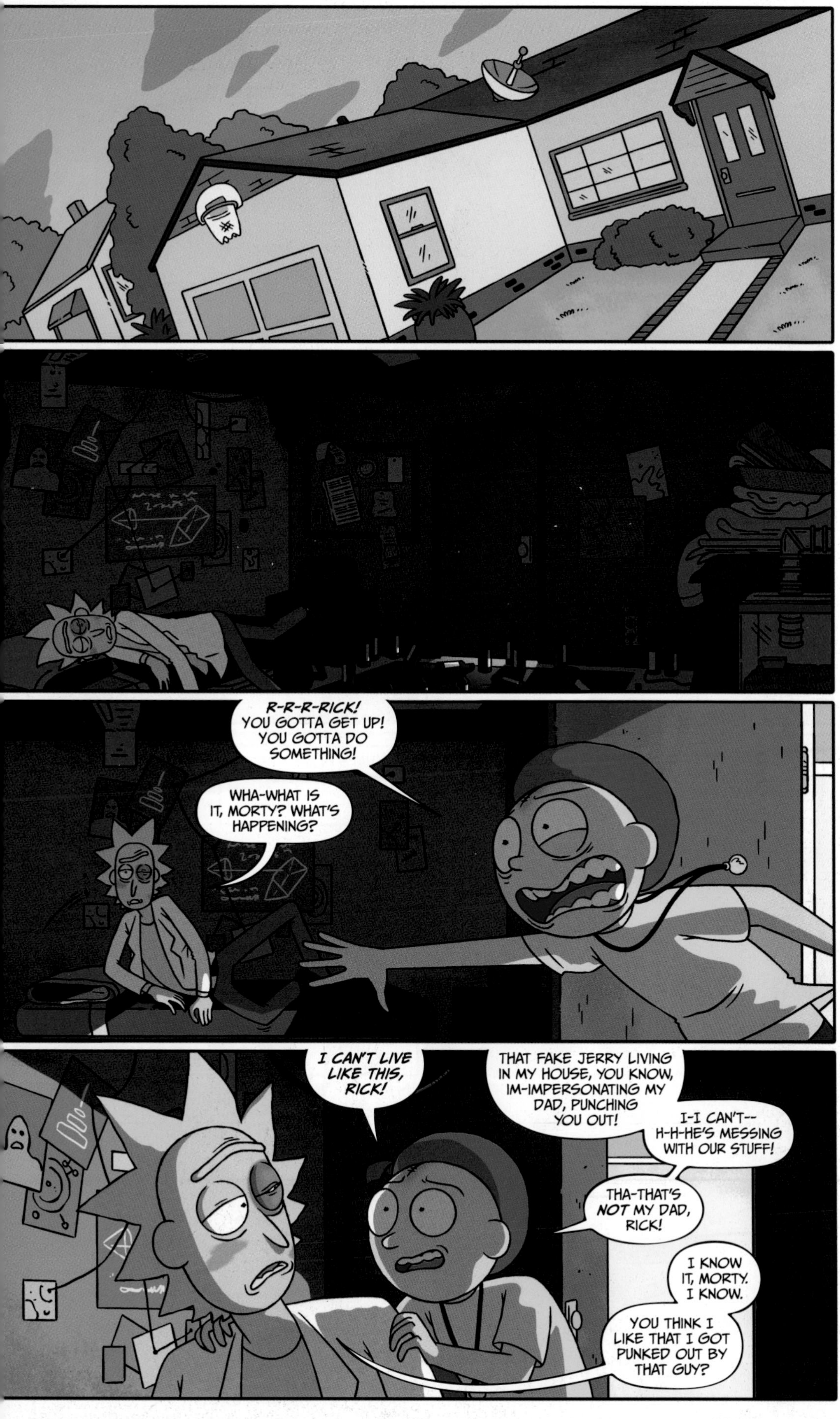
R-R-R-RICK! YOU GOTTA GET UP! YOU GOTTA DO SOMETHING!
WHA-WHAT IS IT, MORTY? WHAT'S HAPPENING?
I CAN'T LIVE LIKE THIS, RICK!
THAT FAKE JERRY LIVING IN MY HOUSE, YOU KNOW, IM-IMPERSONATING MY DAD, PUNCHING YOU OUT!
I-I CAN'T-- H-H-HE'S MESSING WITH OUR STUFF!
THA-THAT'S NOT MY DAD, RICK!
I KNOW IT, MORTY. I KNOW.
YOU THINK I LIKE THAT I GOT PUNKED OUT BY THAT GUY?

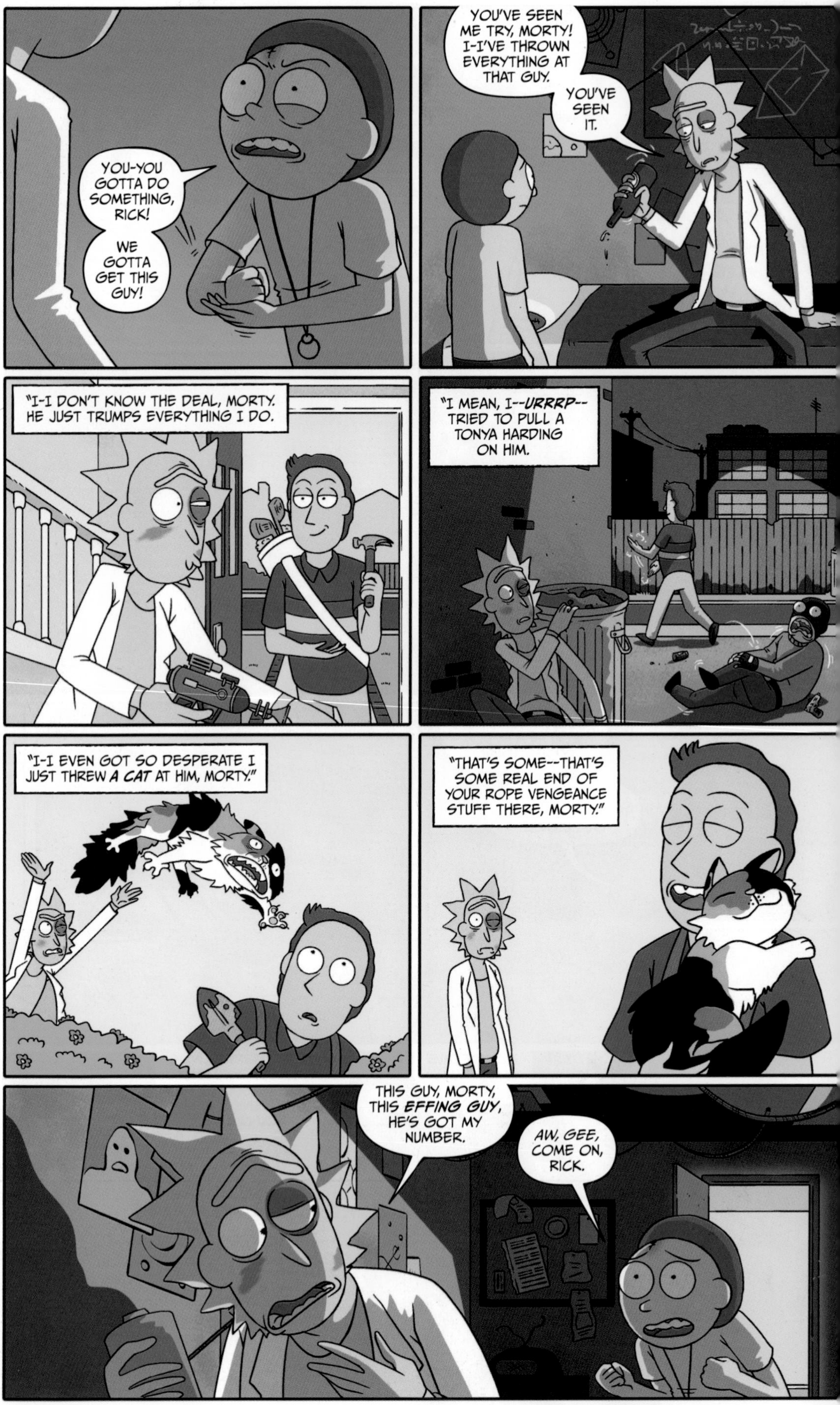
YOU-YOU GOTTA DO SOMETHING, RICK!
WE GOTTA GET THIS GUY!
YOU'VE SEEN ME TRY, MORTY! I-I'VE THROWN EVERYTHING AT THAT GUY.
YOU'VE SEEN IT.
"I-I DON'T KNOW THE DEAL, MORTY. HE JUST TRUMPS EVERYTHING I DO.
"I MEAN, I--*URRRP*--TRIED TO PULL A TONYA HARDING ON HIM.
"I-I EVEN GOT SO DESPERATE I JUST THREW *A CAT* AT HIM, MORTY."
"THAT'S SOME--THAT'S SOME REAL END OF YOUR ROPE VENGEANCE STUFF THERE, MORTY."
THIS GUY, MORTY, THIS *EFFING GUY*, HE'S GOT MY NUMBER.
AW, GEE, COME ON, RICK.

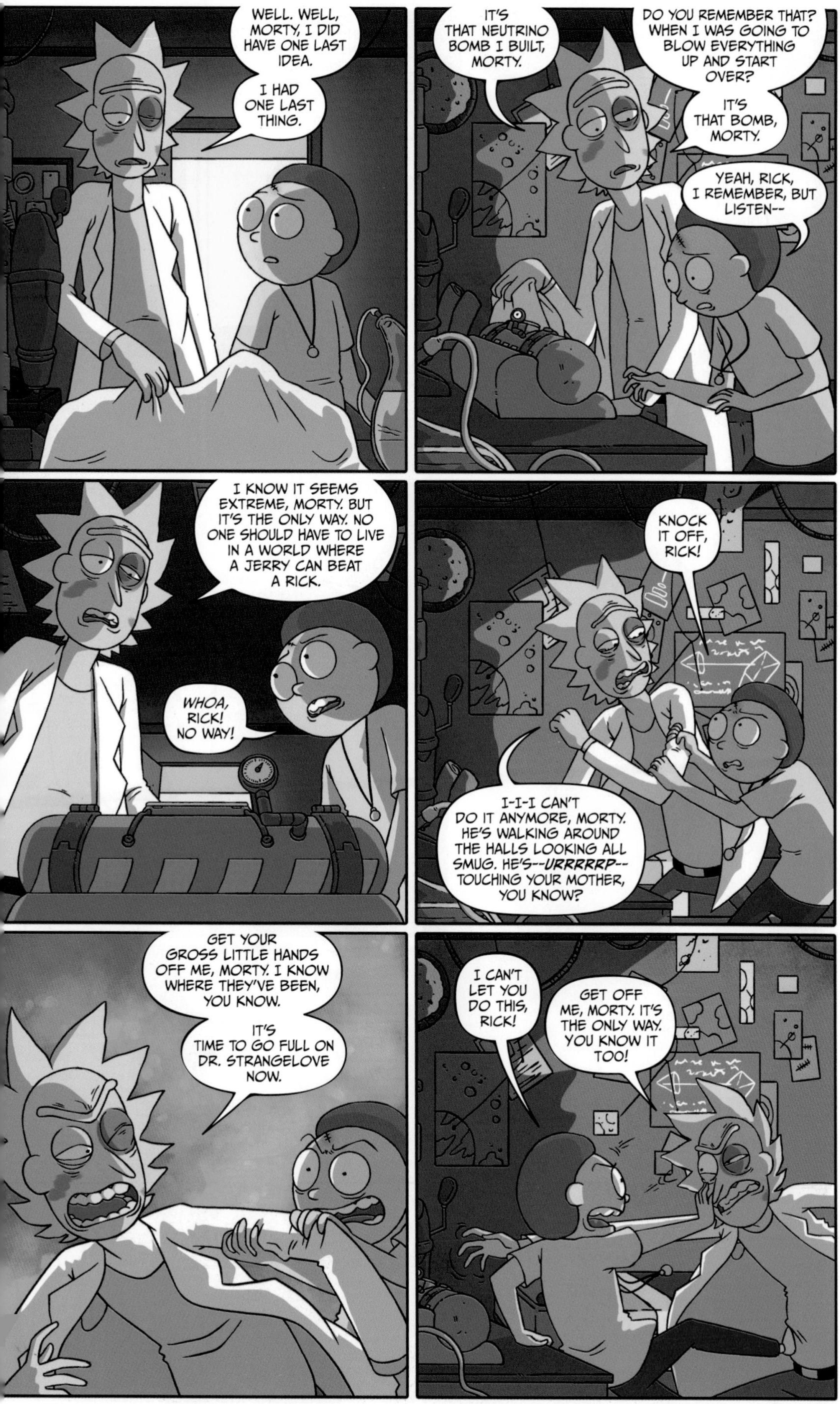
WELL. WELL, MORTY, I DID HAVE ONE LAST IDEA.
I HAD ONE LAST THING.
IT'S THAT NEUTRINO BOMB I BUILT, MORTY.
DO YOU REMEMBER THAT? WHEN I WAS GOING TO BLOW EVERYTHING UP AND START OVER?
IT'S THAT BOMB, MORTY.
YEAH, RICK, I REMEMBER, BUT LISTEN--
I KNOW IT SEEMS EXTREME, MORTY. BUT IT'S THE ONLY WAY. NO ONE SHOULD HAVE TO LIVE IN A WORLD WHERE A JERRY CAN BEAT A RICK.
WHOA, RICK! NO WAY!
KNOCK IT OFF, RICK!
I-I-I CAN'T DO IT ANYMORE, MORTY. HE'S WALKING AROUND THE HALLS LOOKING ALL SMUG. HE'S--URRRRRP-- TOUCHING YOUR MOTHER, YOU KNOW?
GET YOUR GROSS LITTLE HANDS OFF ME, MORTY. I KNOW WHERE THEY'VE BEEN, YOU KNOW.
IT'S TIME TO GO FULL ON DR. STRANGELOVE NOW.
I CAN'T LET YOU DO THIS, RICK!
GET OFF ME, MORTY. IT'S THE ONLY WAY. YOU KNOW IT TOO!

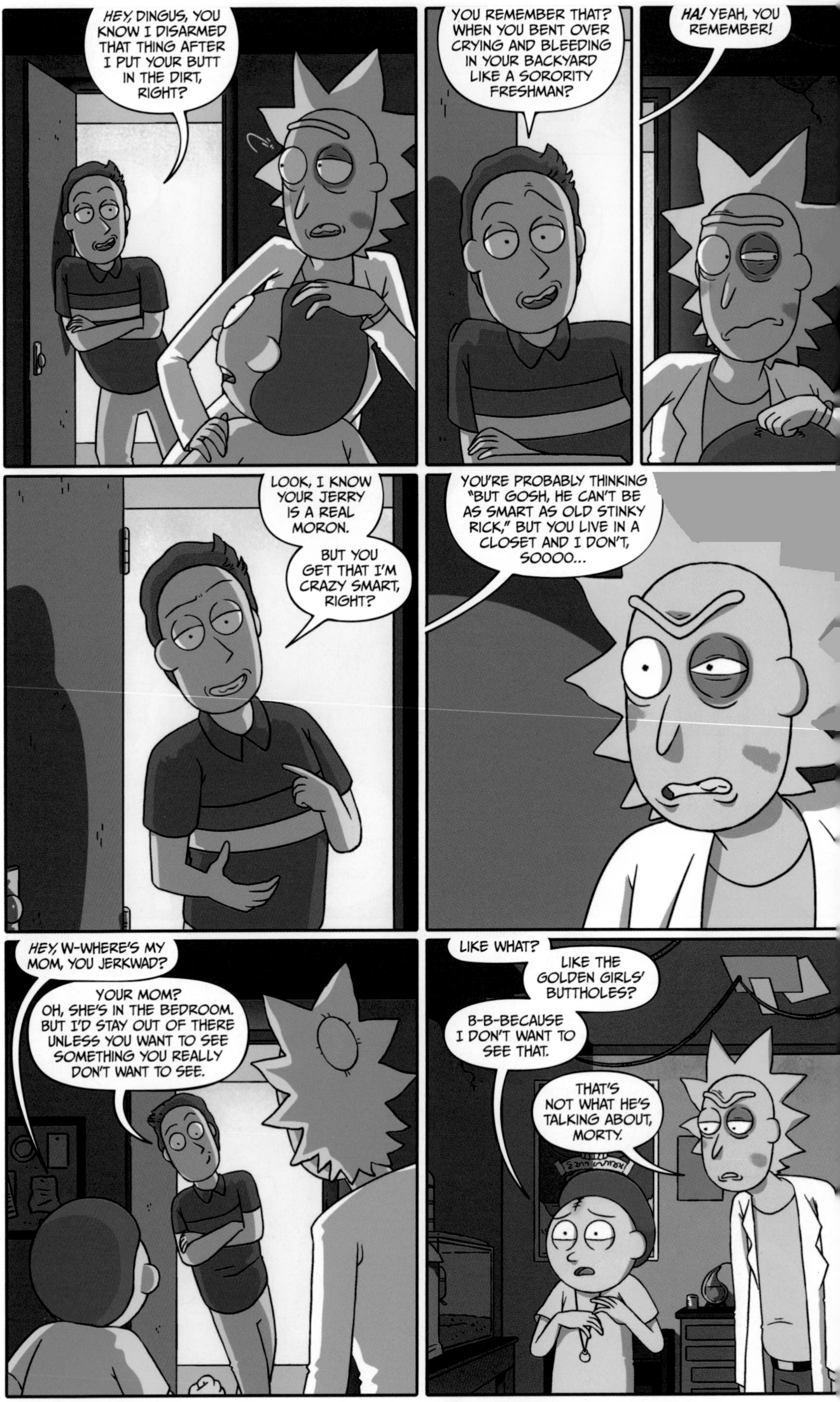
HEY, DINGUS, YOU KNOW I DISARMED THAT THING AFTER I PUT YOUR BUTT IN THE DIRT, RIGHT?
YOU REMEMBER THAT? WHEN YOU BENT OVER CRYING AND BLEEDING IN YOUR BACKYARD LIKE A SORORITY FRESHMAN?
HA! YEAH, YOU REMEMBER!
LOOK, I KNOW YOUR JERRY IS A REAL MORON.
BUT YOU GET THAT I'M CRAZY SMART, RIGHT?
YOU'RE PROBABLY THINKING "BUT GOSH, HE CAN'T BE AS SMART AS OLD STINKY RICK," BUT YOU LIVE IN A CLOSET AND I DON'T, SOOOO...
HEY, W-WHERE'S MY MOM, YOU JERKWAD?
YOUR MOM? OH, SHE'S IN THE BEDROOM. BUT I'D STAY OUT OF THERE UNLESS YOU WANT TO SEE SOMETHING YOU REALLY DON'T WANT TO SEE.
LIKE WHAT?
LIKE THE GOLDEN GIRLS' BUTTHOLES?
B-B-BECAUSE I DON'T WANT TO SEE THAT.
THAT'S NOT WHAT HE'S TALKING ABOUT, MORTY.

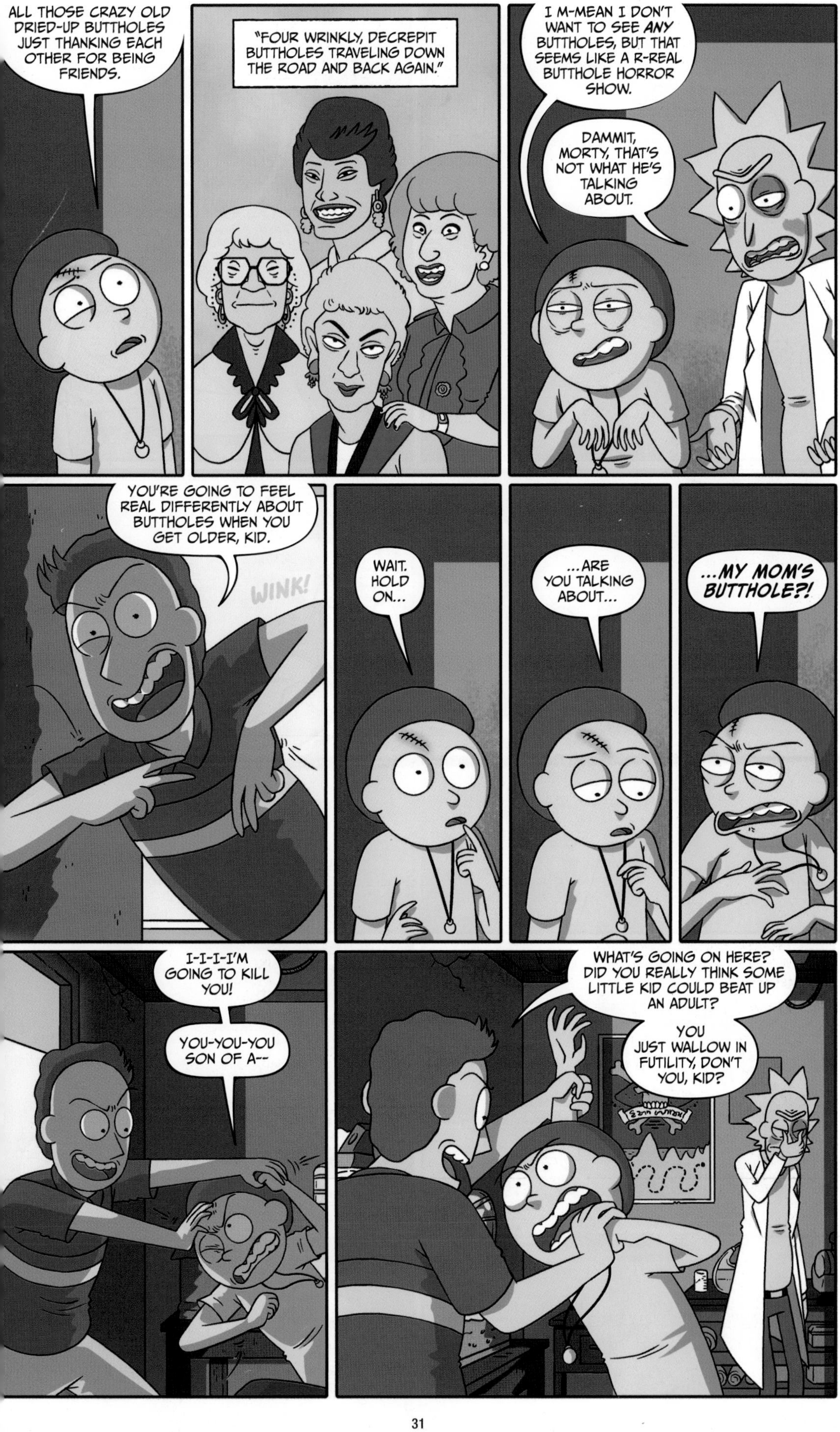
ALL THOSE CRAZY OLD DRIED-UP BUTTHOLES JUST THANKING EACH OTHER FOR BEING FRIENDS.
"FOUR WRINKLY, DECREPIT BUTTHOLES TRAVELING DOWN THE ROAD AND BACK AGAIN."
I M-MEAN I DON'T WANT TO SEE ANY BUTTHOLES, BUT THAT SEEMS LIKE A R-REAL BUTTHOLE HORROR SHOW.
DAMMIT, MORTY, THAT'S NOT WHAT HE'S TALKING ABOUT.
YOU'RE GOING TO FEEL REAL DIFFERENTLY ABOUT BUTTHOLES WHEN YOU GET OLDER, KID.
WINK!
WAIT. HOLD ON...
...ARE YOU TALKING ABOUT...
...MY MOM'S BUTTHOLE?!
I-I-I-I'M GOING TO KILL YOU!
YOU-YOU-YOU SON OF A--
WHAT'S GOING ON HERE? DID YOU REALLY THINK SOME LITTLE KID COULD BEAT UP AN ADULT?
YOU JUST WALLOW IN FUTILITY, DON'T YOU, KID?

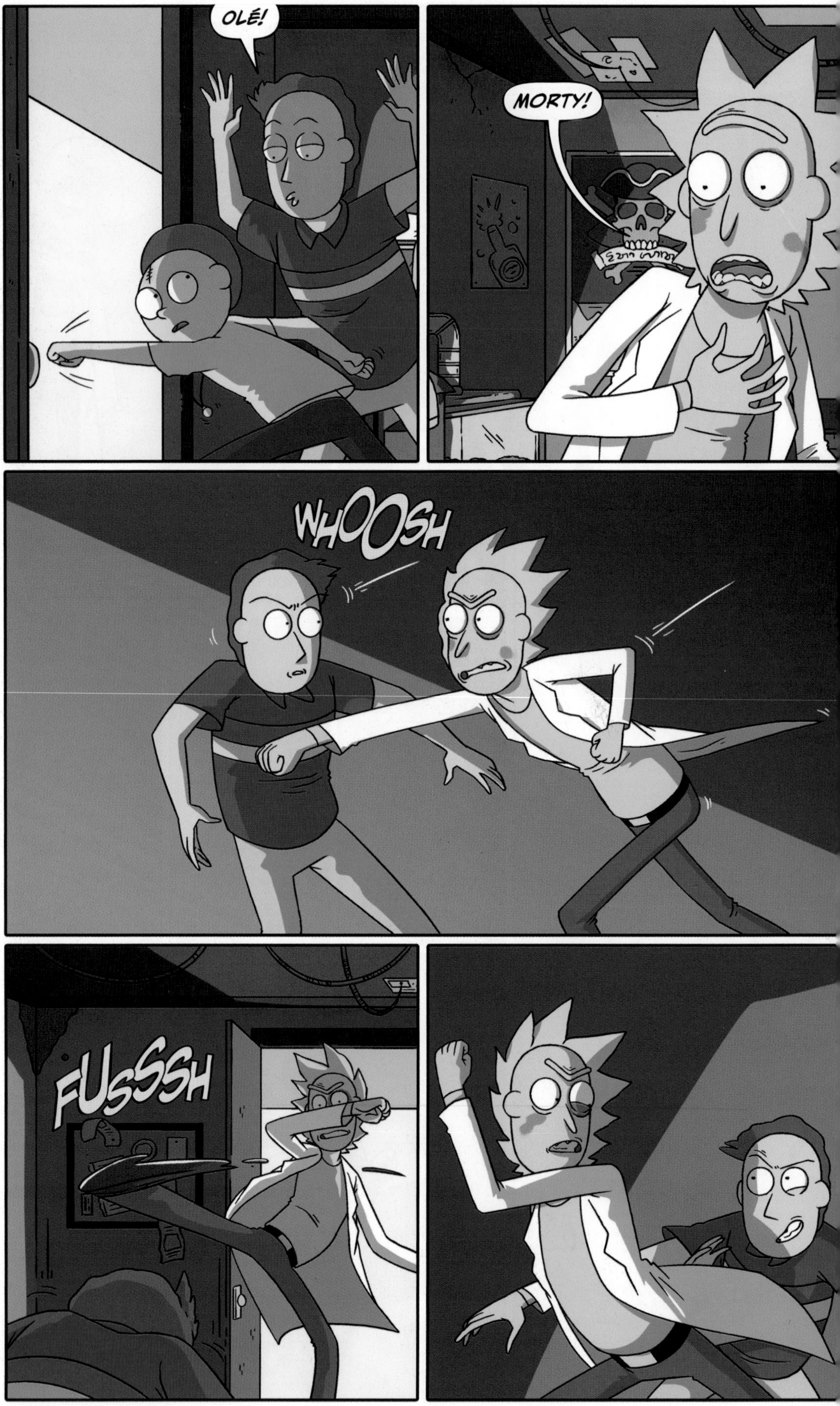
OLÉ!
MORTY!
WHOOSH
FUSSSH

MORTY! GODD**N IT!

AW, GEE! SORRY, RICK!

I CAN'T BELIEVE YOU HAD IT IN YOU TO COME AT ME AGAIN, METHUSELAH. YOU TWO ARE A LAUGH A MINUTE.

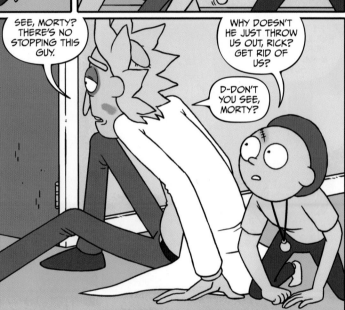

SEE, MORTY? THERE'S NO STOPPING THIS GUY.

WHY DOESN'T HE JUST THROW US OUT, RICK? GET RID OF US?

D-DON'T YOU SEE, MORTY?

"WE'RE NO THREAT TO HIM. WE'RE LESS THAN FLIES.

"WE'RE NOT EVEN WORTH THAT EFFORT."

AT LEAST WE WERE ABLE TO KEEP SUMMER SAFE, MORTY. DOOFUS JERRY WAS LOOKING AT HER LIKE SHE WAS SUNDAY BRUNCH.

ARE YOU SURE SHE'S SAFE IN HERE?

SURE, MORTY. SHE'S SUPER SAFE IN THE LITTLE POCKET DIMENSION I MADE FOR HER.

I-I THOUGHT YOU HAD JUST LIKE SHRUNK HER DOWN, RICK. M-MADE HER A TINY SUMMER.

BEING SMALLER ISN'T SAFER, MORTY. SHE'S IN A SORT OF DIMENSIONAL PANIC ROOM WITH A DOOR ONLY SHE CAN OPEN.

Y-YOU KNOW SHE--URRRP-- DIDN'T WANT TO GO IN THERE, BUT SHE'S GOT A LITTLE FRIDGE, WI-FI, AND SHE CAN SEE OUT, MORTY. SHE-SHE CAN SEE WHAT A DIRE SITUATION IT IS OUT HERE.

OH MAN, UH-OH, SHE CAN SEE OUT HERE FROM THERE?

DIRTY KNOTTY DAWGS, DAWG.

LE DEE'S DOUBLE "D"

WUT WUT IN T HAS A NE

OKAY, HERE WE GO! A LITTLE OF THAT GOOD OLD PRIVATE MORTY TIME.

I'M IN MY HAPPY PLACE. I'M IN MY HAPPY PLACE. I'M IN MY HAPPY PLACE. I'M--

OH BOY, THERE'S THAT CENTERFOLD. SOMEONE'S B-BEEN A NAUGHTY GIRL, ALL RIGHT.

MORTY, THIS GUY IS ON A WHOLE DIFFERENT LEVEL. HE'S MESSING UP THE NATURAL ORDER OF THINGS.

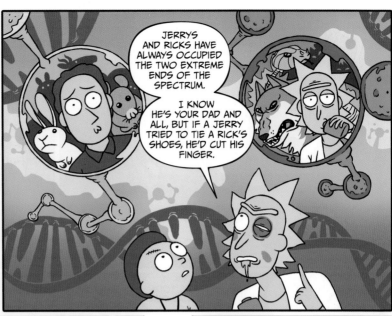

JERRYS AND RICKS HAVE ALWAYS OCCUPIED THE TWO EXTREME ENDS OF THE SPECTRUM.

I KNOW HE'S YOUR DAD AND ALL, BUT IF A JERRY TRIED TO TIE A RICK'S SHOES, HE'D CUT HIS FINGER.

WELL, *UH, GEE*, I MEAN IF A RICK IS ALWAYS THE SOLUTION TO A JERRY, MAYBE WE NEED MORE RICKS?

WH-WH-WHAT ARE YOU SUGGESTING, MORTY?

THE COUNCIL?

NO WAY, MORTY.

IF I WANTED TO HANG OUT WITH A BUNCH OF BUTTHEADS I'D GO BACK TO BETA B-45.

THIS CHILI IS SO DELICIOUS!

I CAN'T BELIEVE THEY SERVED ME WITHOUT A SPOON.

JUST DRINK IT STRAIGHT OUT OF THE BOWL!

OH MAN. HA HA. HERE WE GO!

SLURP

HOLY CRAP, YOU'RE GETTING IT ALL OVER YOU!

LOOK AT THIS MESS!

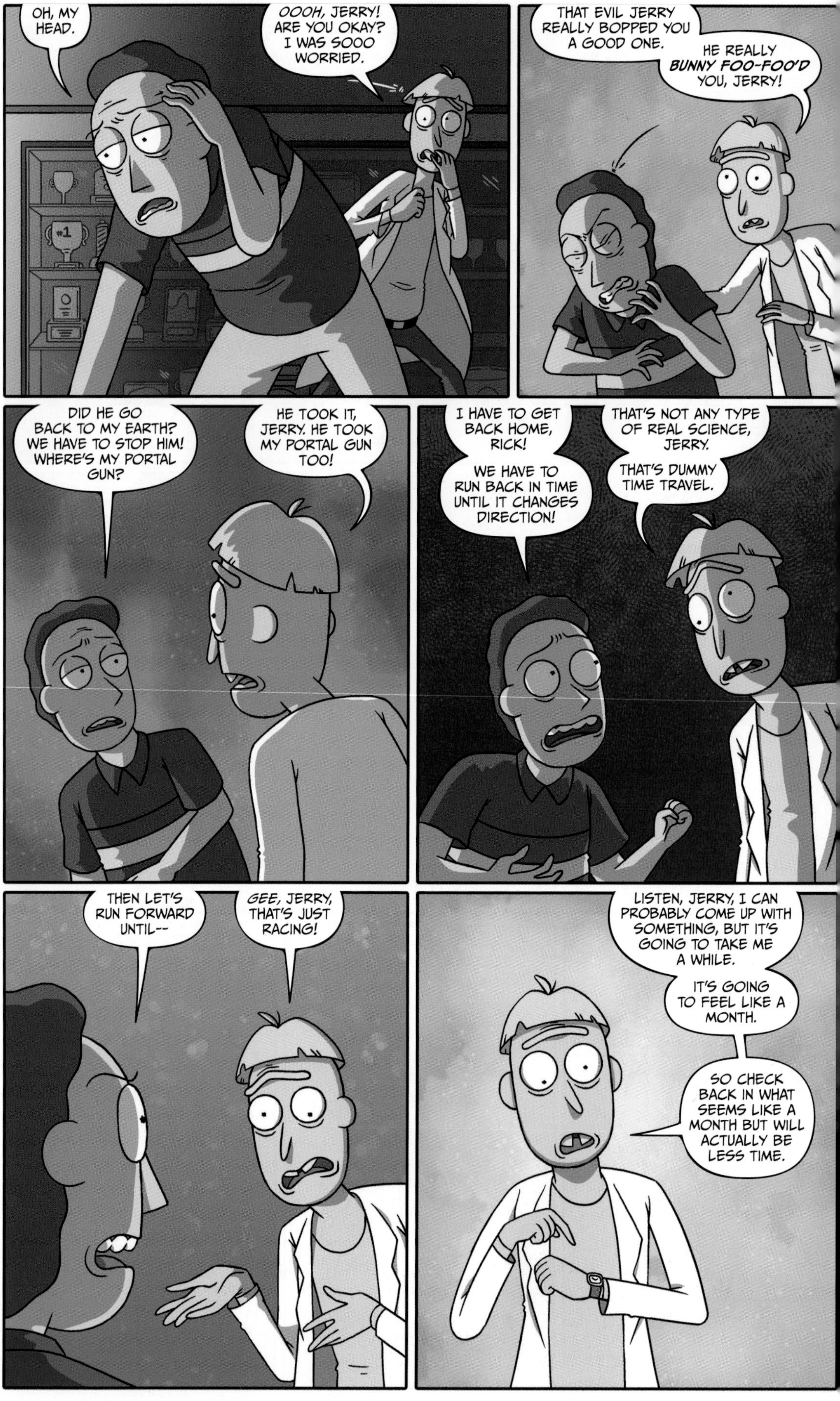

OH, MY HEAD.
OOOH, JERRY! ARE YOU OKAY? I WAS SOOO WORRIED.
THAT EVIL JERRY REALLY BOPPED YOU A GOOD ONE.
HE REALLY BUNNY FOO-FOO'D YOU, JERRY!
DID HE GO BACK TO MY EARTH? WE HAVE TO STOP HIM! WHERE'S MY PORTAL GUN?
HE TOOK IT, JERRY. HE TOOK MY PORTAL GUN TOO!
I HAVE TO GET BACK HOME, RICK!
WE HAVE TO RUN BACK IN TIME UNTIL IT CHANGES DIRECTION!
THAT'S NOT ANY TYPE OF REAL SCIENCE, JERRY.
THAT'S DUMMY TIME TRAVEL.
THEN LET'S RUN FORWARD UNTIL--
GEE, JERRY, THAT'S JUST RACING!
LISTEN, JERRY, I CAN PROBABLY COME UP WITH SOMETHING, BUT IT'S GOING TO TAKE ME A WHILE.
IT'S GOING TO FEEL LIKE A MONTH.
SO CHECK BACK IN WHAT SEEMS LIKE A MONTH BUT WILL ACTUALLY BE LESS TIME.

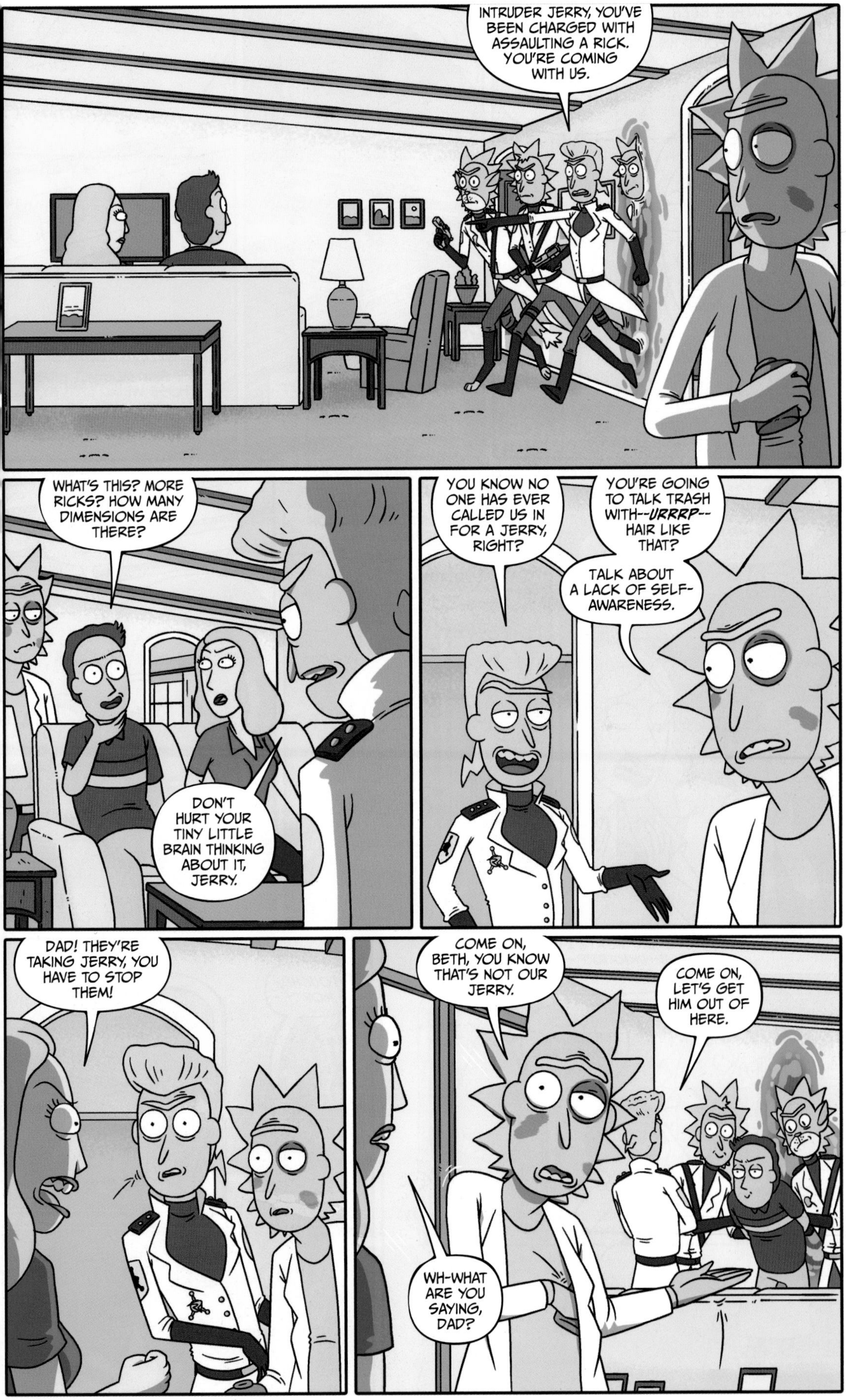
INTRUDER JERRY, YOU'VE BEEN CHARGED WITH ASSAULTING A RICK. YOU'RE COMING WITH US.
WHAT'S THIS? MORE RICKS? HOW MANY DIMENSIONS ARE THERE?
DON'T HURT YOUR TINY LITTLE BRAIN THINKING ABOUT IT, JERRY.
YOU KNOW NO ONE HAS EVER CALLED US IN FOR A JERRY, RIGHT?
YOU'RE GOING TO TALK TRASH WITH--URRRP-- HAIR LIKE THAT?
TALK ABOUT A LACK OF SELF-AWARENESS.
DAD! THEY'RE TAKING JERRY, YOU HAVE TO STOP THEM!
COME ON, BETH, YOU KNOW THAT'S NOT OUR JERRY.
COME ON, LET'S GET HIM OUT OF HERE.
WH-WHAT ARE YOU SAYING, DAD?

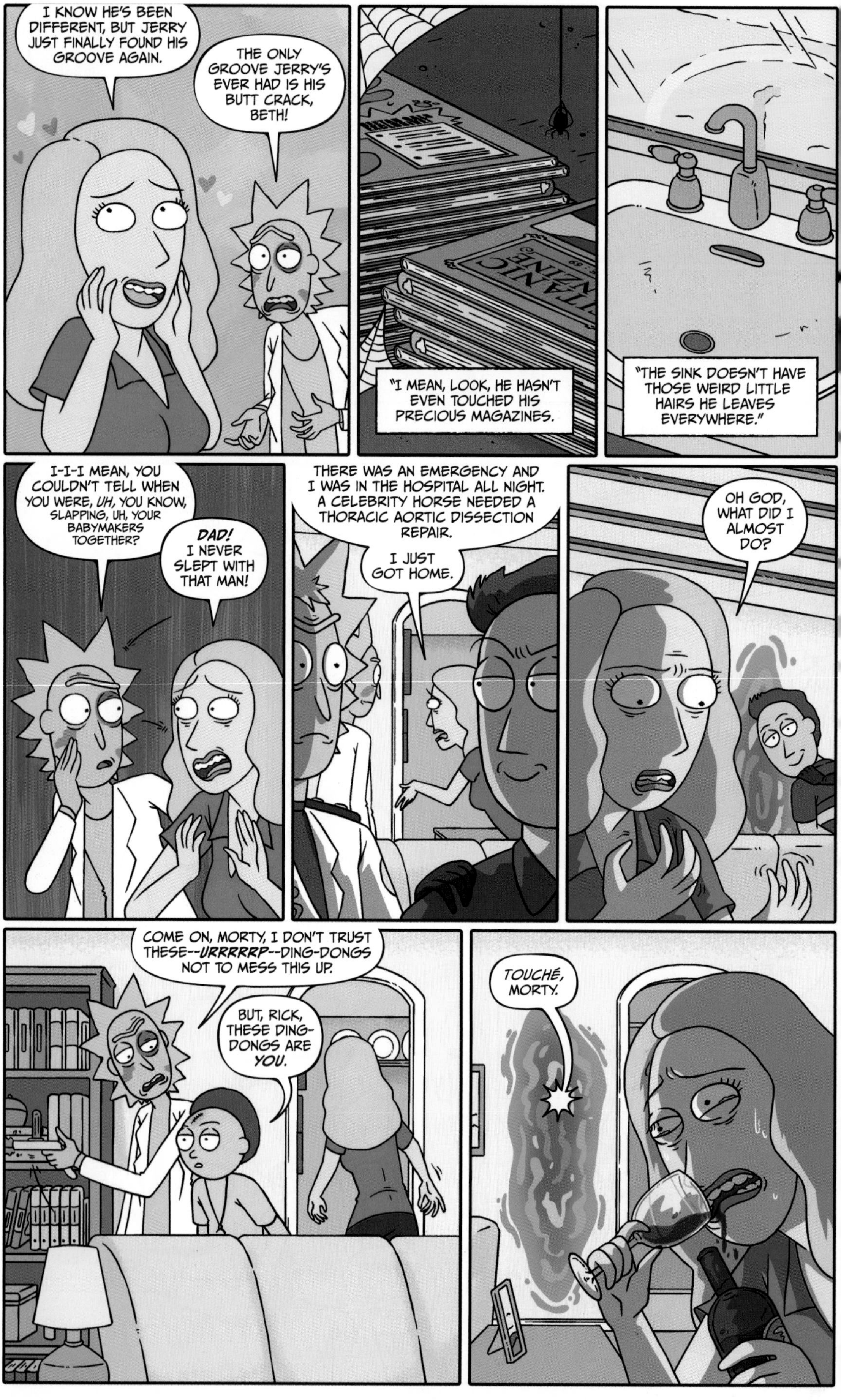
I KNOW HE'S BEEN DIFFERENT, BUT JERRY JUST FINALLY FOUND HIS GROOVE AGAIN.
THE ONLY GROOVE JERRY'S EVER HAD IS HIS BUTT CRACK, BETH!
"I MEAN, LOOK, HE HASN'T EVEN TOUCHED HIS PRECIOUS MAGAZINES.
"THE SINK DOESN'T HAVE THOSE WEIRD LITTLE HAIRS HE LEAVES EVERYWHERE."
I-I-I MEAN, YOU COULDN'T TELL WHEN YOU WERE, *UH,* YOU KNOW, SLAPPING, UH, YOUR BABYMAKERS TOGETHER?
DAD! I NEVER SLEPT WITH THAT MAN!
THERE WAS AN EMERGENCY AND I WAS IN THE HOSPITAL ALL NIGHT. A CELEBRITY HORSE NEEDED A THORACIC AORTIC DISSECTION REPAIR.
I JUST GOT HOME.
OH GOD, WHAT DID I ALMOST DO?
COME ON, MORTY, I DON'T TRUST THESE--***URRRRRP***--DING-DONGS NOT TO MESS THIS UP.
BUT, RICK, THESE DING-DONGS ARE ***YOU.***
TOUCHÉ, MORTY.

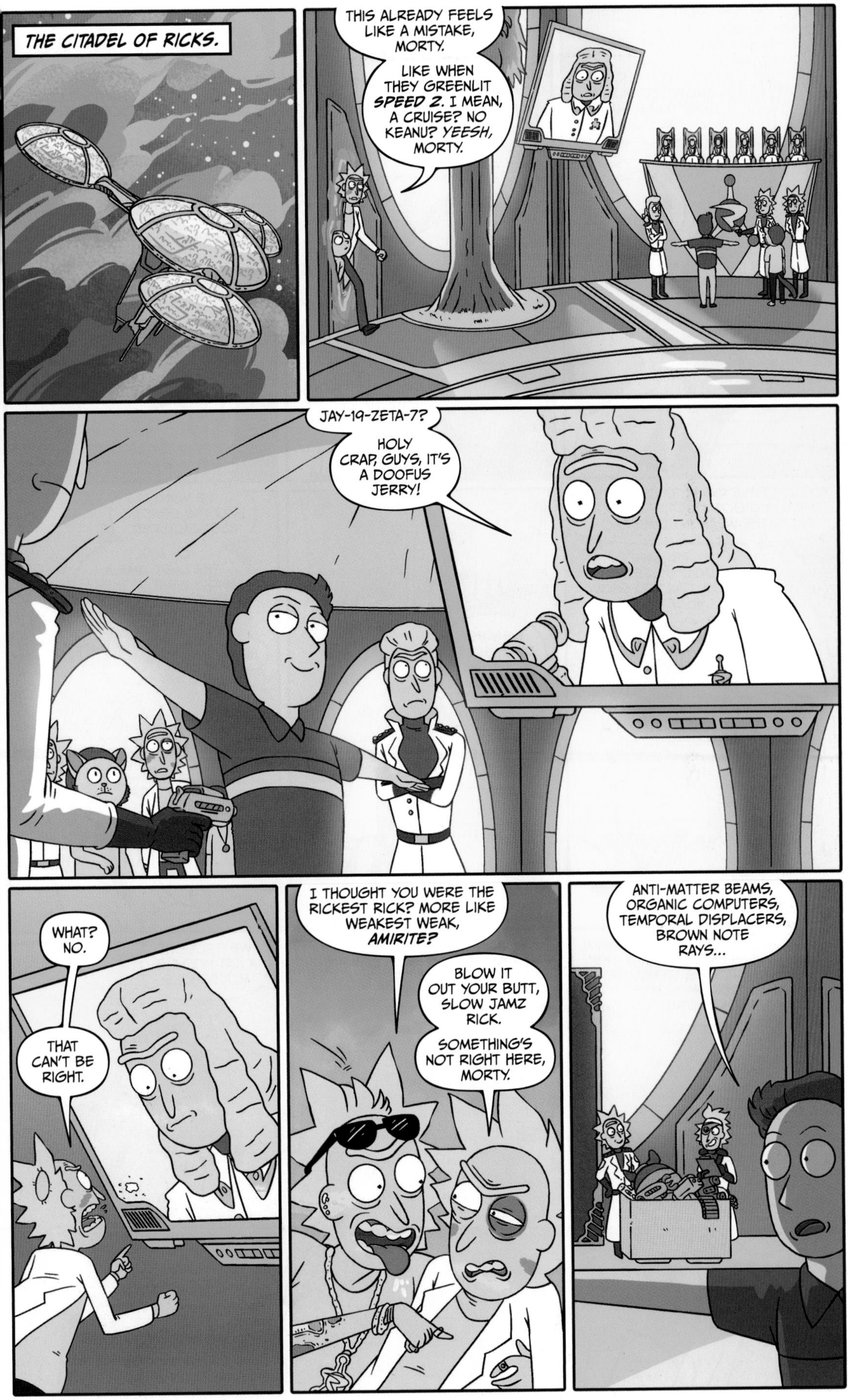
THE CITADEL OF RICKS.
THIS ALREADY FEELS LIKE A MISTAKE, MORTY.
LIKE WHEN THEY GREENLIT SPEED 2. I MEAN, A CRUISE? NO KEANU? YEESH, MORTY.
JAY-19-ZETA-7?
HOLY CRAP, GUYS, IT'S A DOOFUS JERRY!
WHAT? NO.
THAT CAN'T BE RIGHT.
I THOUGHT YOU WERE THE RICKEST RICK? MORE LIKE WEAKEST WEAK, AMIRITE?
BLOW IT OUT YOUR BUTT, SLOW JAMZ RICK.
SOMETHING'S NOT RIGHT HERE, MORTY.
ANTI-MATTER BEAMS, ORGANIC COMPUTERS, TEMPORAL DISPLACERS, BROWN NOTE RAYS...

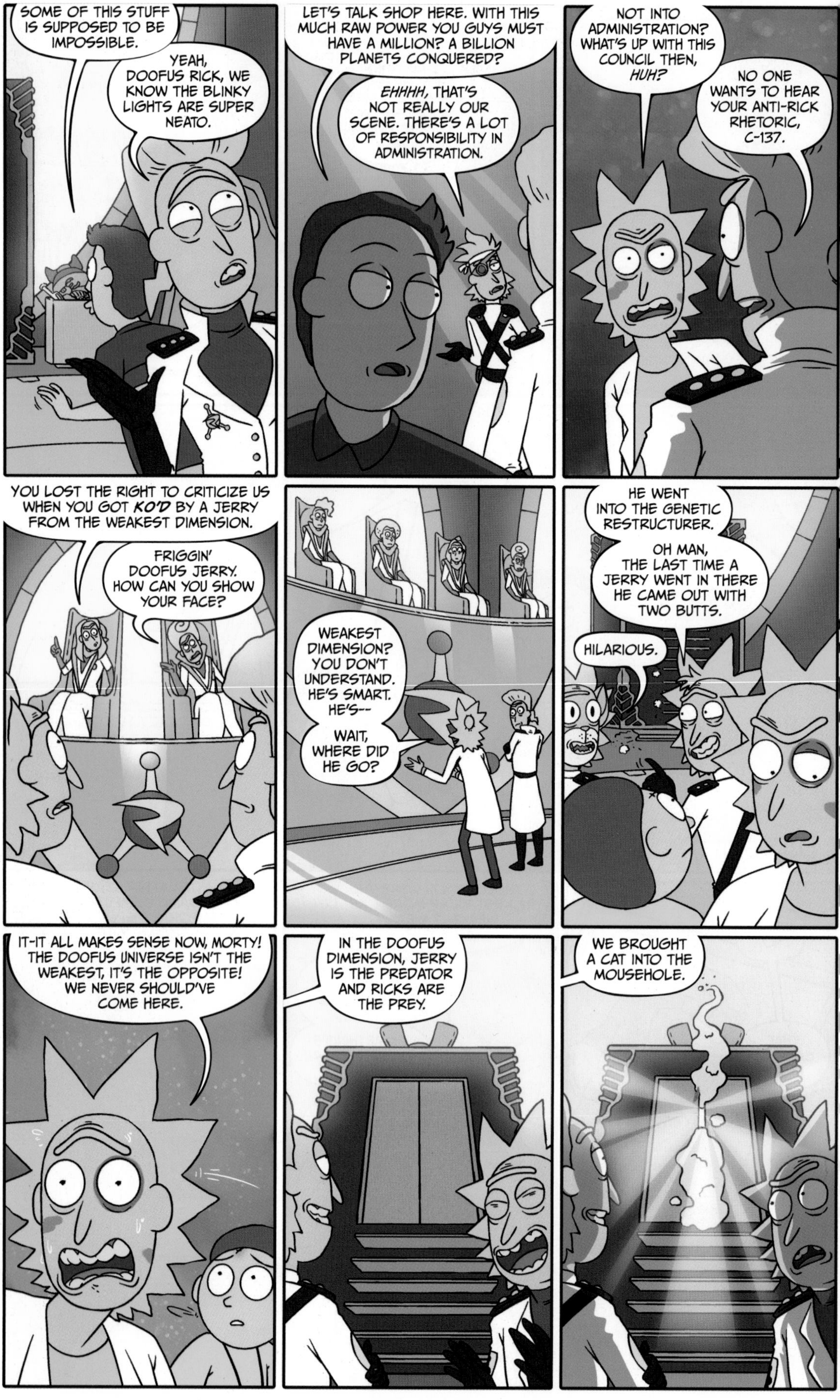
SOME OF THIS STUFF IS SUPPOSED TO BE IMPOSSIBLE.
YEAH, DOOFUS RICK, WE KNOW THE BLINKY LIGHTS ARE SUPER NEATO.
LET'S TALK SHOP HERE. WITH THIS MUCH RAW POWER YOU GUYS MUST HAVE A MILLION? A BILLION PLANETS CONQUERED?
EHHHH, THAT'S NOT REALLY OUR SCENE. THERE'S A LOT OF RESPONSIBILITY IN ADMINISTRATION.
NOT INTO ADMINISTRATION? WHAT'S UP WITH THIS COUNCIL THEN, *HUH?*
NO ONE WANTS TO HEAR YOUR ANTI-RICK RHETORIC, C-137.
YOU LOST THE RIGHT TO CRITICIZE US WHEN YOU GOT ***KO'D*** BY A JERRY FROM THE WEAKEST DIMENSION.
FRIGGIN' DOOFUS JERRY. HOW CAN YOU SHOW YOUR FACE?
WEAKEST DIMENSION? YOU DON'T UNDERSTAND. HE'S SMART. HE'S--
WAIT, WHERE DID HE GO?
HE WENT INTO THE GENETIC RESTRUCTURER.
OH MAN, THE LAST TIME A JERRY WENT IN THERE HE CAME OUT WITH TWO BUTTS.
HILARIOUS.
IT-IT ALL MAKES SENSE NOW, MORTY! THE DOOFUS UNIVERSE ISN'T THE WEAKEST, IT'S THE OPPOSITE! WE NEVER SHOULD'VE COME HERE.
IN THE DOOFUS DIMENSION, JERRY IS THE PREDATOR AND RICKS ARE THE PREY.
WE BROUGHT A CAT INTO THE MOUSEHOLE.

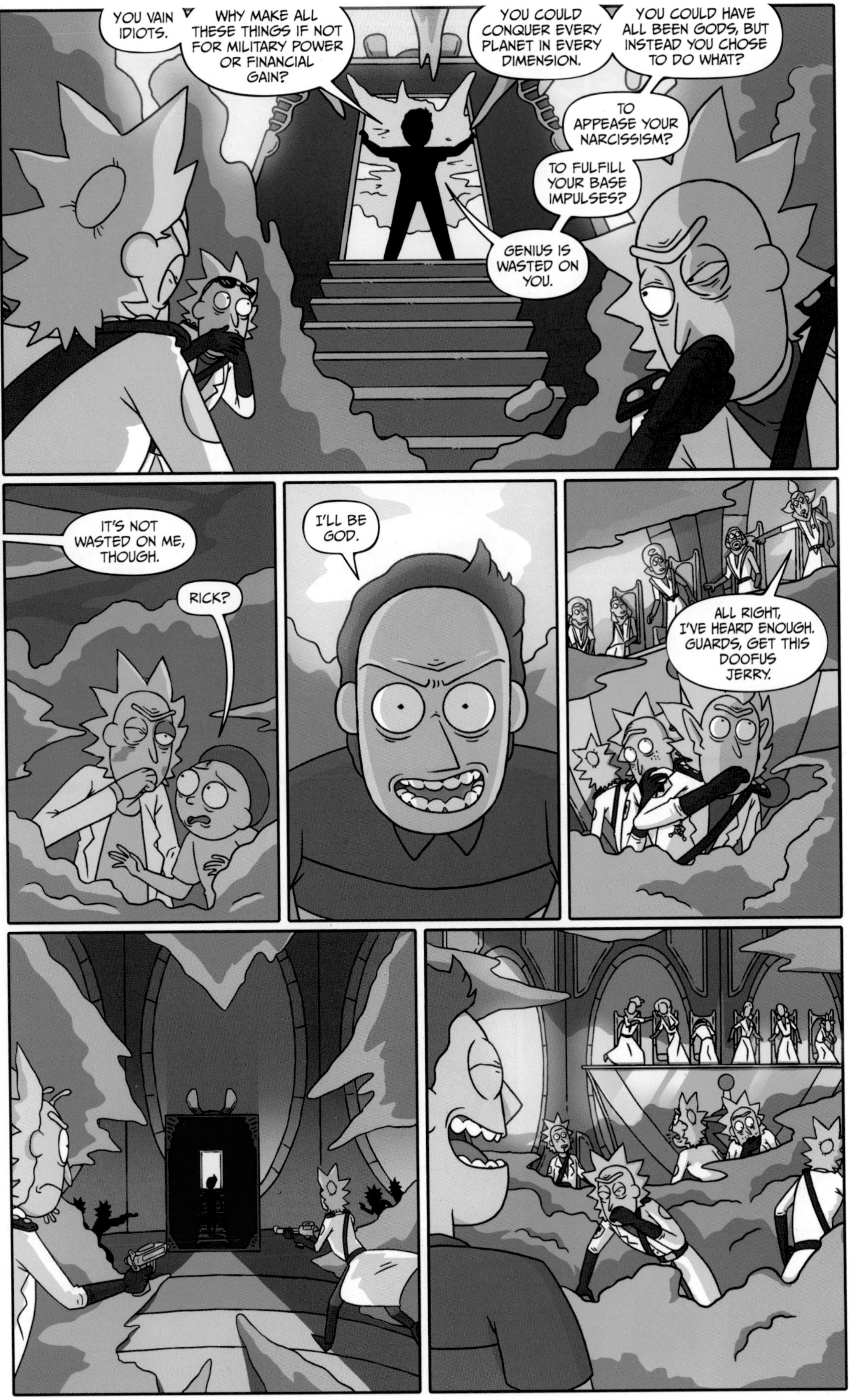
YOU VAIN IDIOTS.
WHY MAKE ALL THESE THINGS IF NOT FOR MILITARY POWER OR FINANCIAL GAIN?
YOU COULD CONQUER EVERY PLANET IN EVERY DIMENSION.
YOU COULD HAVE ALL BEEN GODS, BUT INSTEAD YOU CHOSE TO DO WHAT?
TO APPEASE YOUR NARCISSISM?
TO FULFILL YOUR BASE IMPULSES?
GENIUS IS WASTED ON YOU.
IT'S NOT WASTED ON ME, THOUGH.
RICK?
I'LL BE GOD.
ALL RIGHT, I'VE HEARD ENOUGH. GUARDS, GET THIS DOOFUS JERRY.

IN MY DIMENSION, WE HAD AN INFESTATION OF JAPANESE BEETLES.

IT THREATENED TO ERADICATE EVERYTHING. FOOD SUPPLIES, FORESTS.

WE DISCOVERED, QUITE BY ACCIDENT, THAT THE WHITE GERANIUM CREATED A TOXIN THAT WAS PARTICULARLY TOXIC TO THE JAPANESE BEETLE.

WHAT'S HAPPENING TO US?

WHAT IS =COUGH= THIS?

SO I WEAPONIZED THAT TOXIN AND ERADICATED THE BEETLE.

RIGHT NOW I'M DOING THE SAME TO YOU.

I'VE ALTERED MY PHEROMONES TO BE PARTICULARLY POISONOUS TO RICKS.

HE'S KILLING US WITH HIS SKIN FARTS!

I'M WALKING DEATH TO YOU ALL NOW.

AW, GEEZ, RICK. OH NO!

DING DING DING

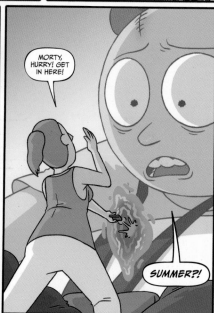

MORTY, HURRY! GET IN HERE!

SUMMER?!

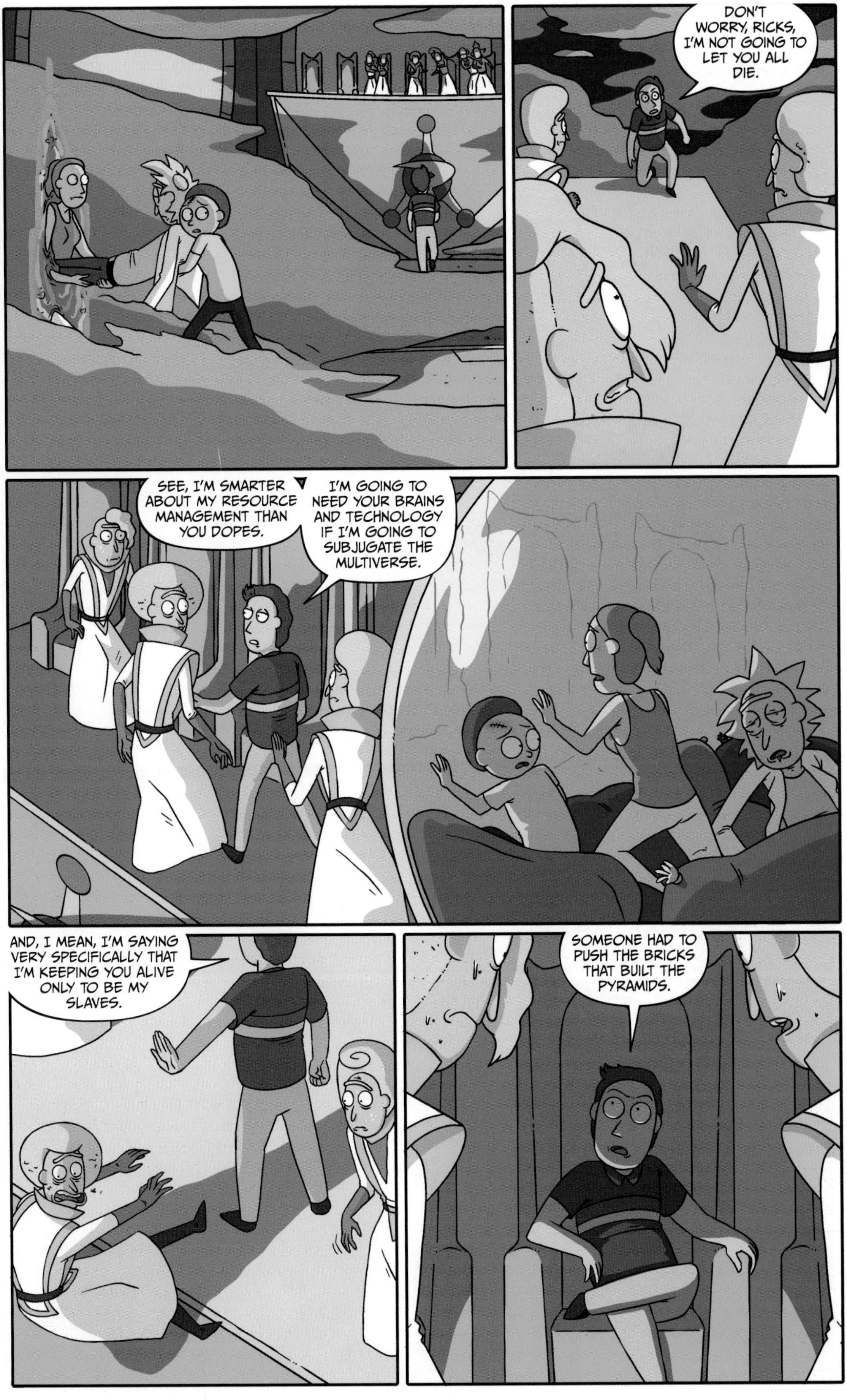
DON'T WORRY, RICKS, I'M NOT GOING TO LET YOU ALL DIE.
SEE, I'M SMARTER ABOUT MY RESOURCE MANAGEMENT THAN YOU DOPES.
I'M GOING TO NEED YOUR BRAINS AND TECHNOLOGY IF I'M GOING TO SUBJUGATE THE MULTIVERSE.
AND, I MEAN, I'M SAYING VERY SPECIFICALLY THAT I'M KEEPING YOU ALIVE ONLY TO BE MY SLAVES.
SOMEONE HAD TO PUSH THE BRICKS THAT BUILT THE PYRAMIDS.

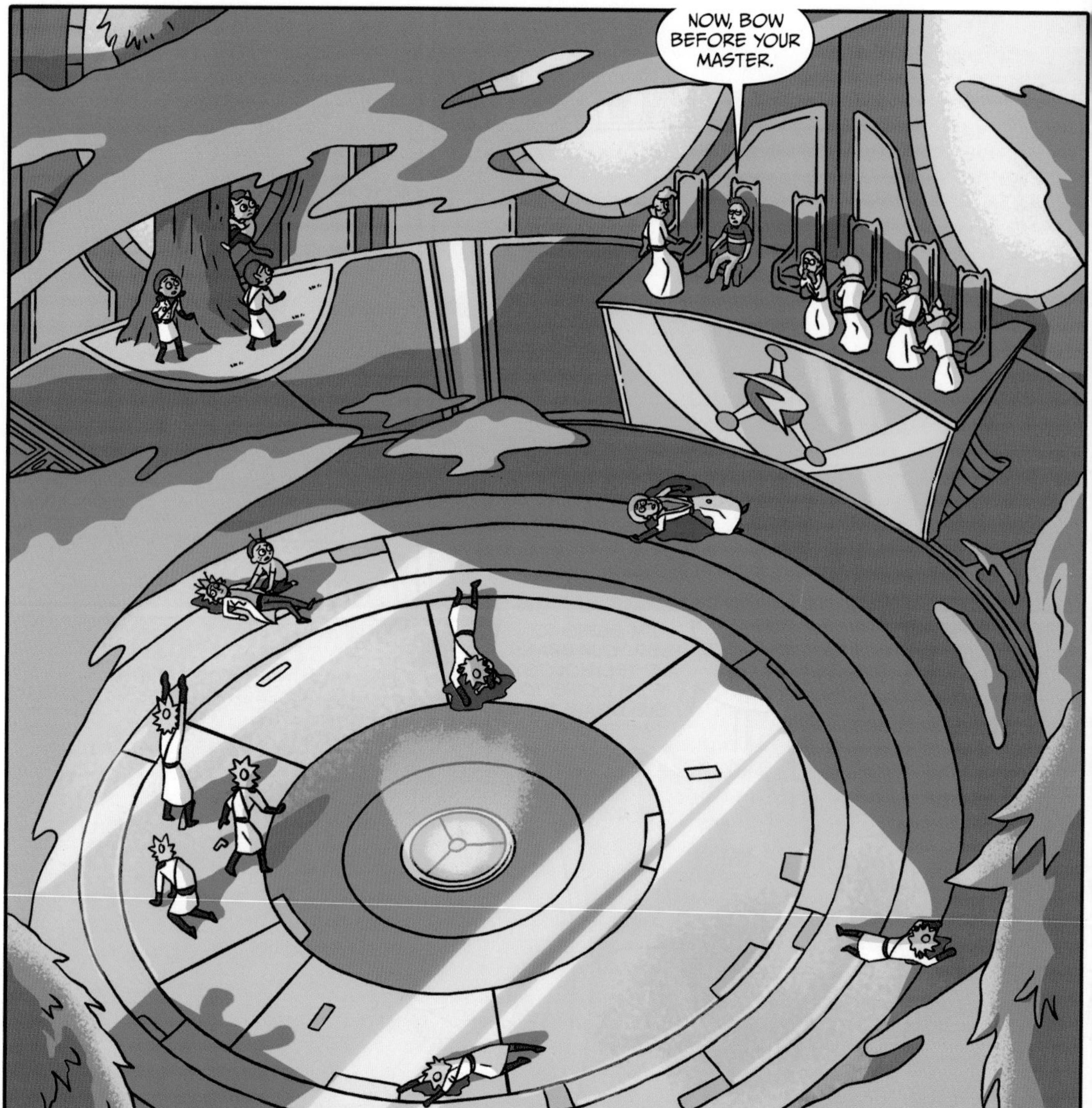
NOW, BOW BEFORE YOUR MASTER.

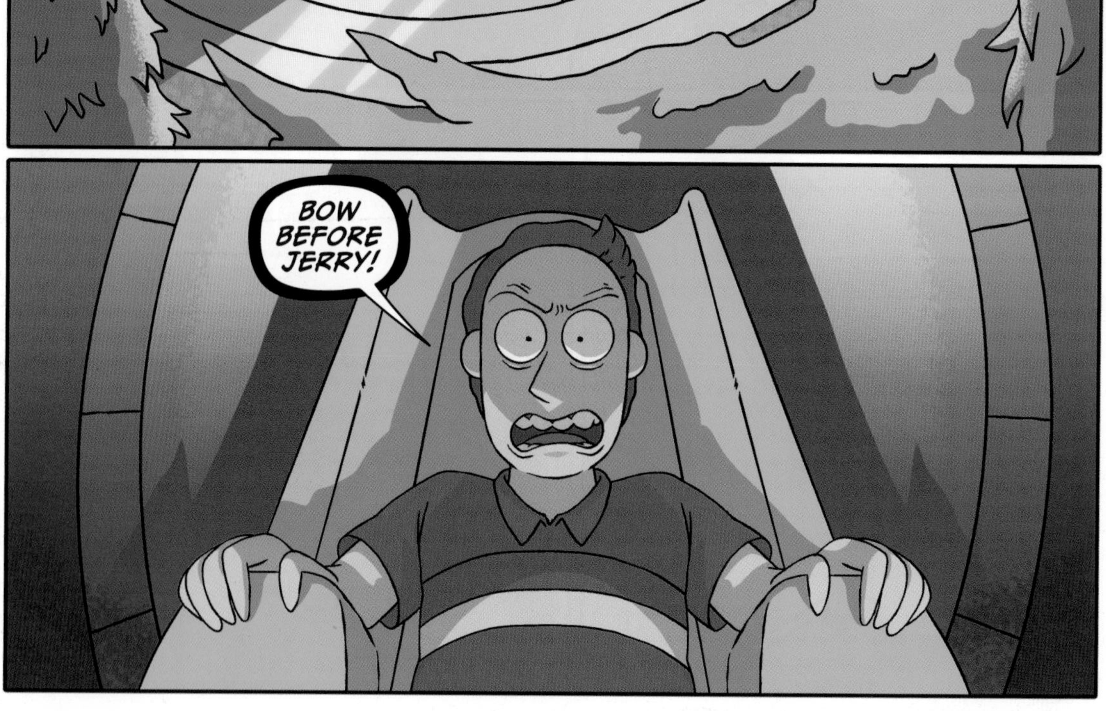
BOW BEFORE JERRY!

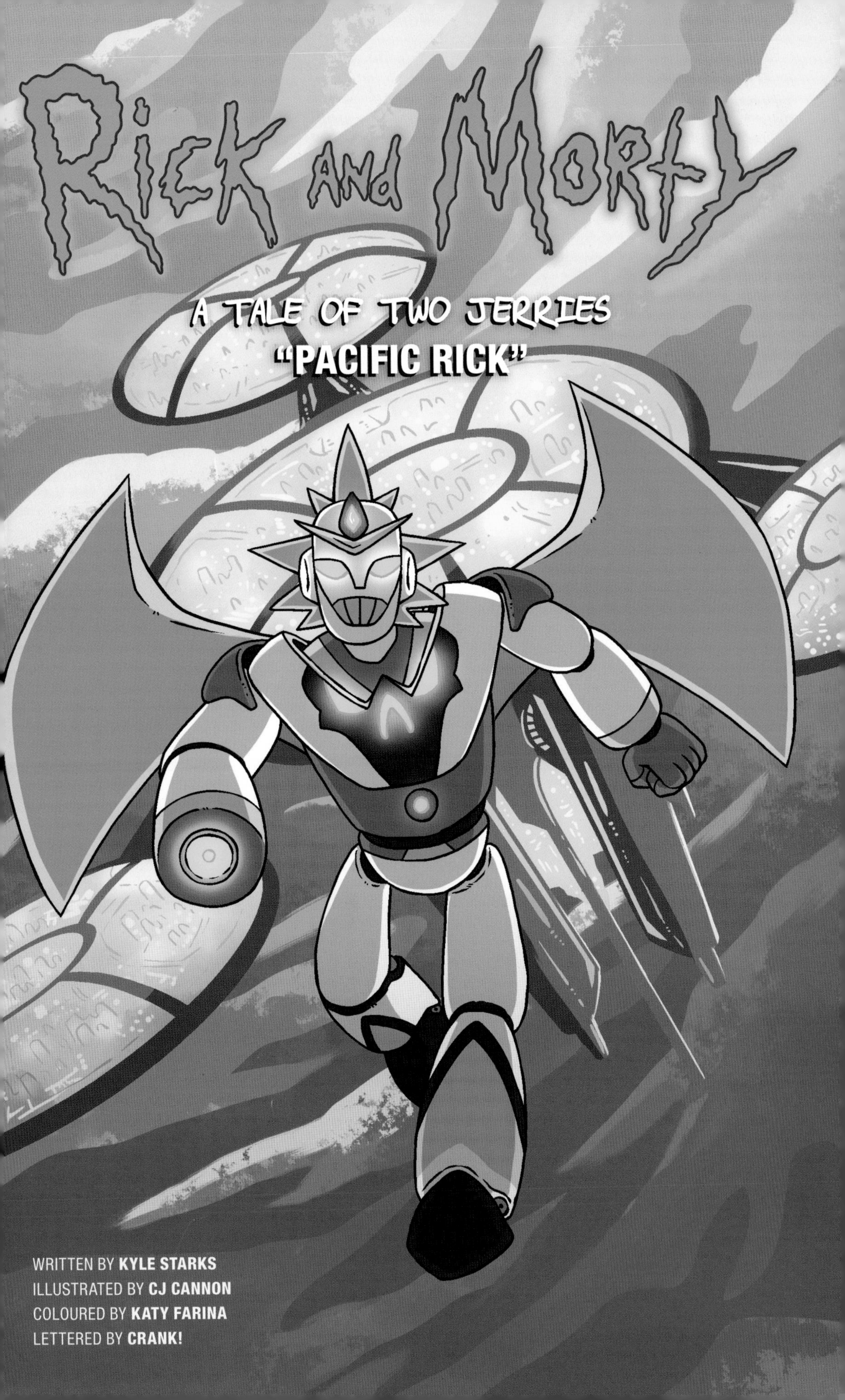
RICK AND MORTY
A TALE OF TWO JERRIES
"PACIFIC RICK"
WRITTEN BY KYLE STARKS
ILLUSTRATED BY CJ CANNON
COLOURED BY KATY FARINA
LETTERED BY CRANK!

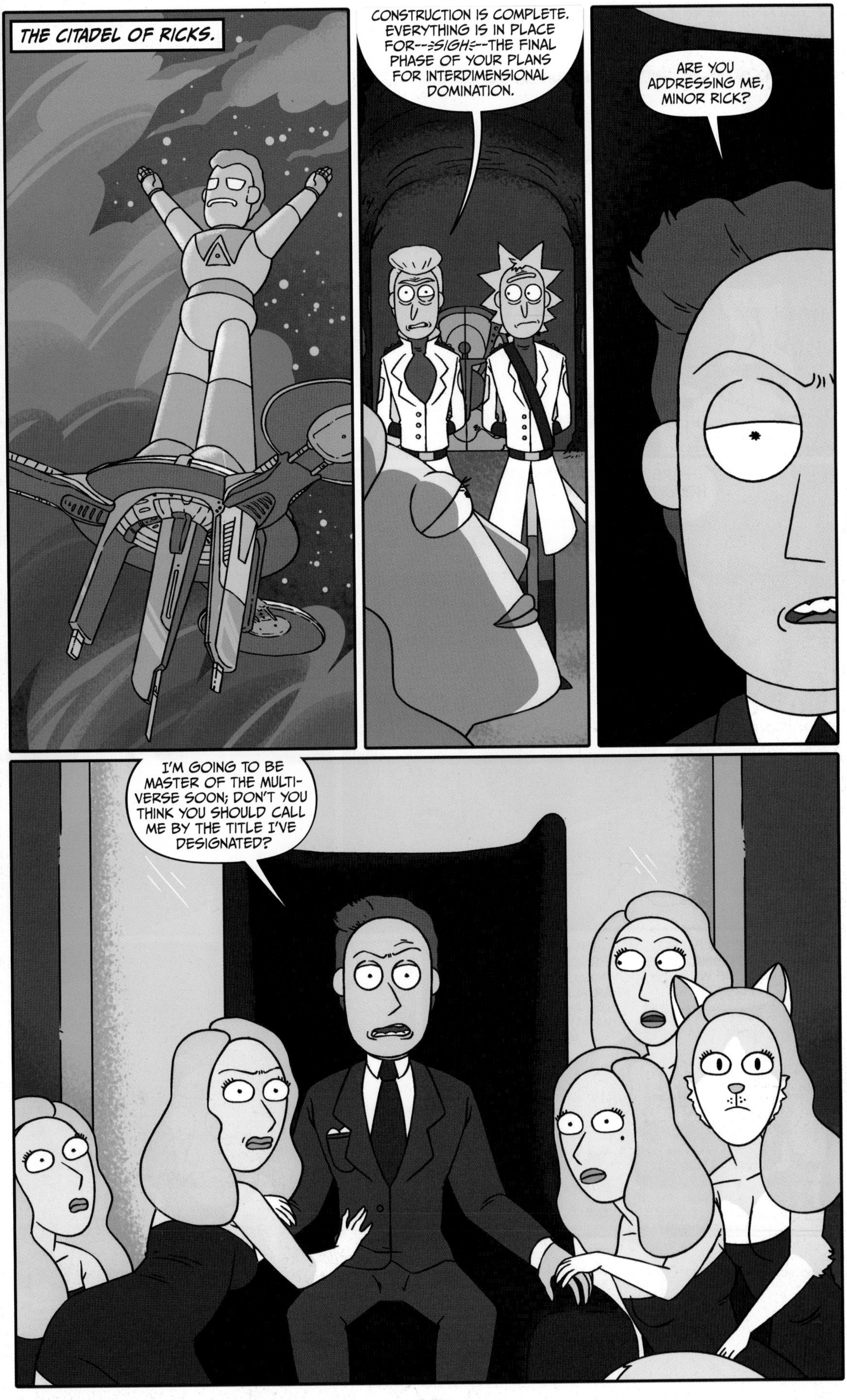
THE CITADEL OF RICKS.
CONSTRUCTION IS COMPLETE. EVERYTHING IS IN PLACE FOR--SIGH--THE FINAL PHASE OF YOUR PLANS FOR INTERDIMENSIONAL DOMINATION.
ARE YOU ADDRESSING ME, MINOR RICK?
I'M GOING TO BE MASTER OF THE MULTI-VERSE SOON; DON'T YOU THINK YOU SHOULD CALL ME BY THE TITLE I'VE DESIGNATED?

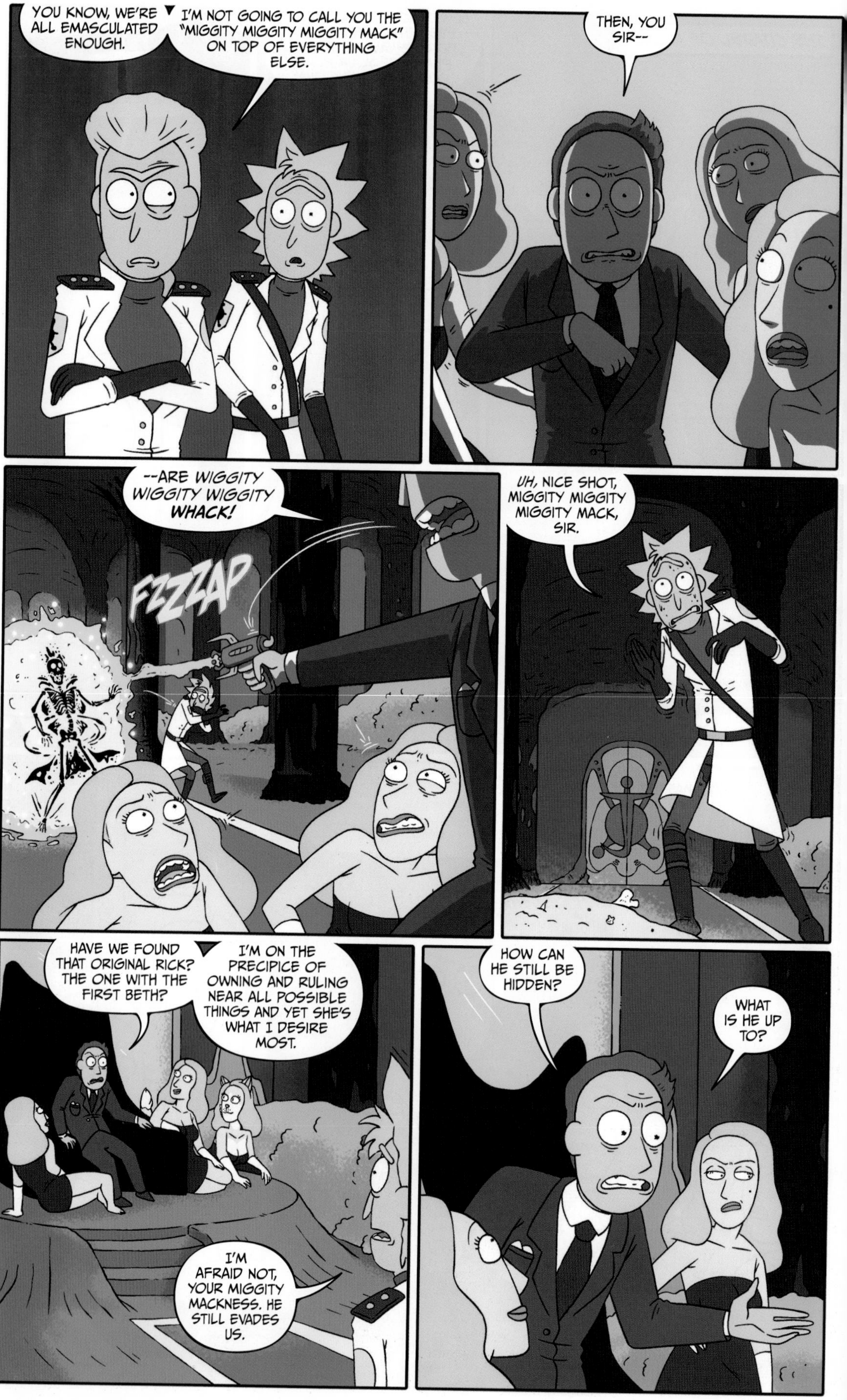
YOU KNOW, WE'RE ALL EMASCULATED ENOUGH.
I'M NOT GOING TO CALL YOU THE "MIGGITY MIGGITY MIGGITY MACK" ON TOP OF EVERYTHING ELSE.
THEN, YOU SIR--
--ARE *WIGGITY WIGGITY WIGGITY* **WHACK!**
FZZZAP
UH, NICE SHOT, MIGGITY MIGGITY MIGGITY MACK, SIR.
HAVE WE FOUND THAT ORIGINAL RICK? THE ONE WITH THE FIRST BETH?
I'M ON THE PRECIPICE OF OWNING AND RULING NEAR ALL POSSIBLE THINGS AND YET SHE'S WHAT I DESIRE MOST.
I'M AFRAID NOT, YOUR MIGGITY MACKNESS. HE STILL EVADES US.
HOW CAN HE STILL BE HIDDEN?
WHAT IS HE UP TO?

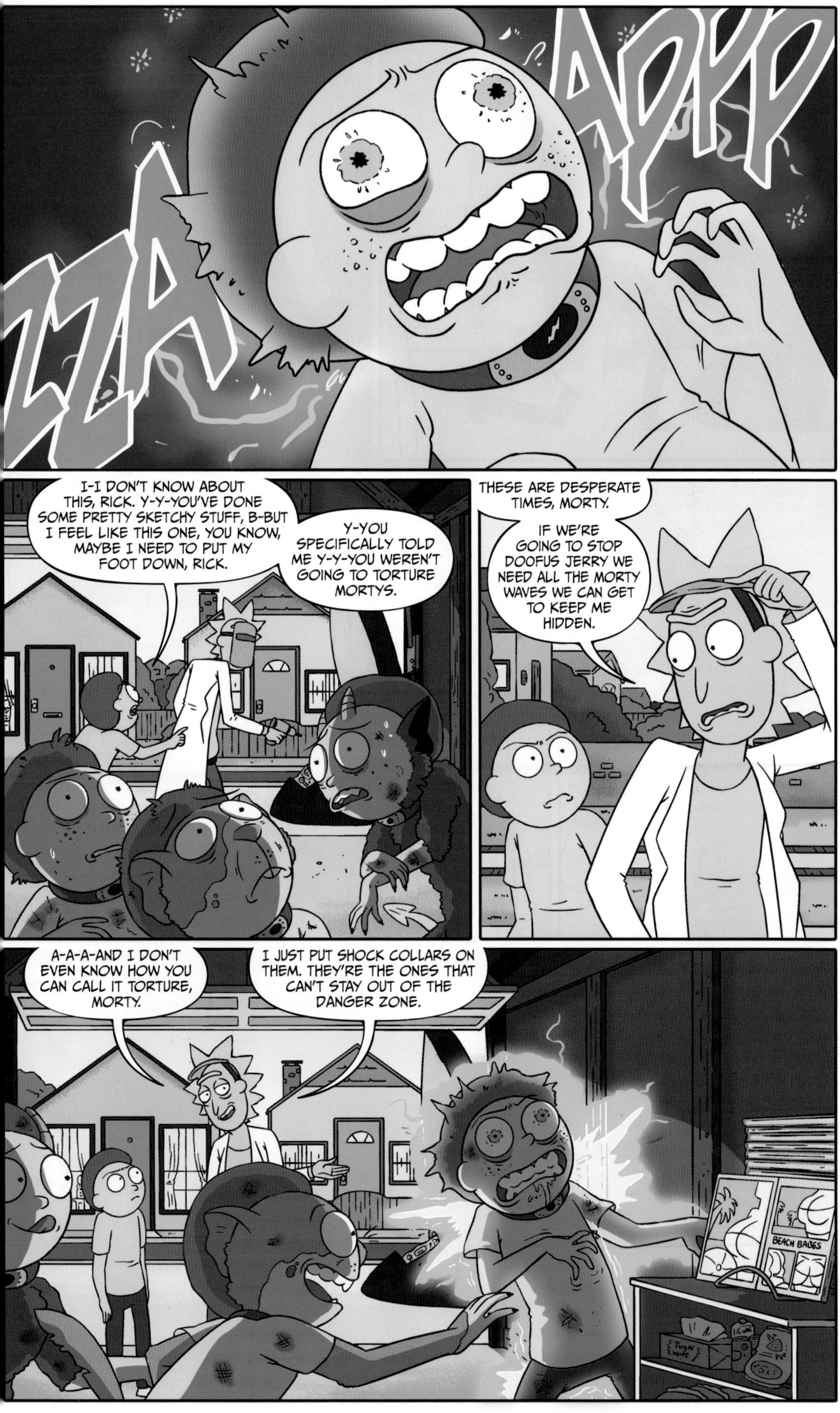
ZZZA
ADDD
I-I DON'T KNOW ABOUT THIS, RICK. Y-Y-YOU'VE DONE SOME PRETTY SKETCHY STUFF, B-BUT I FEEL LIKE THIS ONE, YOU KNOW, MAYBE I NEED TO PUT MY FOOT DOWN, RICK.
Y-YOU SPECIFICALLY TOLD ME Y-Y-YOU WEREN'T GOING TO TORTURE MORTYS.
THESE ARE DESPERATE TIMES, MORTY.
IF WE'RE GOING TO STOP DOOFUS JERRY WE NEED ALL THE MORTY WAVES WE CAN GET TO KEEP ME HIDDEN.
A-A-A-AND I DON'T EVEN KNOW HOW YOU CAN CALL IT TORTURE, MORTY.
I JUST PUT SHOCK COLLARS ON THEM. THEY'RE THE ONES THAT CAN'T STAY OUT OF THE DANGER ZONE.
BEACH BABES

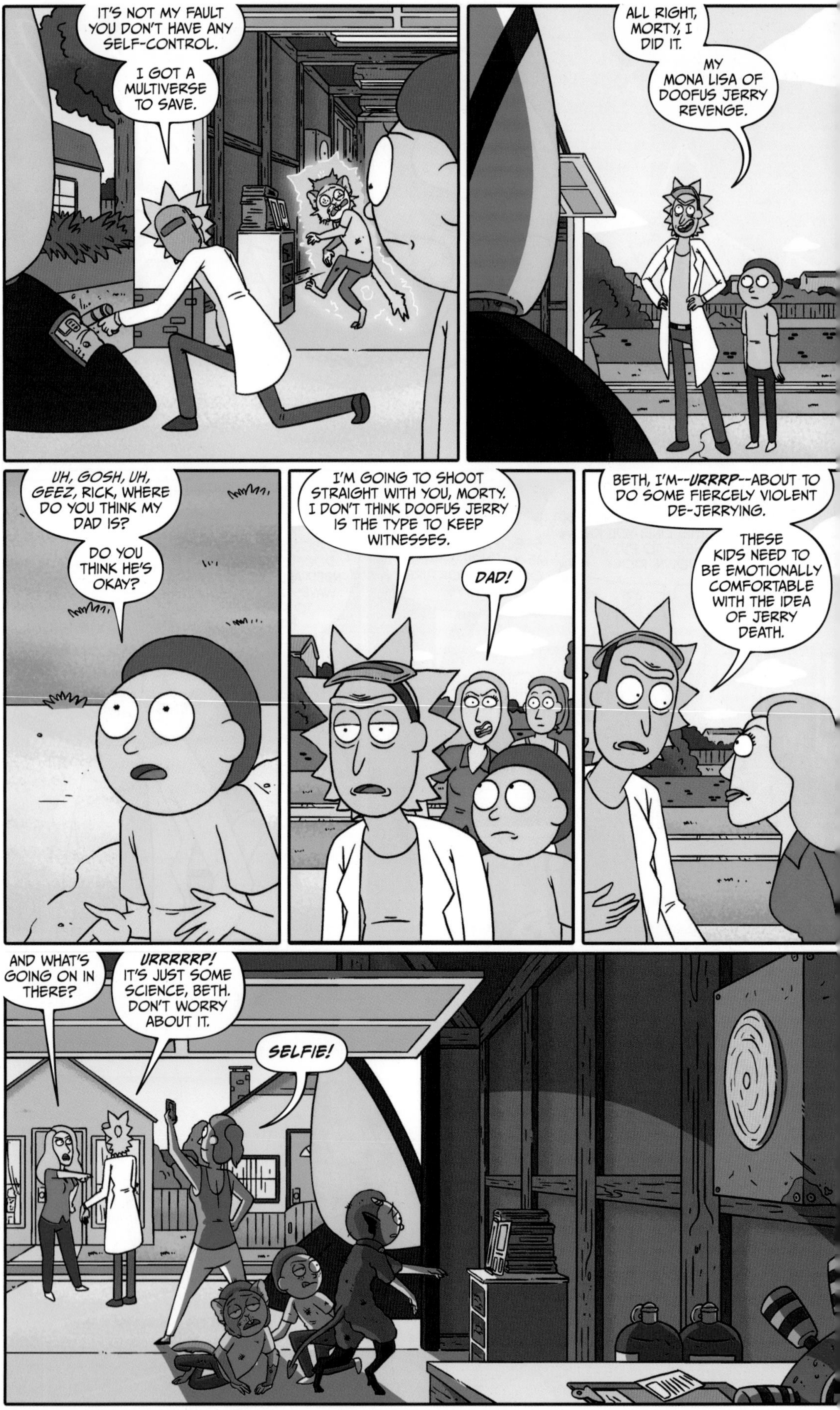

IT'S NOT MY FAULT YOU DON'T HAVE ANY SELF-CONTROL.
I GOT A MULTIVERSE TO SAVE.
ALL RIGHT, MORTY, I DID IT.
MY MONA LISA OF DOOFUS JERRY REVENGE.
UH, GOSH, UH, GEEZ, RICK, WHERE DO YOU THINK MY DAD IS?
DO YOU THINK HE'S OKAY?
I'M GOING TO SHOOT STRAIGHT WITH YOU, MORTY. I DON'T THINK DOOFUS JERRY IS THE TYPE TO KEEP WITNESSES.
DAD!
BETH, I'M--URRRP--ABOUT TO DO SOME FIERCELY VIOLENT DE-JERRYING.
THESE KIDS NEED TO BE EMOTIONALLY COMFORTABLE WITH THE IDEA OF JERRY DEATH.
AND WHAT'S GOING ON IN THERE?
URRRRRP! IT'S JUST SOME SCIENCE, BETH. DON'T WORRY ABOUT IT.
SELFIE!

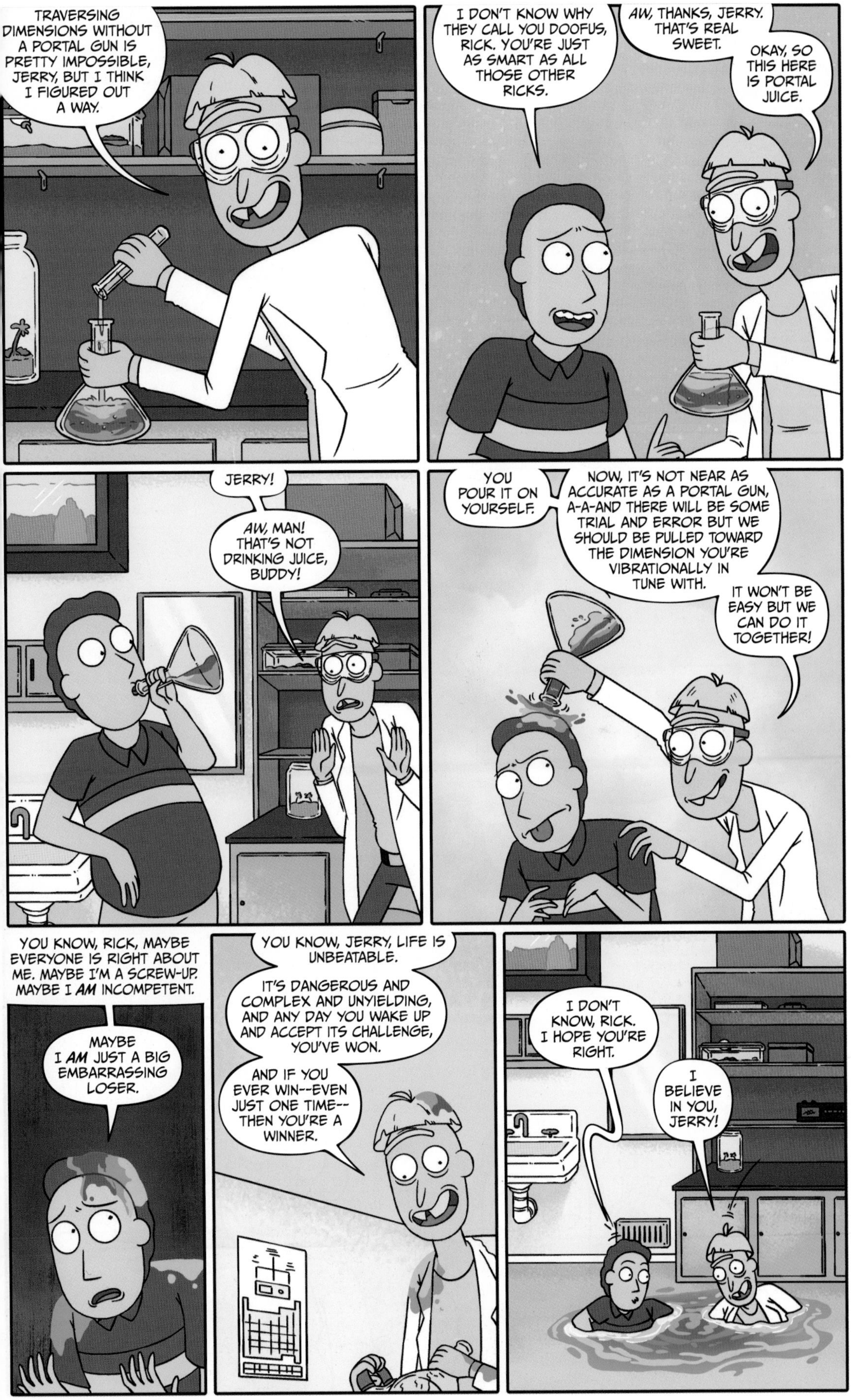
TRAVERSING DIMENSIONS WITHOUT A PORTAL GUN IS PRETTY IMPOSSIBLE, JERRY, BUT I THINK I FIGURED OUT A WAY.
I DON'T KNOW WHY THEY CALL YOU DOOFUS, RICK. YOU'RE JUST AS SMART AS ALL THOSE OTHER RICKS.
AW, THANKS, JERRY. THAT'S REAL SWEET.
OKAY, SO THIS HERE IS PORTAL JUICE.
JERRY!
AW, MAN! THAT'S NOT DRINKING JUICE, BUDDY!
YOU POUR IT ON YOURSELF.
NOW, IT'S NOT NEAR AS ACCURATE AS A PORTAL GUN, A-A-AND THERE WILL BE SOME TRIAL AND ERROR BUT WE SHOULD BE PULLED TOWARD THE DIMENSION YOU'RE VIBRATIONALLY IN TUNE WITH.
IT WON'T BE EASY BUT WE CAN DO IT TOGETHER!
YOU KNOW, RICK, MAYBE EVERYONE IS RIGHT ABOUT ME. MAYBE I'M A SCREW-UP. MAYBE I AM INCOMPETENT.
MAYBE I AM JUST A BIG EMBARRASSING LOSER.
YOU KNOW, JERRY, LIFE IS UNBEATABLE.
IT'S DANGEROUS AND COMPLEX AND UNYIELDING, AND ANY DAY YOU WAKE UP AND ACCEPT ITS CHALLENGE, YOU'VE WON.
AND IF YOU EVER WIN--EVEN JUST ONE TIME--THEN YOU'RE A WINNER.
I DON'T KNOW, RICK. I HOPE YOU'RE RIGHT.
I BELIEVE IN YOU, JERRY!

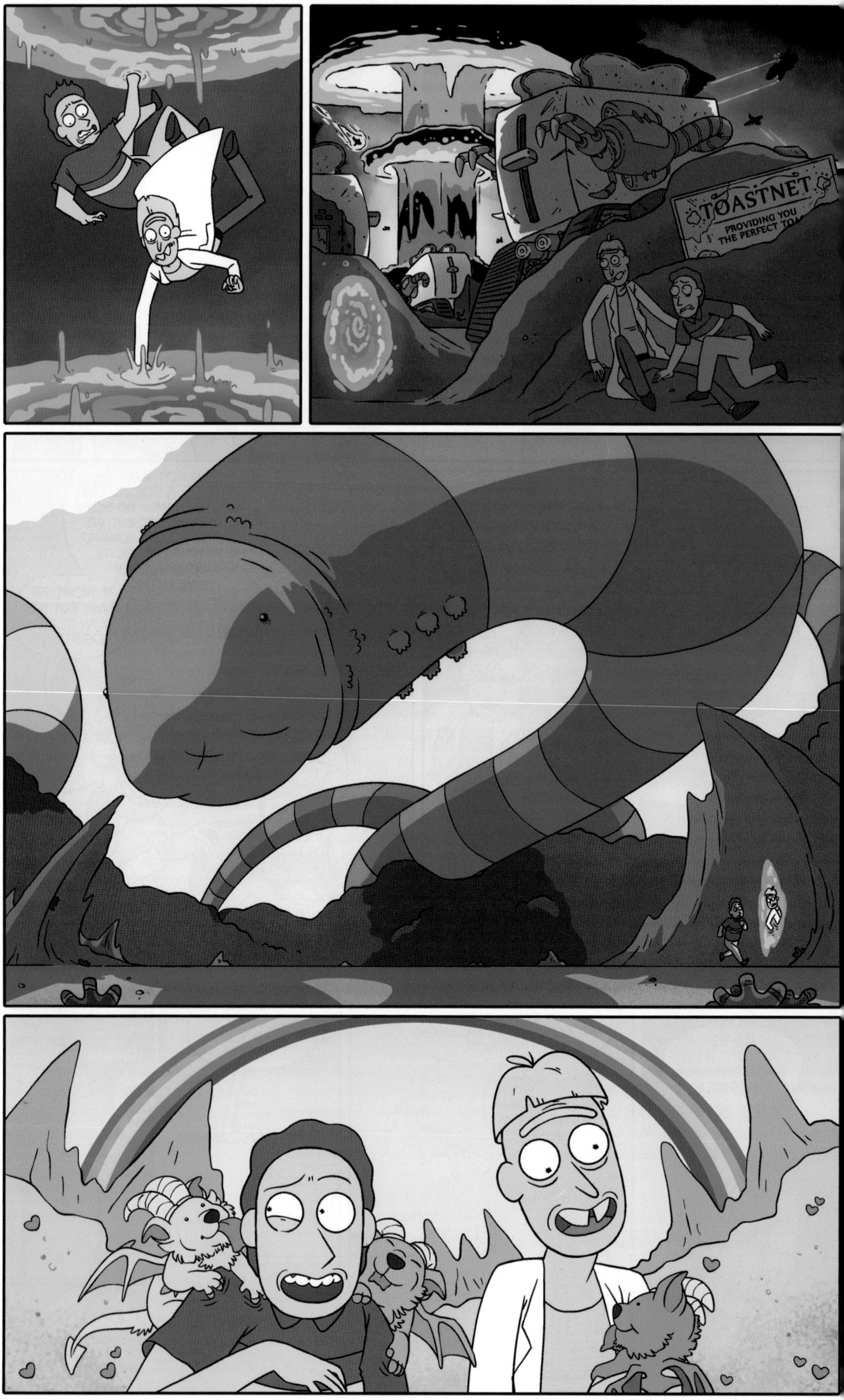
TOASTNET
PROVIDING YOU
THE PERFECT

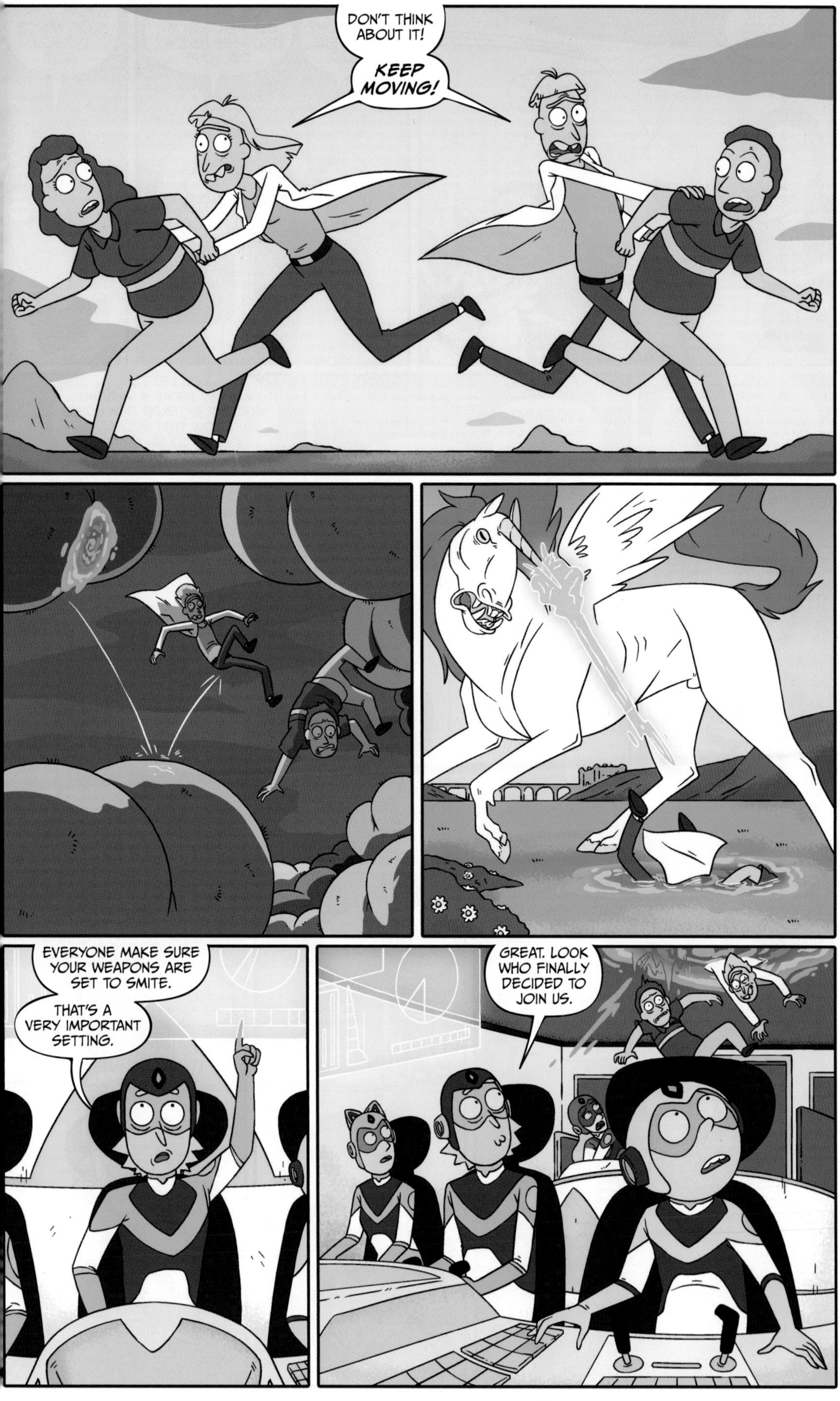
DON'T THINK ABOUT IT!
KEEP MOVING!
EVERYONE MAKE SURE YOUR WEAPONS ARE SET TO SMITE.
THAT'S A VERY IMPORTANT SETTING.
GREAT. LOOK WHO FINALLY DECIDED TO JOIN US.

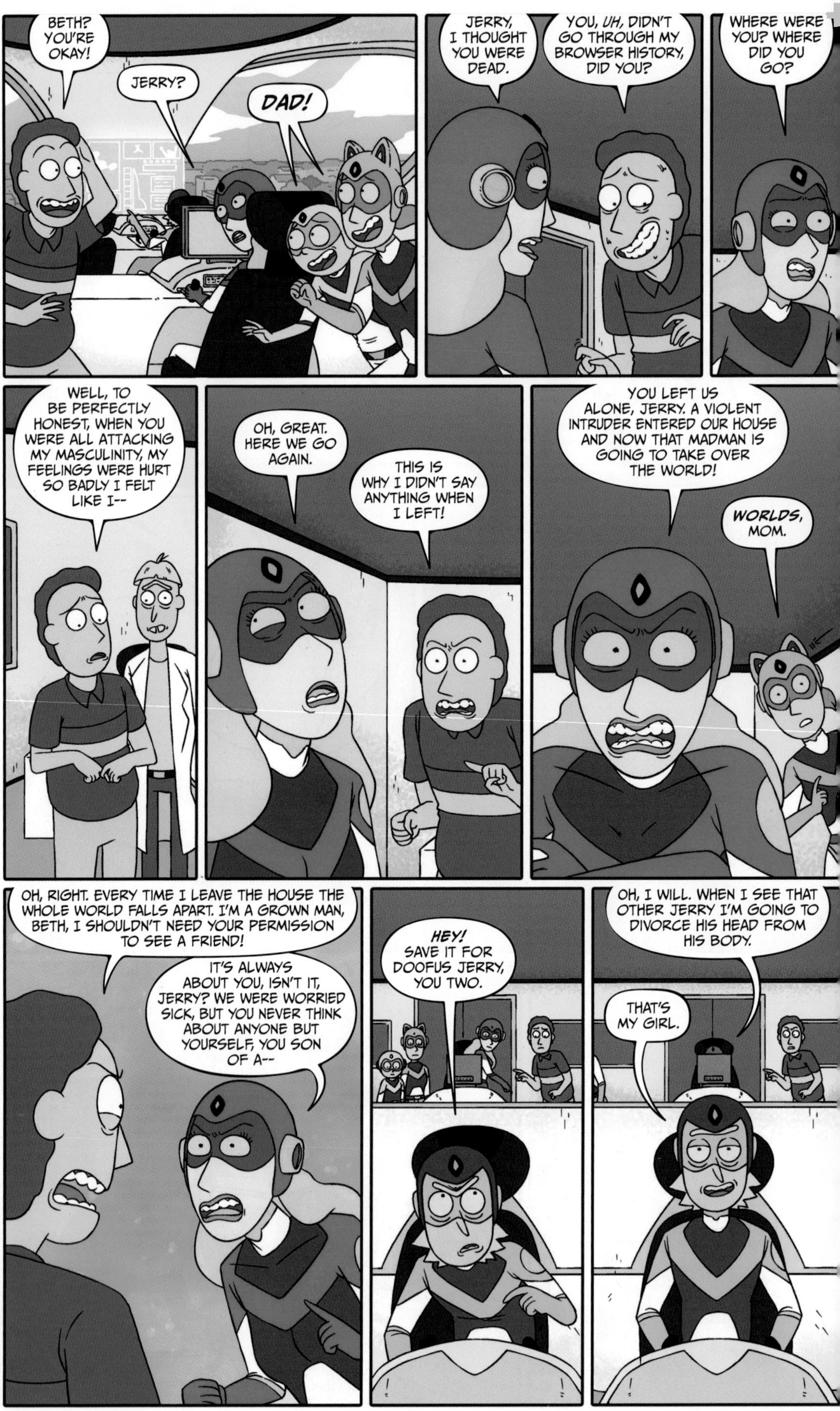
BETH? YOU'RE OKAY!
JERRY?
DAD!
JERRY, I THOUGHT YOU WERE DEAD.
YOU, UH, DIDN'T GO THROUGH MY BROWSER HISTORY, DID YOU?
WHERE WERE YOU? WHERE DID YOU GO?
WELL, TO BE PERFECTLY HONEST, WHEN YOU WERE ALL ATTACKING MY MASCULINITY, MY FEELINGS WERE HURT SO BADLY I FELT LIKE I--
OH, GREAT. HERE WE GO AGAIN.
THIS IS WHY I DIDN'T SAY ANYTHING WHEN I LEFT!
YOU LEFT US ALONE, JERRY. A VIOLENT INTRUDER ENTERED OUR HOUSE AND NOW THAT MADMAN IS GOING TO TAKE OVER THE WORLD!
WORLDS, MOM.
OH, RIGHT. EVERY TIME I LEAVE THE HOUSE THE WHOLE WORLD FALLS APART. I'M A GROWN MAN, BETH, I SHOULDN'T NEED YOUR PERMISSION TO SEE A FRIEND!
IT'S ALWAYS ABOUT YOU, ISN'T IT, JERRY? WE WERE WORRIED SICK, BUT YOU NEVER THINK ABOUT ANYONE BUT YOURSELF, YOU SON OF A--
HEY! SAVE IT FOR DOOFUS JERRY, YOU TWO.
OH, I WILL. WHEN I SEE THAT OTHER JERRY I'M GOING TO DIVORCE HIS HEAD FROM HIS BODY.
THAT'S MY GIRL.

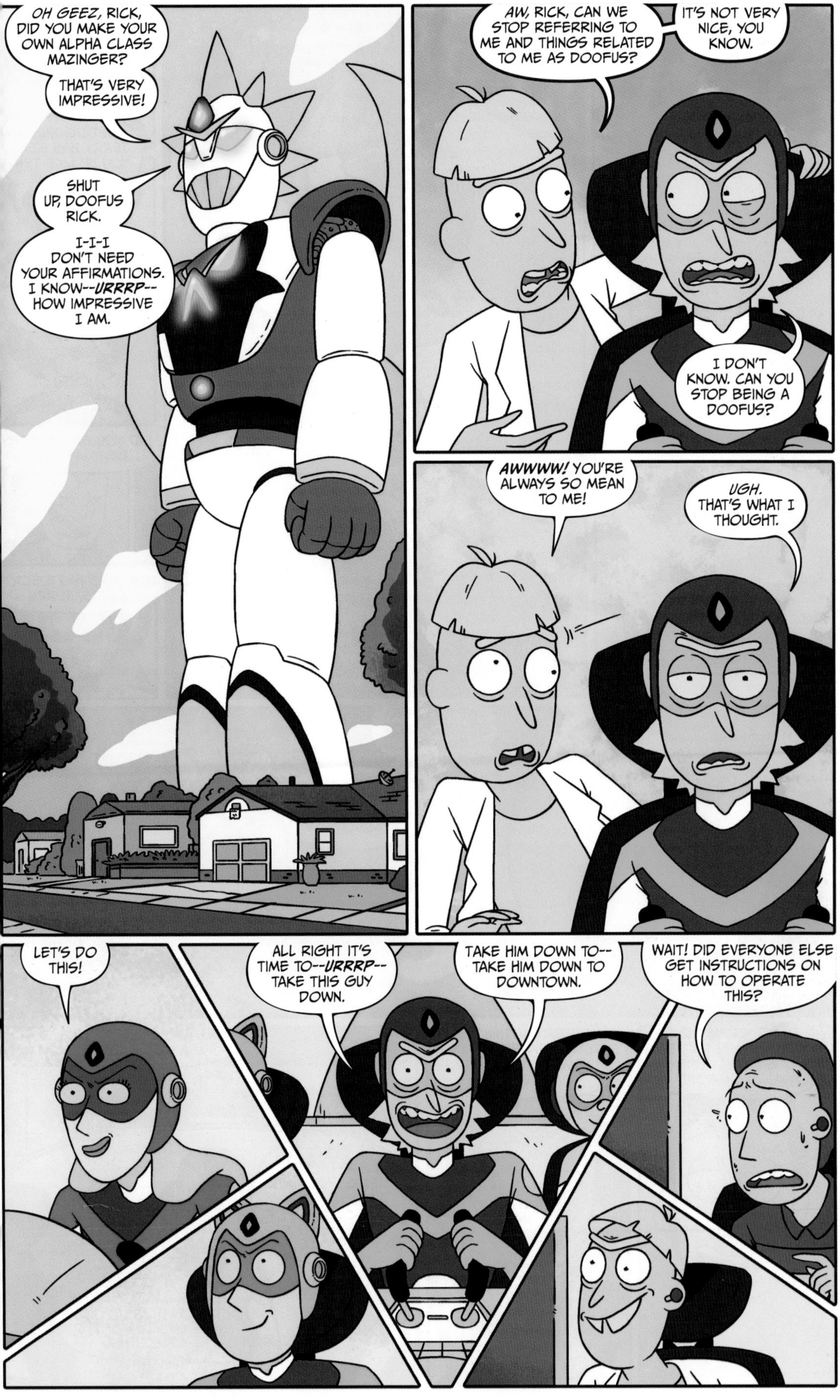
OH GEEZ, RICK, DID YOU MAKE YOUR OWN ALPHA CLASS MAZINGER?
THAT'S VERY IMPRESSIVE!
SHUT UP, DOOFUS RICK.
I-I-I DON'T NEED YOUR AFFIRMATIONS. I KNOW--URRRP--HOW IMPRESSIVE I AM.
AW, RICK, CAN WE STOP REFERRING TO ME AND THINGS RELATED TO ME AS DOOFUS?
IT'S NOT VERY NICE, YOU KNOW.
I DON'T KNOW. CAN YOU STOP BEING A DOOFUS?
AWWWW! YOU'RE ALWAYS SO MEAN TO ME!
UGH. THAT'S WHAT I THOUGHT.
LET'S DO THIS!
ALL RIGHT IT'S TIME TO--URRRP--TAKE THIS GUY DOWN.
TAKE HIM DOWN TO--TAKE HIM DOWN TO DOWNTOWN.
WAIT! DID EVERYONE ELSE GET INSTRUCTIONS ON HOW TO OPERATE THIS?

GEEZ, RICK, A-ARE YOU SURE A GIANT ROBOT IS THE SOLUTION TO ALL THIS?

I'M ALWAYS SURE, MORTY. GIANT ROBOTS ARE HOW UNIVERSE-LEVEL THREATS ARE DEALT WITH.

AND MY ROBOT IS THE BIGGEST.

BUT DOOFUS JERRY HAS BEAT YOU UP LIKE TEN TIMES NOW!

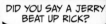

BIGGEST ROBOT, MORTY!

DID YOU SAY A JERRY BEAT UP RICK?

THIS THING HAS EJECTOR SEATS, JERRY.

WE'RE HERE. BE READY FOR ANYTHING.

HOLY CRAP, THIS GUY BUILT A GIANT STATUE OF HIMSELF.

I DON'T KNOW, GUYS. MAYBE IT WOULDN'T BE SO BAD IF A JERRY WAS IN CHARGE?

YEAH, JERRY, NOTHING SAYS STRONG LEADERSHIP LIKE UNEMPLOYMENT AND DAILY BATHS.

HEY, WHO DOESN'T LIKE A NICE BATH?

DON'T LISTEN TO HIM, JERRY. YOU HAVE A BIG HEART AND THAT COUNTS FOR A LOT IN THIS WORLD.

IT COUNTS FOR CARDIOMEGALY. NOW BOTH OF YOU SHUT YOUR STUPID MOUTHS.

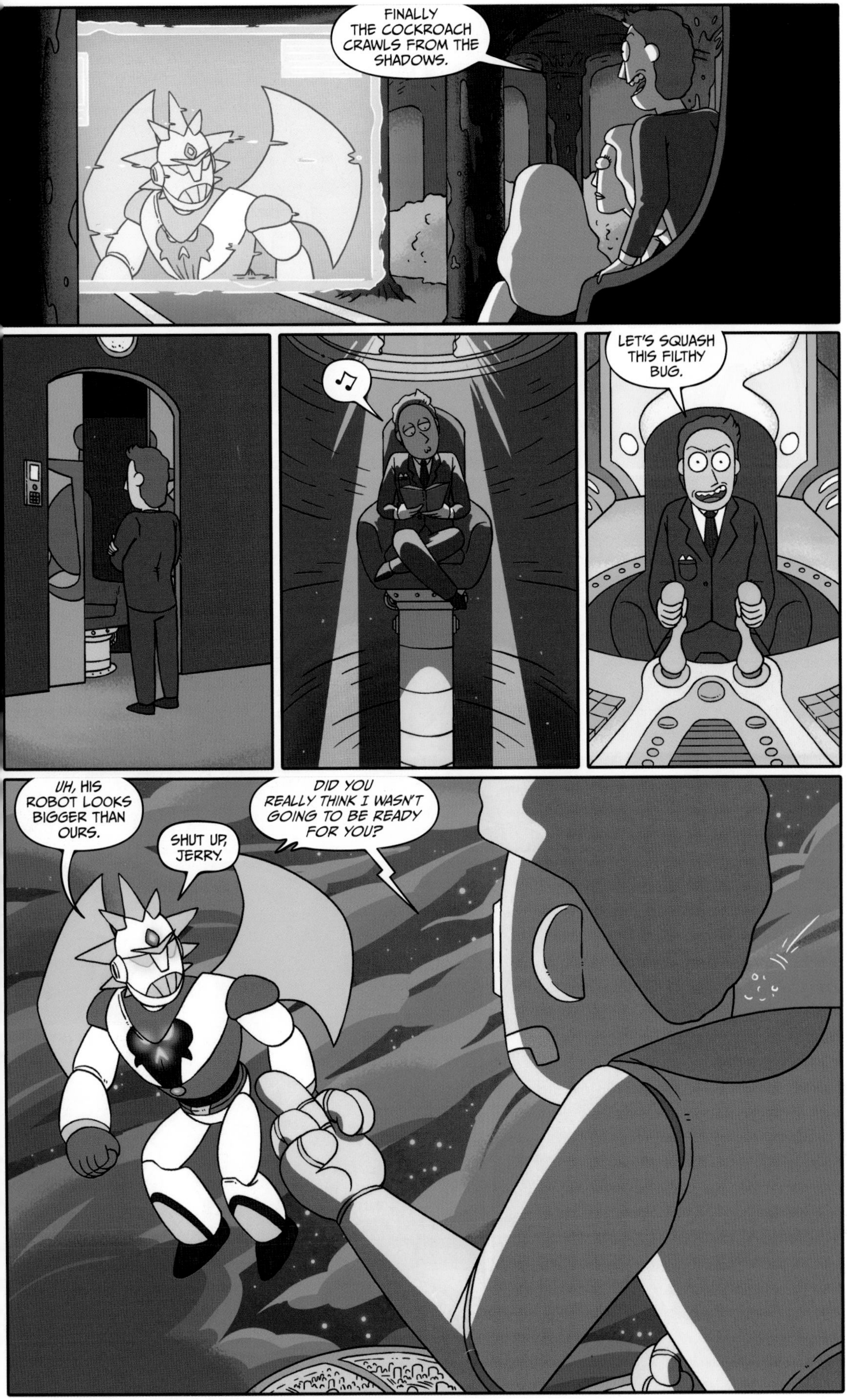
FINALLY THE COCKROACH CRAWLS FROM THE SHADOWS.
♫
LET'S SQUASH THIS FILTHY BUG.
UH, HIS ROBOT LOOKS BIGGER THAN OURS.
SHUT UP, JERRY.
DID YOU REALLY THINK I WASN'T GOING TO BE READY FOR YOU?

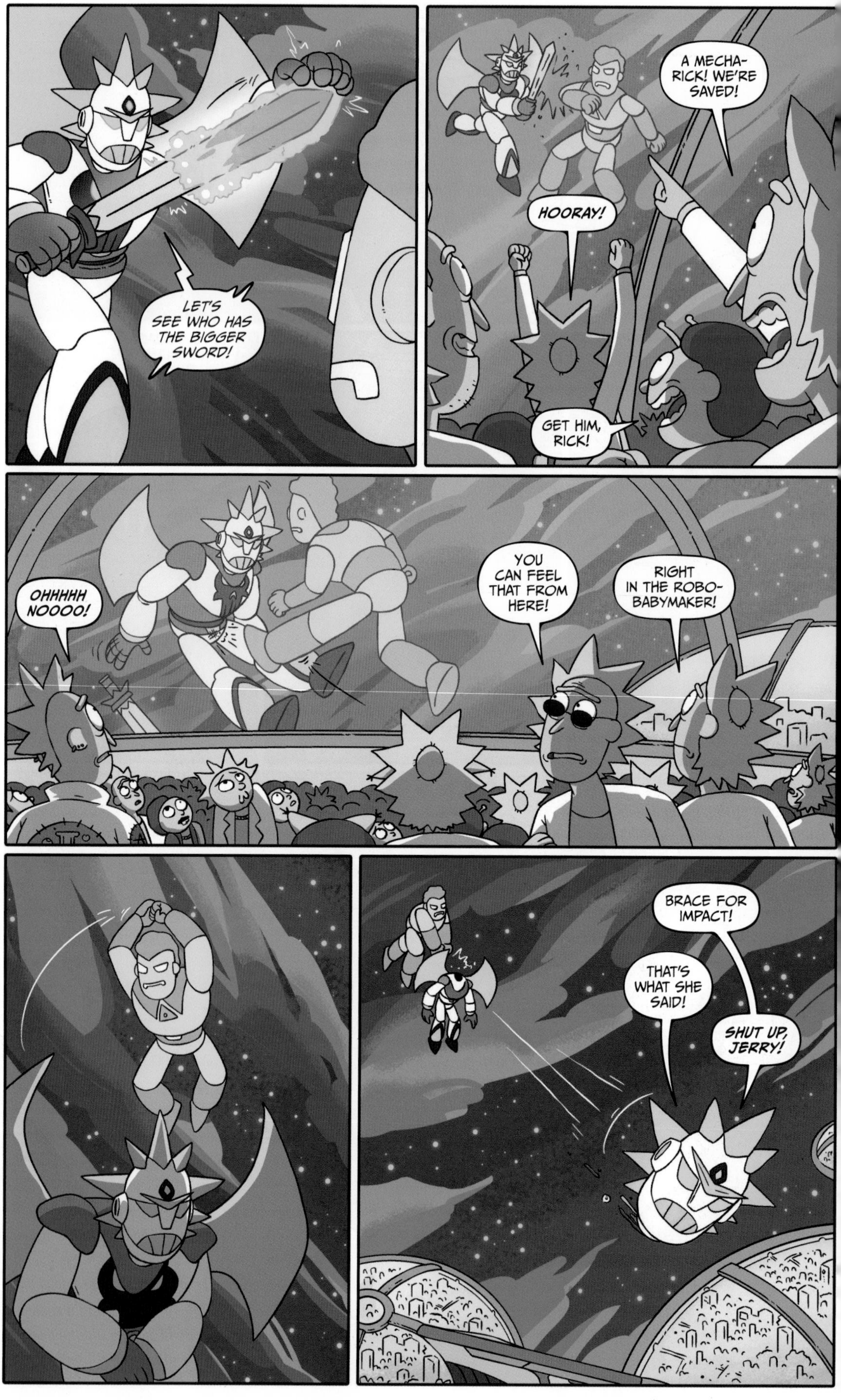
LET'S SEE WHO HAS THE BIGGER SWORD!
A MECHA-RICK! WE'RE SAVED!
HOORAY!
GET HIM, RICK!
OHHHHH NOOOO!
YOU CAN FEEL THAT FROM HERE!
RIGHT IN THE ROBO-BABYMAKER!
BRACE FOR IMPACT!
THAT'S WHAT SHE SAID!
SHUT UP, JERRY!

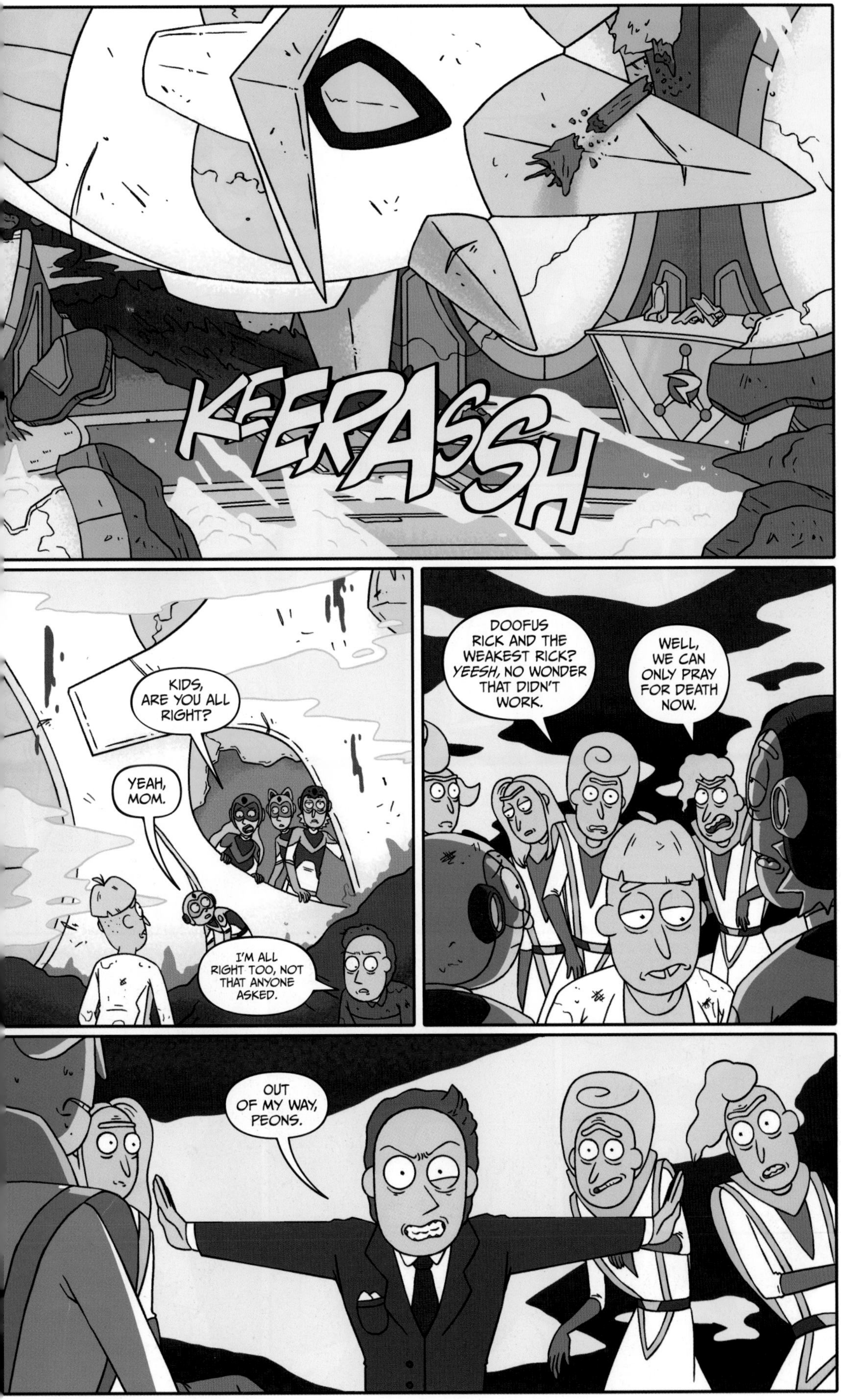
KEERASSH
KIDS, ARE YOU ALL RIGHT?
YEAH, MOM.
I'M ALL RIGHT TOO, NOT THAT ANYONE ASKED.
DOOFUS RICK AND THE WEAKEST RICK? *YEESH,* NO WONDER THAT DIDN'T WORK.
WELL, WE CAN ONLY PRAY FOR DEATH NOW.
OUT OF MY WAY, PEONS.

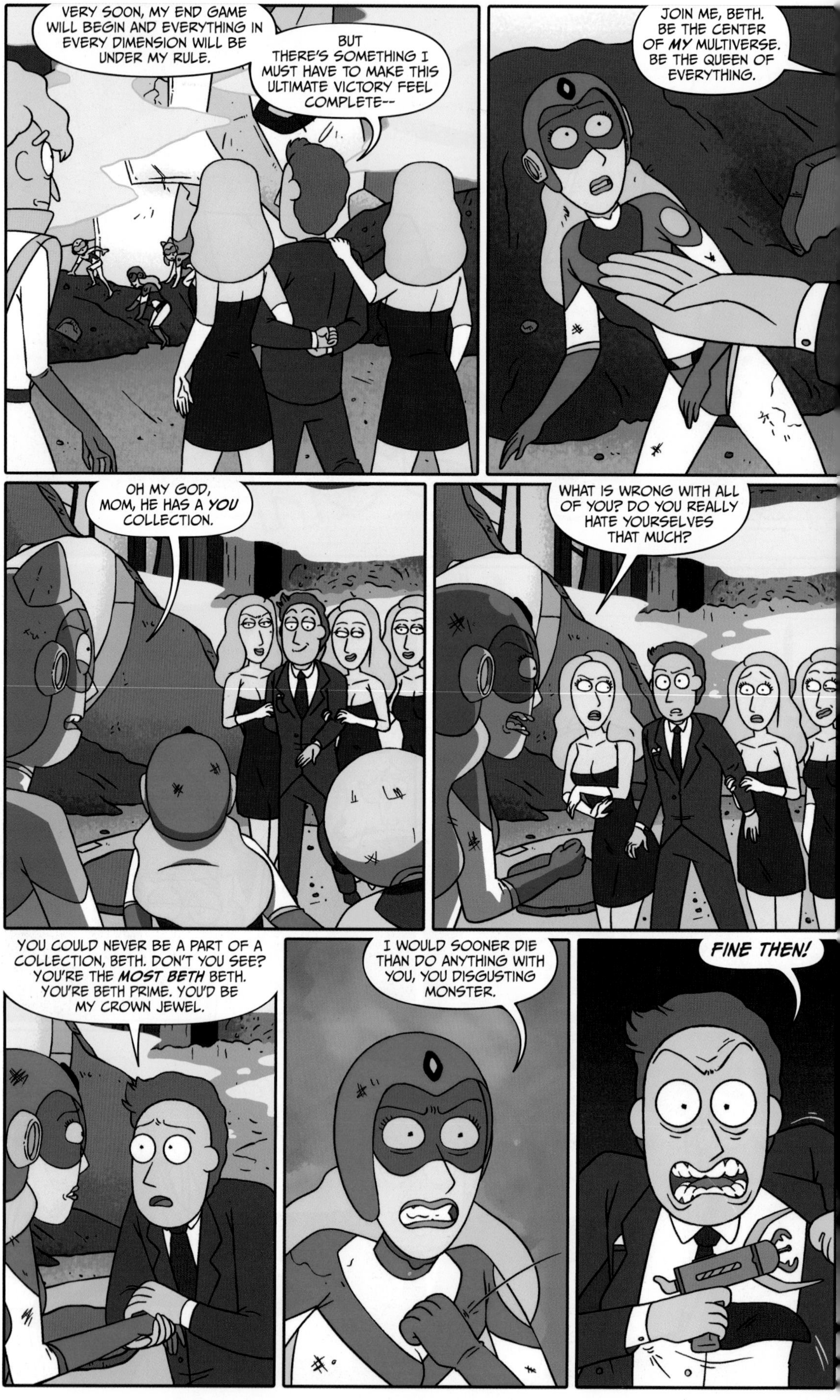
VERY SOON, MY END GAME WILL BEGIN AND EVERYTHING IN EVERY DIMENSION WILL BE UNDER MY RULE.
BUT THERE'S SOMETHING I MUST HAVE TO MAKE THIS ULTIMATE VICTORY FEEL COMPLETE--
JOIN ME, BETH. BE THE CENTER OF *MY* MULTIVERSE. BE THE QUEEN OF EVERYTHING.
OH MY GOD, MOM, HE HAS A *YOU* COLLECTION.
WHAT IS WRONG WITH ALL OF YOU? DO YOU REALLY HATE YOURSELVES THAT MUCH?
YOU COULD NEVER BE A PART OF A COLLECTION, BETH. DON'T YOU SEE? YOU'RE THE *MOST BETH* BETH. YOU'RE BETH PRIME. YOU'D BE MY CROWN JEWEL.
I WOULD SOONER DIE THAN DO ANYTHING WITH YOU, YOU DISGUSTING MONSTER.
FINE THEN!

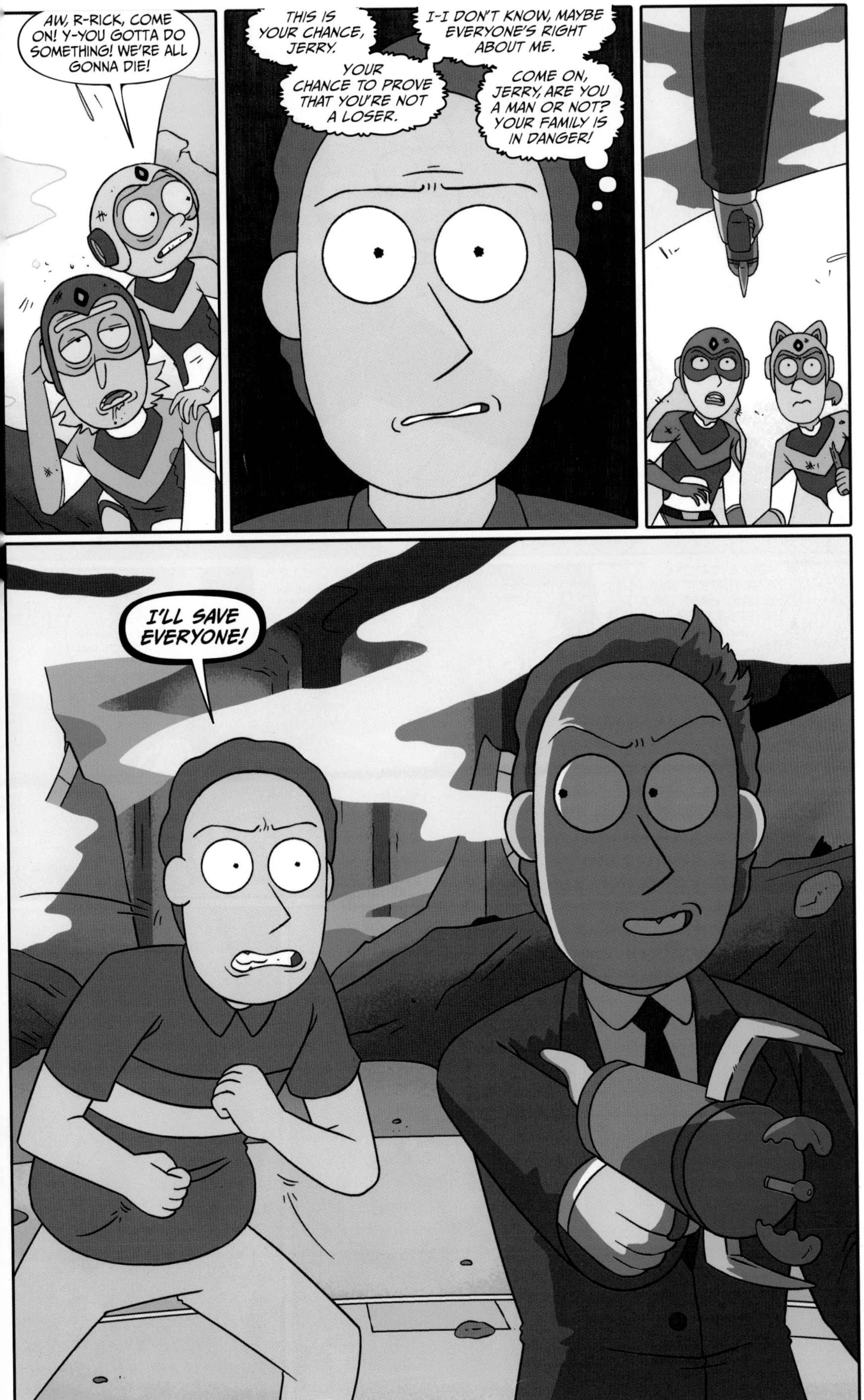
AW, R-RICK, COME ON! Y-YOU GOTTA DO SOMETHING! WE'RE ALL GONNA DIE!
THIS IS YOUR CHANCE, JERRY.
YOUR CHANCE TO PROVE THAT YOU'RE NOT A LOSER.
I-I DON'T KNOW, MAYBE EVERYONE'S RIGHT ABOUT ME.
COME ON, JERRY, ARE YOU A MAN OR NOT? YOUR FAMILY IS IN DANGER!
I'LL SAVE EVERYONE!

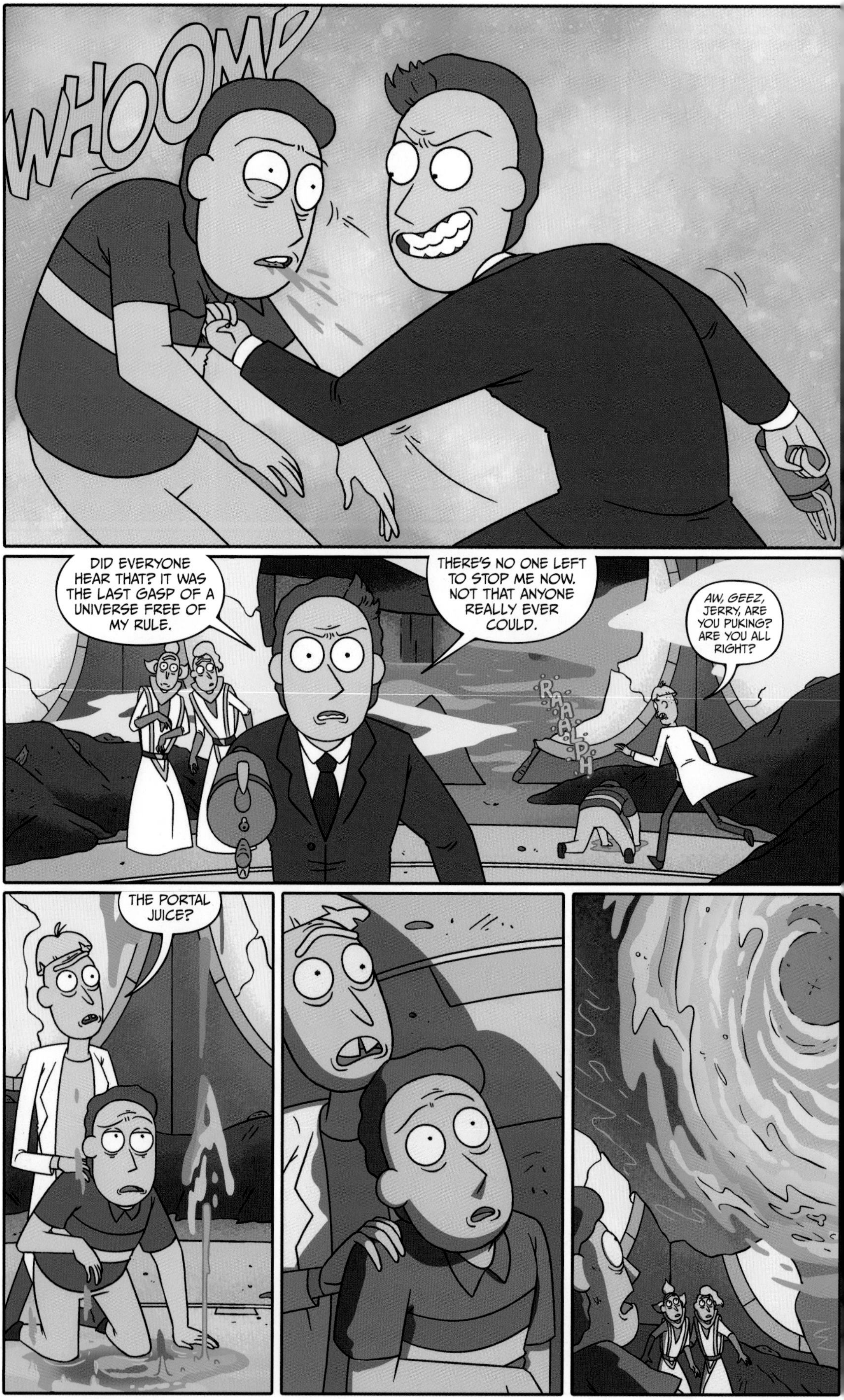
WHOOMP
DID EVERYONE HEAR THAT? IT WAS THE LAST GASP OF A UNIVERSE FREE OF MY RULE.
THERE'S NO ONE LEFT TO STOP ME NOW. NOT THAT ANYONE REALLY EVER COULD.
RAAALPH
AW, GEEZ, JERRY, ARE YOU PUKING? ARE YOU ALL RIGHT?
THE PORTAL JUICE?

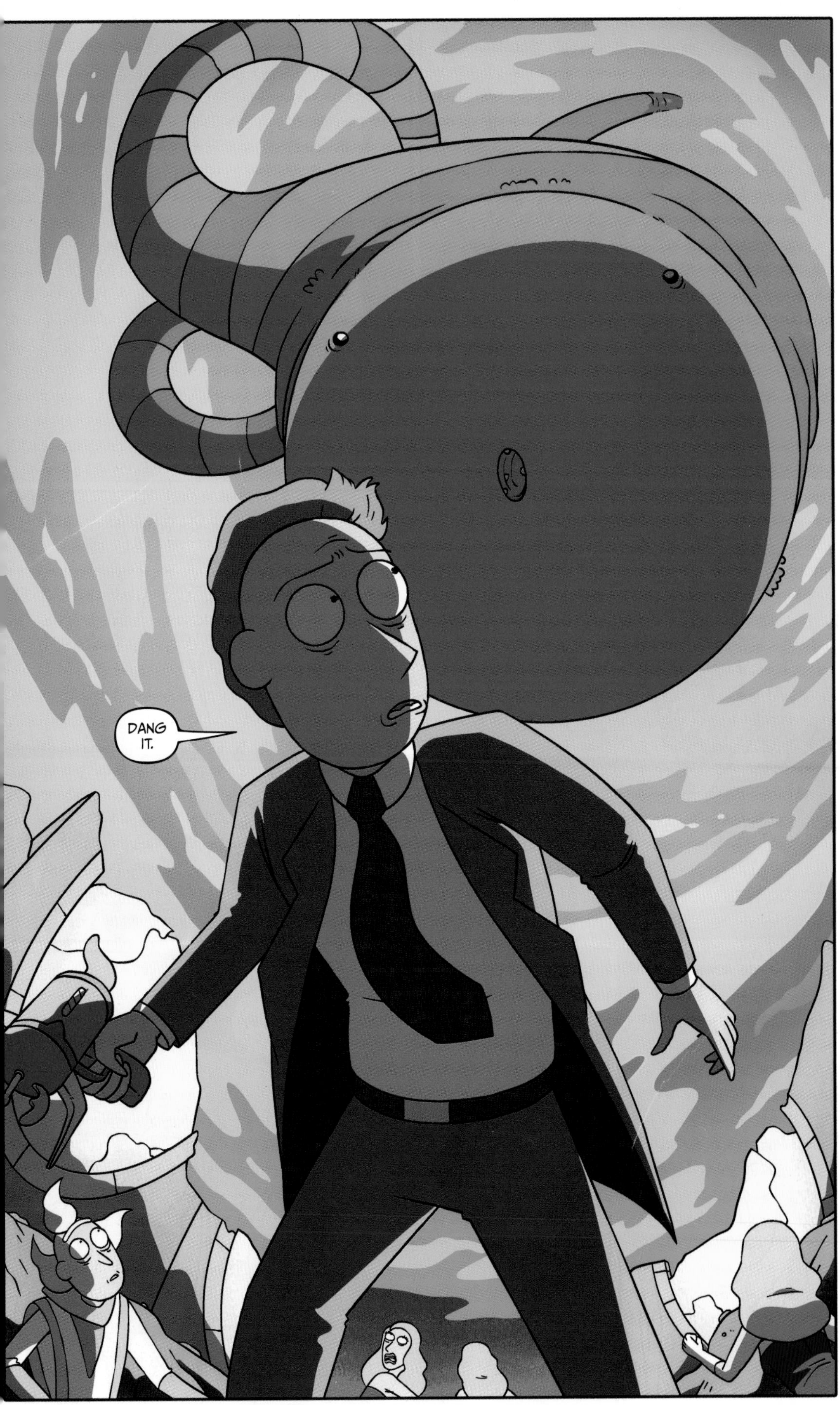
DANG IT.

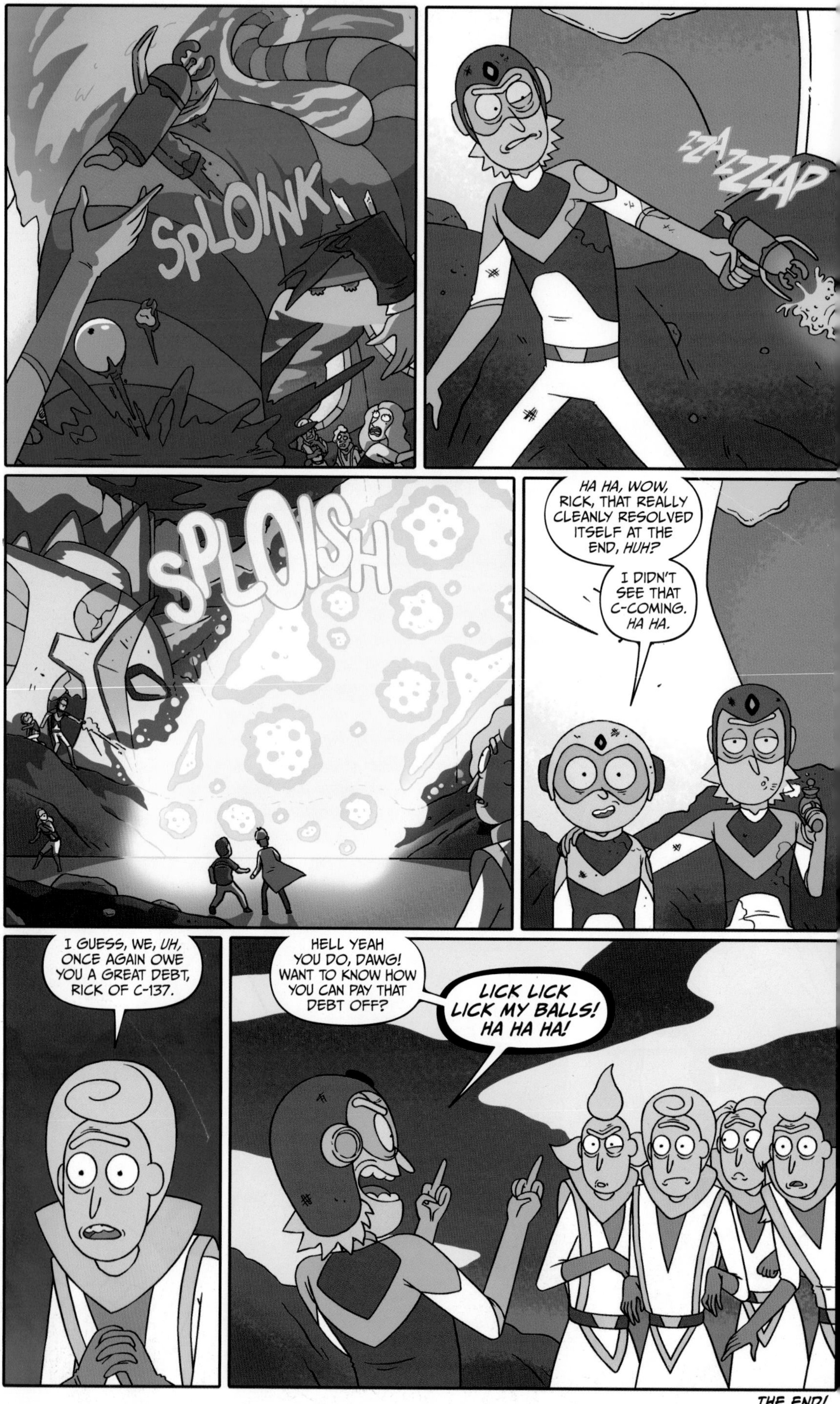
SPLOINK
ZZAZZZAP
SPLOISH
HA HA, WOW, RICK, THAT REALLY CLEANLY RESOLVED ITSELF AT THE END, *HUH?*
I DIDN'T SEE THAT C-COMING. HA HA.
I GUESS, WE, *UH,* ONCE AGAIN OWE YOU A GREAT DEBT, RICK OF C-137.
HELL YEAH YOU DO, DAWG! WANT TO KNOW HOW YOU CAN PAY THAT DEBT OFF?
LICK LICK LICK MY BALLS! HA HA HA!

THE END!

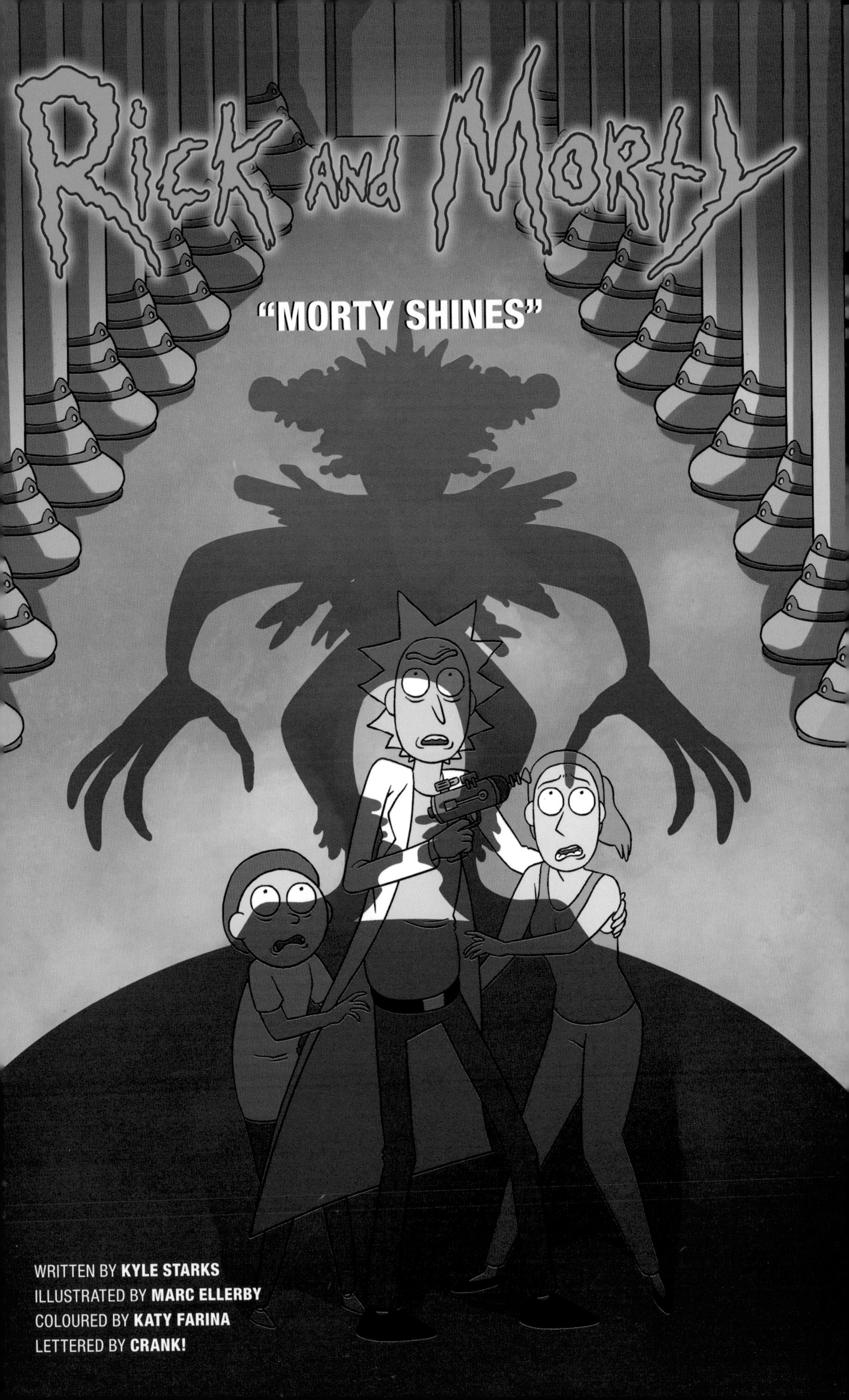
Rick and Morty
"MORTY SHINES"

WRITTEN BY **KYLE STARKS**
ILLUSTRATED BY **MARC ELLERBY**
COLOURED BY **KATY FARINA**
LETTERED BY **CRANK!**

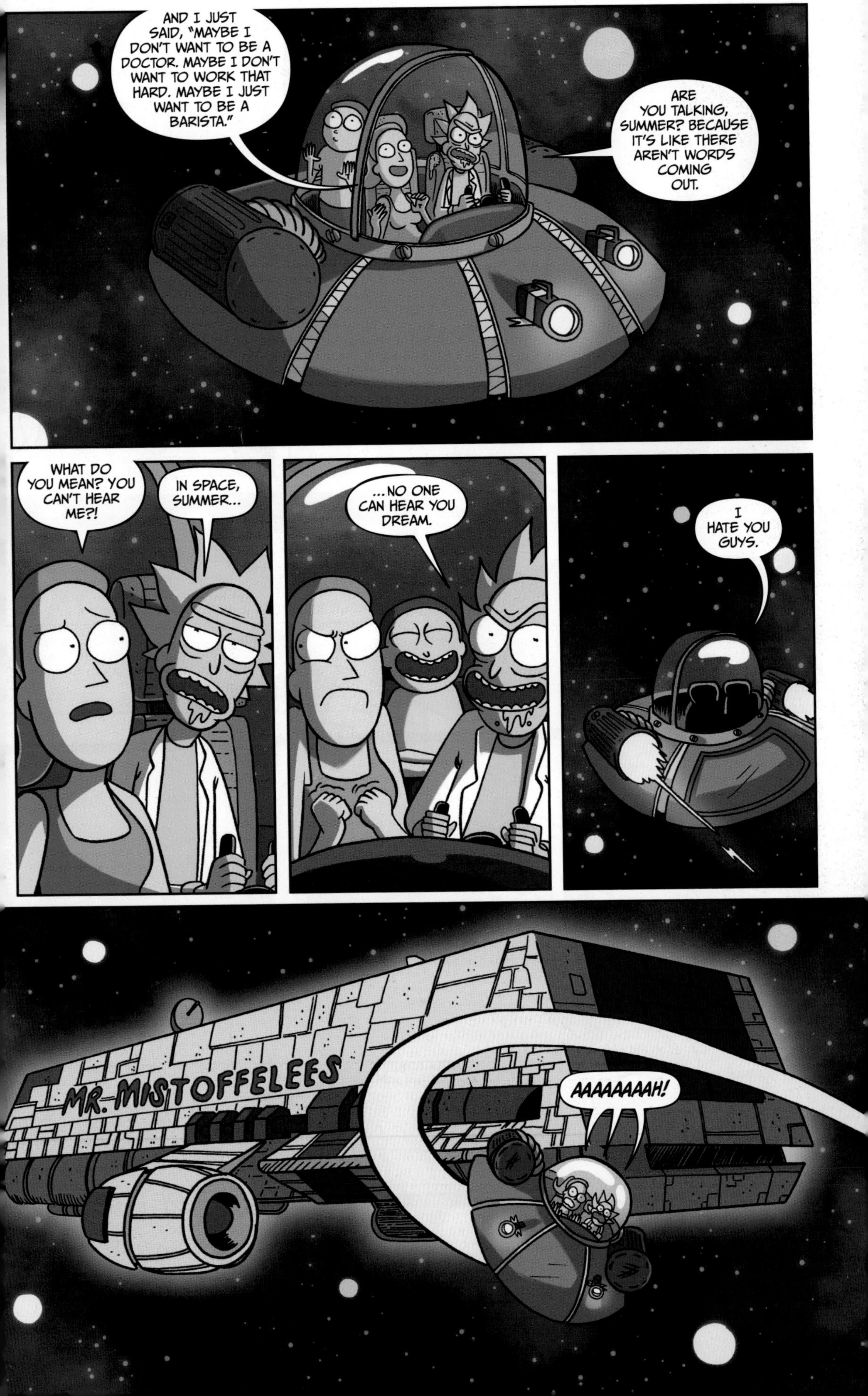
AND I JUST SAID, "MAYBE I DON'T WANT TO BE A DOCTOR. MAYBE I DON'T WANT TO WORK THAT HARD. MAYBE I JUST WANT TO BE A BARISTA."
ARE YOU TALKING, SUMMER? BECAUSE IT'S LIKE THERE AREN'T WORDS COMING OUT.
WHAT DO YOU MEAN? YOU CAN'T HEAR ME?!
IN SPACE, SUMMER...
...NO ONE CAN HEAR YOU DREAM.
I HATE YOU GUYS.
MR. MISTOFFELEES
AAAAAAAAH!

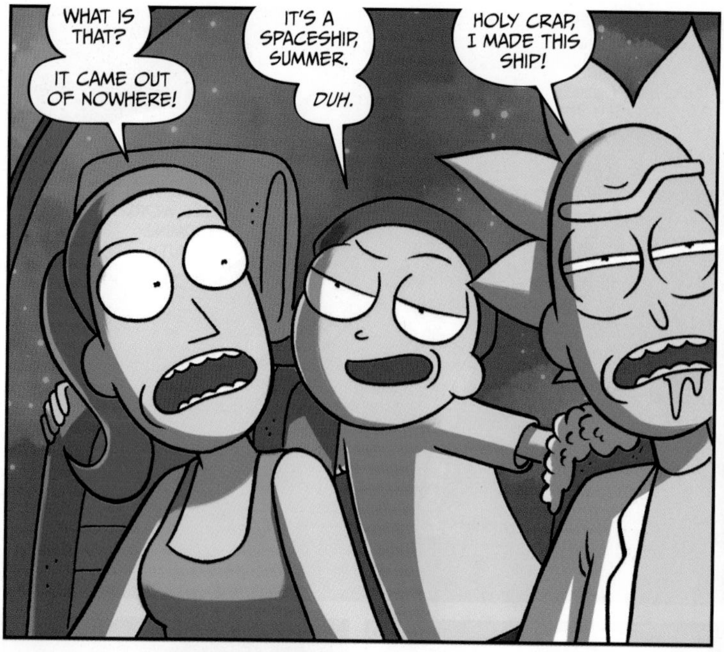
WHAT IS THAT?
IT CAME OUT OF NOWHERE!
IT'S A SPACESHIP, SUMMER.
DUH.
HOLY CRAP, I MADE THIS SHIP!

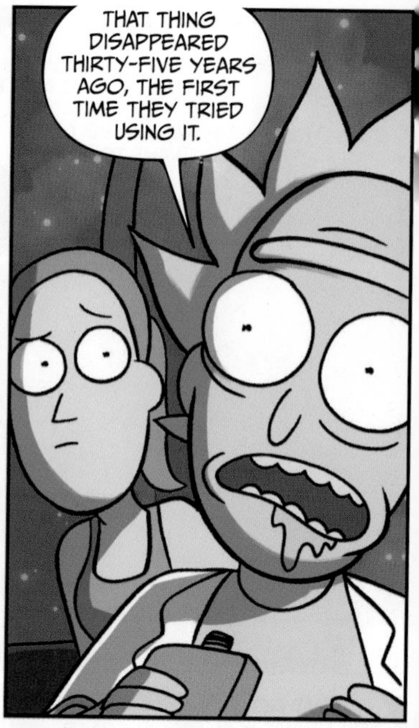
THAT THING DISAPPEARED THIRTY-FIVE YEARS AGO, THE FIRST TIME THEY TRIED USING IT.

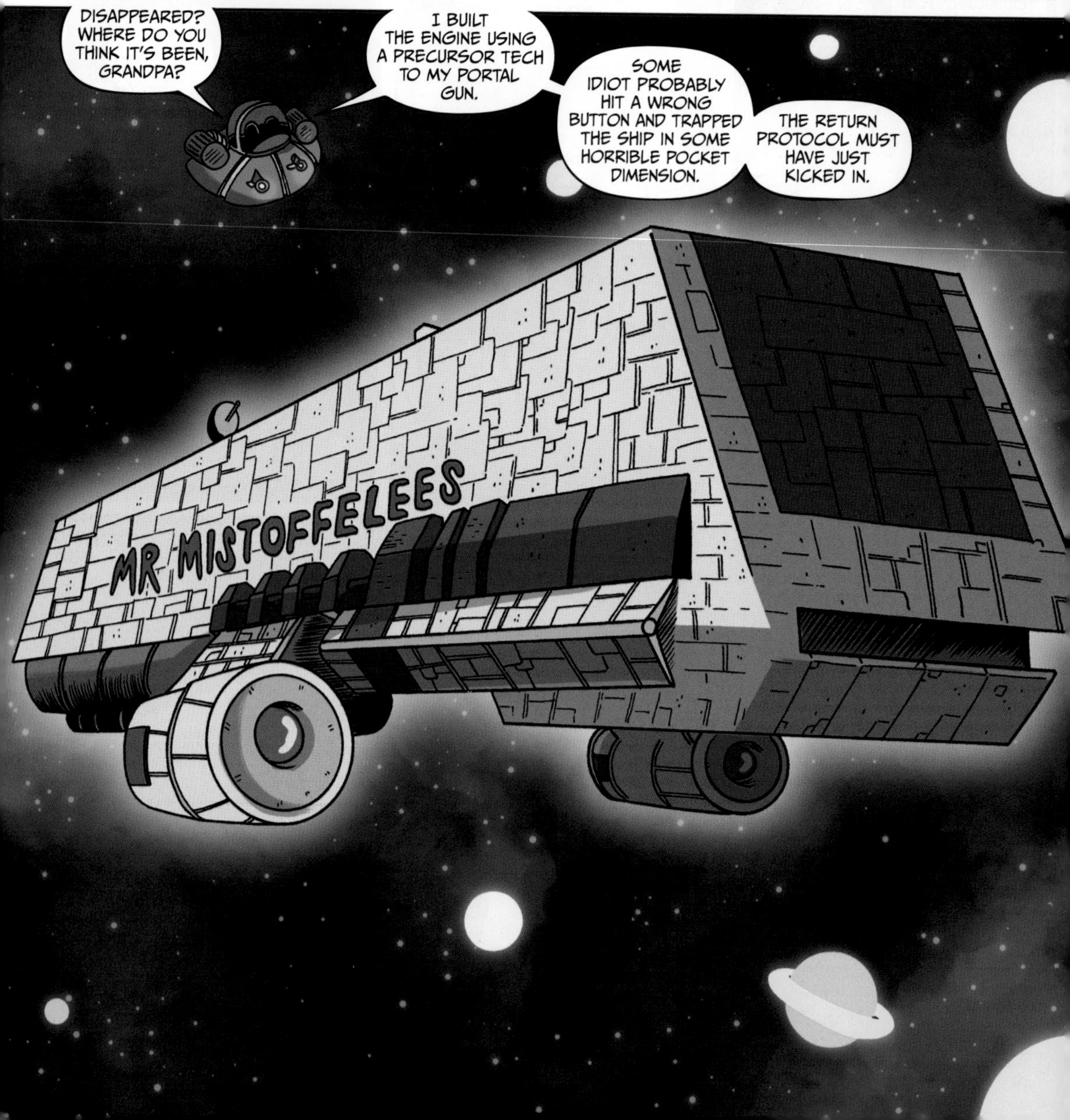
DISAPPEARED? WHERE DO YOU THINK IT'S BEEN, GRANDPA?
I BUILT THE ENGINE USING A PRECURSOR TECH TO MY PORTAL GUN.
SOME IDIOT PROBABLY HIT A WRONG BUTTON AND TRAPPED THE SHIP IN SOME HORRIBLE POCKET DIMENSION.
THE RETURN PROTOCOL MUST HAVE JUST KICKED IN.
MR MISTOFFELEES

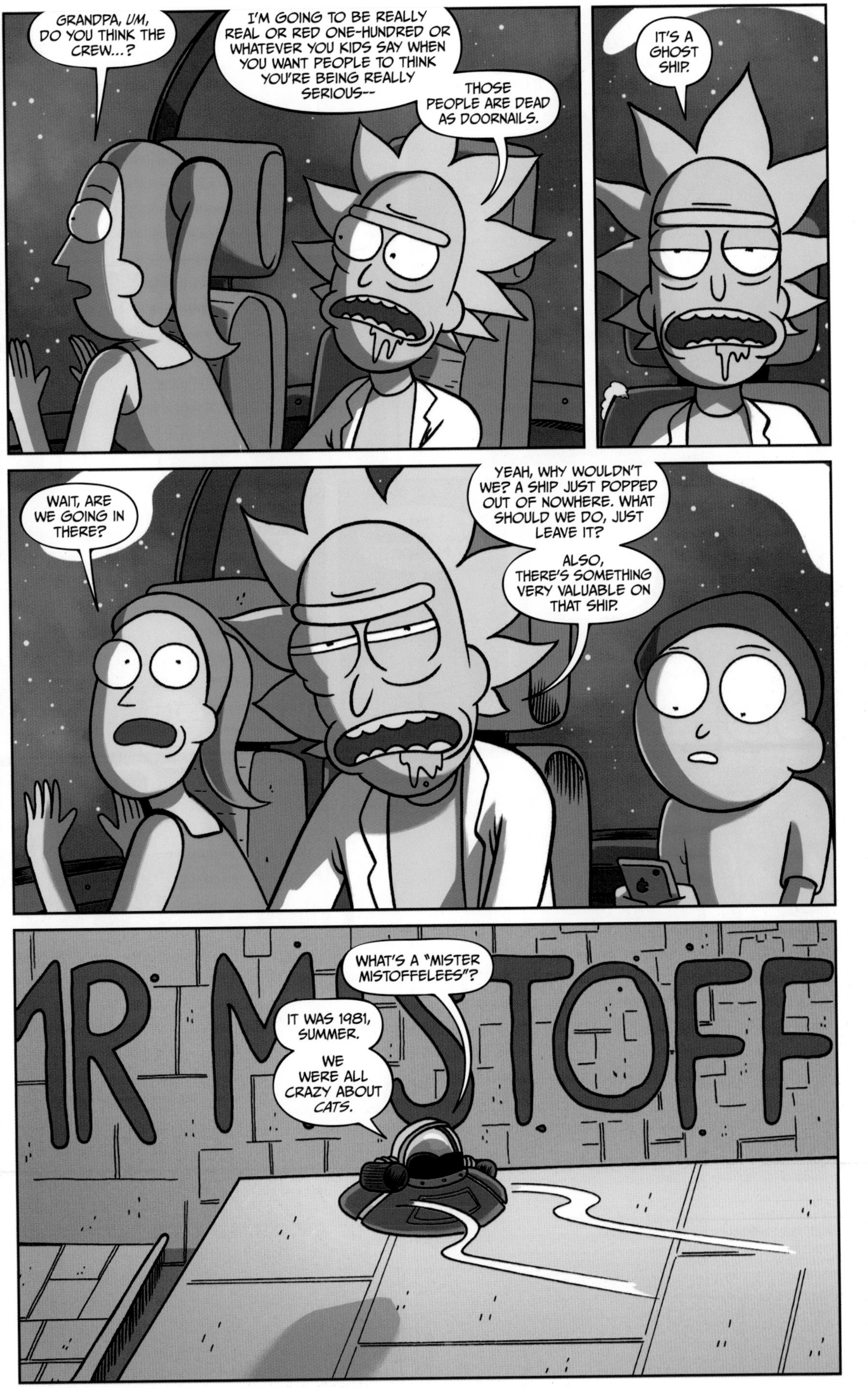
GRANDPA, UM, DO YOU THINK THE CREW...?
I'M GOING TO BE REALLY REAL OR RED ONE-HUNDRED OR WHATEVER YOU KIDS SAY WHEN YOU WANT PEOPLE TO THINK YOU'RE BEING REALLY SERIOUS--
THOSE PEOPLE ARE DEAD AS DOORNAILS.
IT'S A GHOST SHIP.
WAIT, ARE WE GOING IN THERE?
YEAH, WHY WOULDN'T WE? A SHIP JUST POPPED OUT OF NOWHERE. WHAT SHOULD WE DO, JUST LEAVE IT?
ALSO, THERE'S SOMETHING VERY VALUABLE ON THAT SHIP.
MR MISTOFF
WHAT'S A "MISTER MISTOFFELEES"?
IT WAS 1981, SUMMER.
WE WERE ALL CRAZY ABOUT CATS.

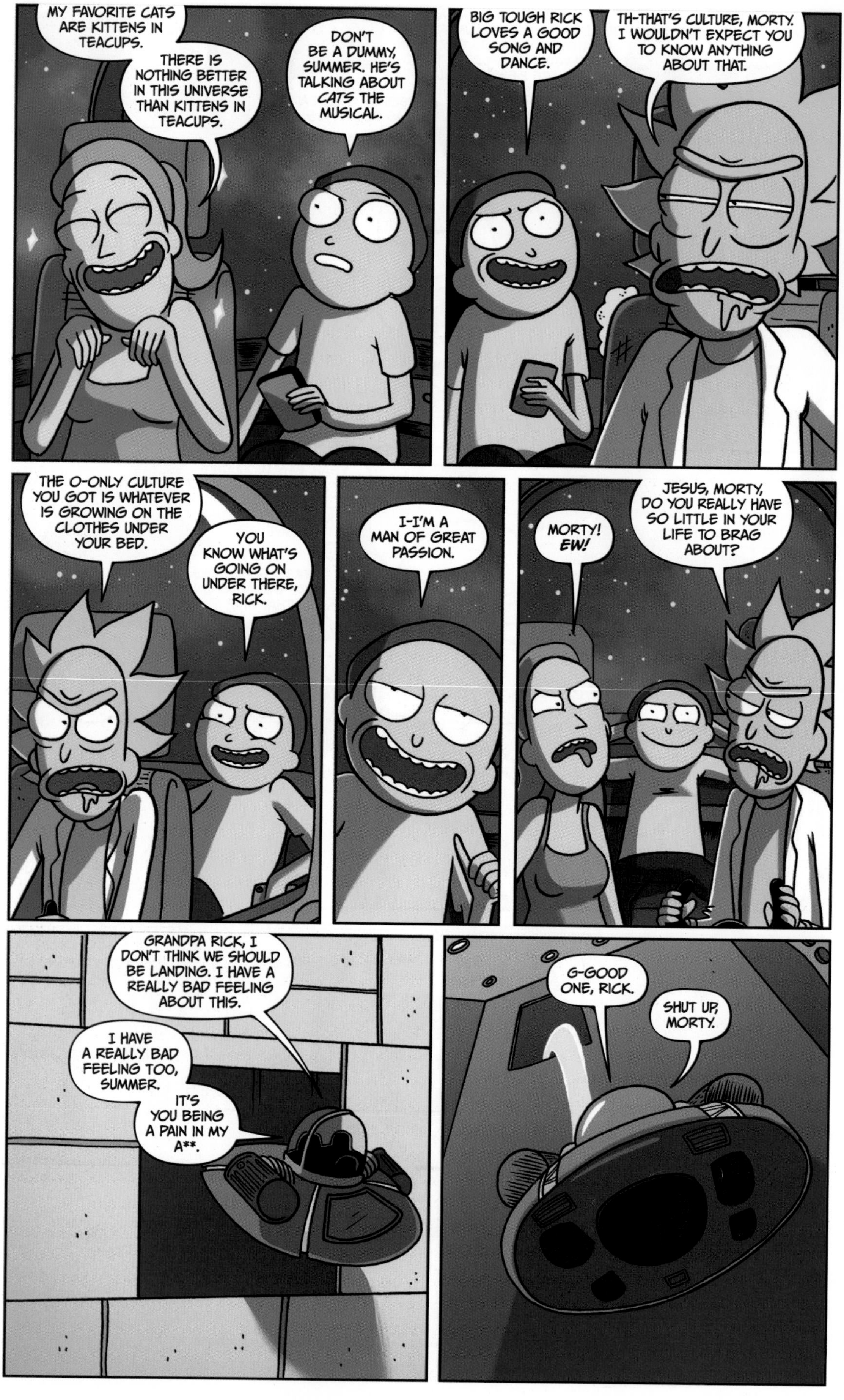
MY FAVORITE CATS ARE KITTENS IN TEACUPS.
THERE IS NOTHING BETTER IN THIS UNIVERSE THAN KITTENS IN TEACUPS.
DON'T BE A DUMMY, SUMMER. HE'S TALKING ABOUT CATS THE MUSICAL.
BIG TOUGH RICK LOVES A GOOD SONG AND DANCE.
TH-THAT'S CULTURE, MORTY. I WOULDN'T EXPECT YOU TO KNOW ANYTHING ABOUT THAT.
THE O-ONLY CULTURE YOU GOT IS WHATEVER IS GROWING ON THE CLOTHES UNDER YOUR BED.
YOU KNOW WHAT'S GOING ON UNDER THERE, RICK.
I-I'M A MAN OF GREAT PASSION.
MORTY! EW!
JESUS, MORTY, DO YOU REALLY HAVE SO LITTLE IN YOUR LIFE TO BRAG ABOUT?
GRANDPA RICK, I DON'T THINK WE SHOULD BE LANDING. I HAVE A REALLY BAD FEELING ABOUT THIS.
I HAVE A REALLY BAD FEELING TOO, SUMMER.
IT'S YOU BEING A PAIN IN MY A**.
G-GOOD ONE, RICK.
SHUT UP, MORTY.

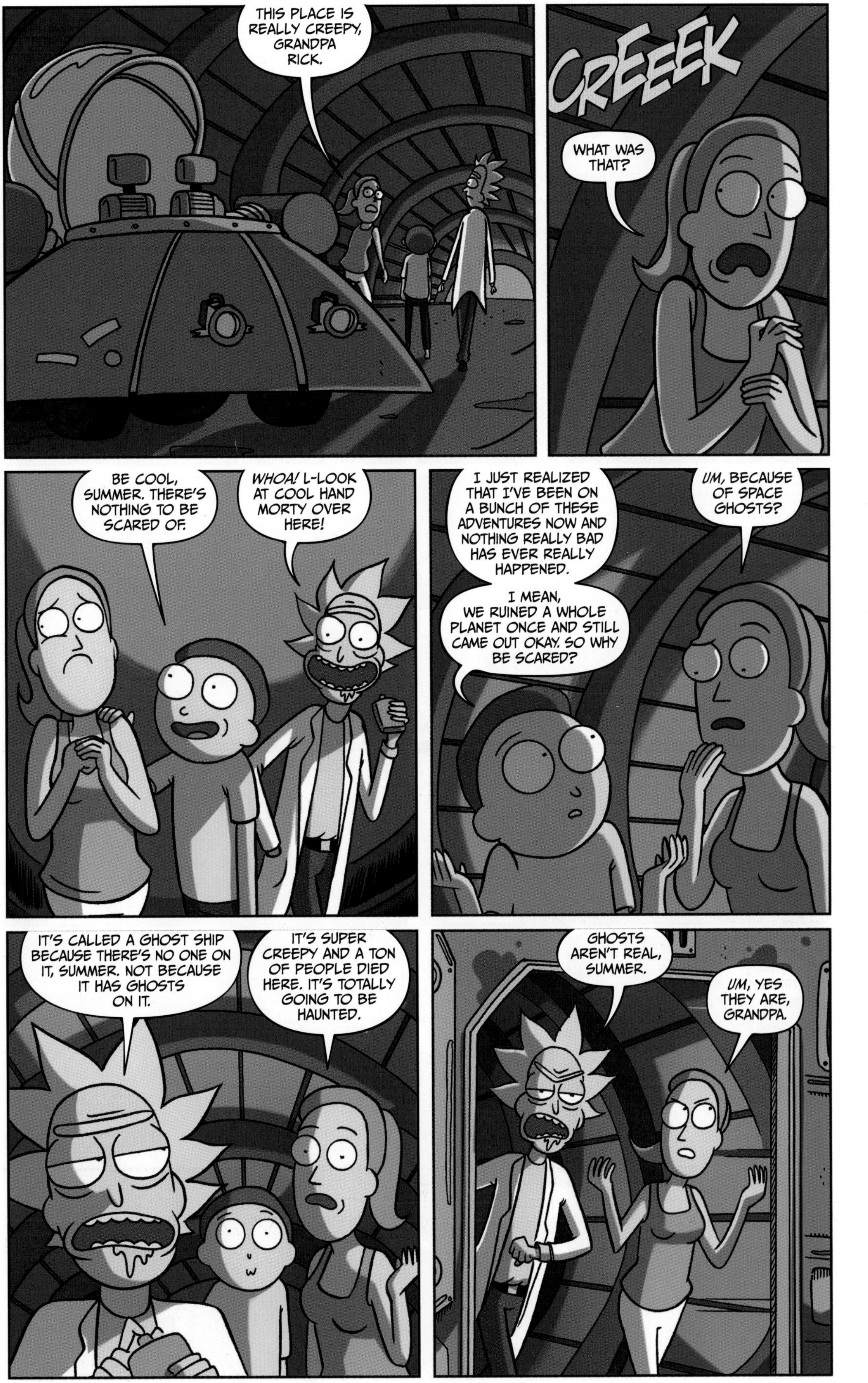

THIS PLACE IS REALLY CREEPY, GRANDPA RICK.
CREEEK
WHAT WAS THAT?
BE COOL, SUMMER. THERE'S NOTHING TO BE SCARED OF.
WHOA! L-LOOK AT COOL HAND MORTY OVER HERE!
I JUST REALIZED THAT I'VE BEEN ON A BUNCH OF THESE ADVENTURES NOW AND NOTHING REALLY BAD HAS EVER REALLY HAPPENED.
UM, BECAUSE OF SPACE GHOSTS?
I MEAN, WE RUINED A WHOLE PLANET ONCE AND STILL CAME OUT OKAY. SO WHY BE SCARED?
IT'S CALLED A GHOST SHIP BECAUSE THERE'S NO ONE ON IT, SUMMER. NOT BECAUSE IT HAS GHOSTS ON IT.
IT'S SUPER CREEPY AND A TON OF PEOPLE DIED HERE. IT'S TOTALLY GOING TO BE HAUNTED.
GHOSTS AREN'T REAL, SUMMER.
UM, YES THEY ARE, GRANDPA.

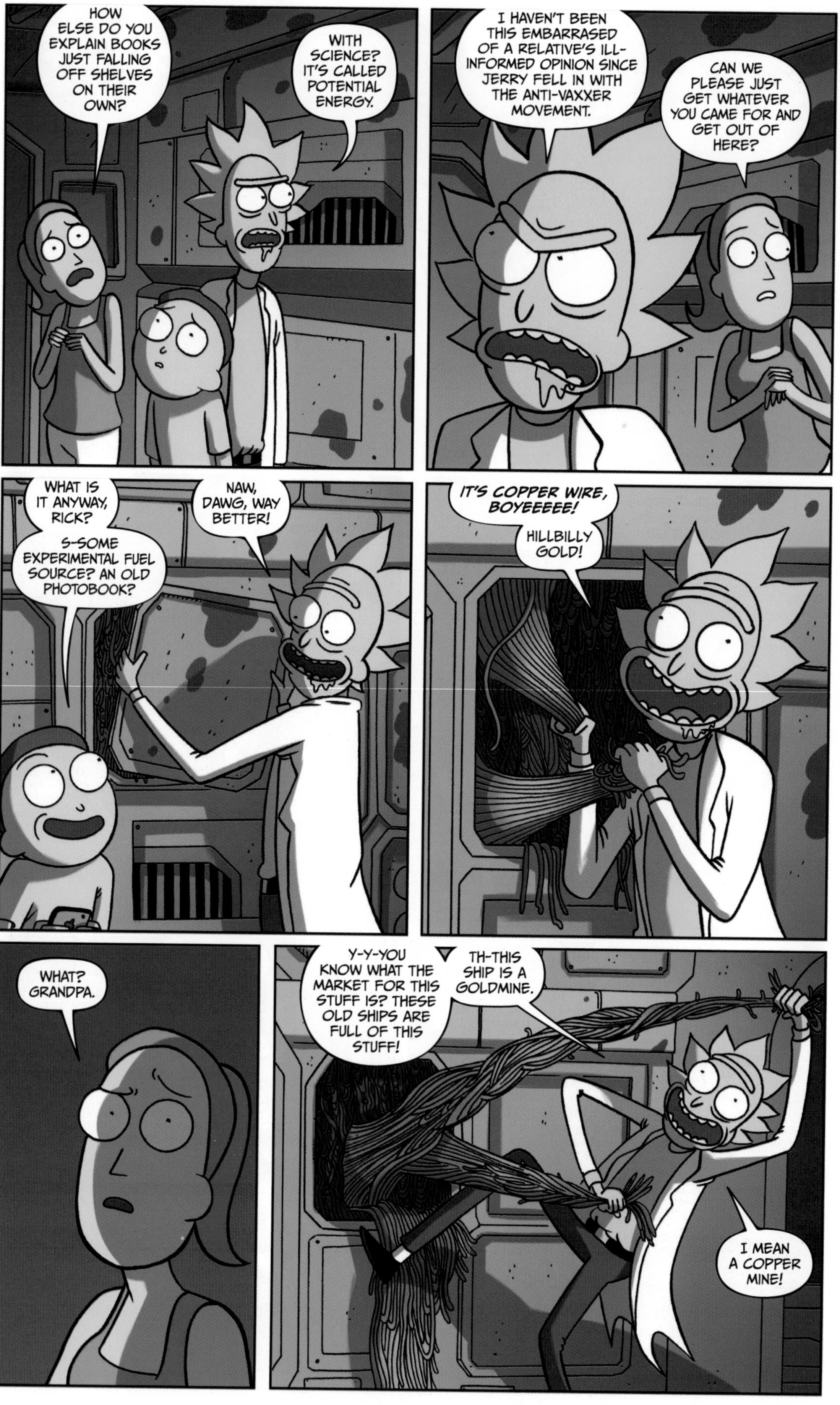
HOW ELSE DO YOU EXPLAIN BOOKS JUST FALLING OFF SHELVES ON THEIR OWN?
WITH SCIENCE? IT'S CALLED POTENTIAL ENERGY.
I HAVEN'T BEEN THIS EMBARRASED OF A RELATIVE'S ILL-INFORMED OPINION SINCE JERRY FELL IN WITH THE ANTI-VAXXER MOVEMENT.
CAN WE PLEASE JUST GET WHATEVER YOU CAME FOR AND GET OUT OF HERE?
WHAT IS IT ANYWAY, RICK?
S-SOME EXPERIMENTAL FUEL SOURCE? AN OLD PHOTOBOOK?
NAW, DAWG, WAY BETTER!
IT'S COPPER WIRE, BOYEEEEE!
HILLBILLY GOLD!
WHAT? GRANDPA.
Y-Y-YOU KNOW WHAT THE MARKET FOR THIS STUFF IS? THESE OLD SHIPS ARE FULL OF THIS STUFF!
TH-THIS SHIP IS A GOLDMINE.
I MEAN A COPPER MINE!

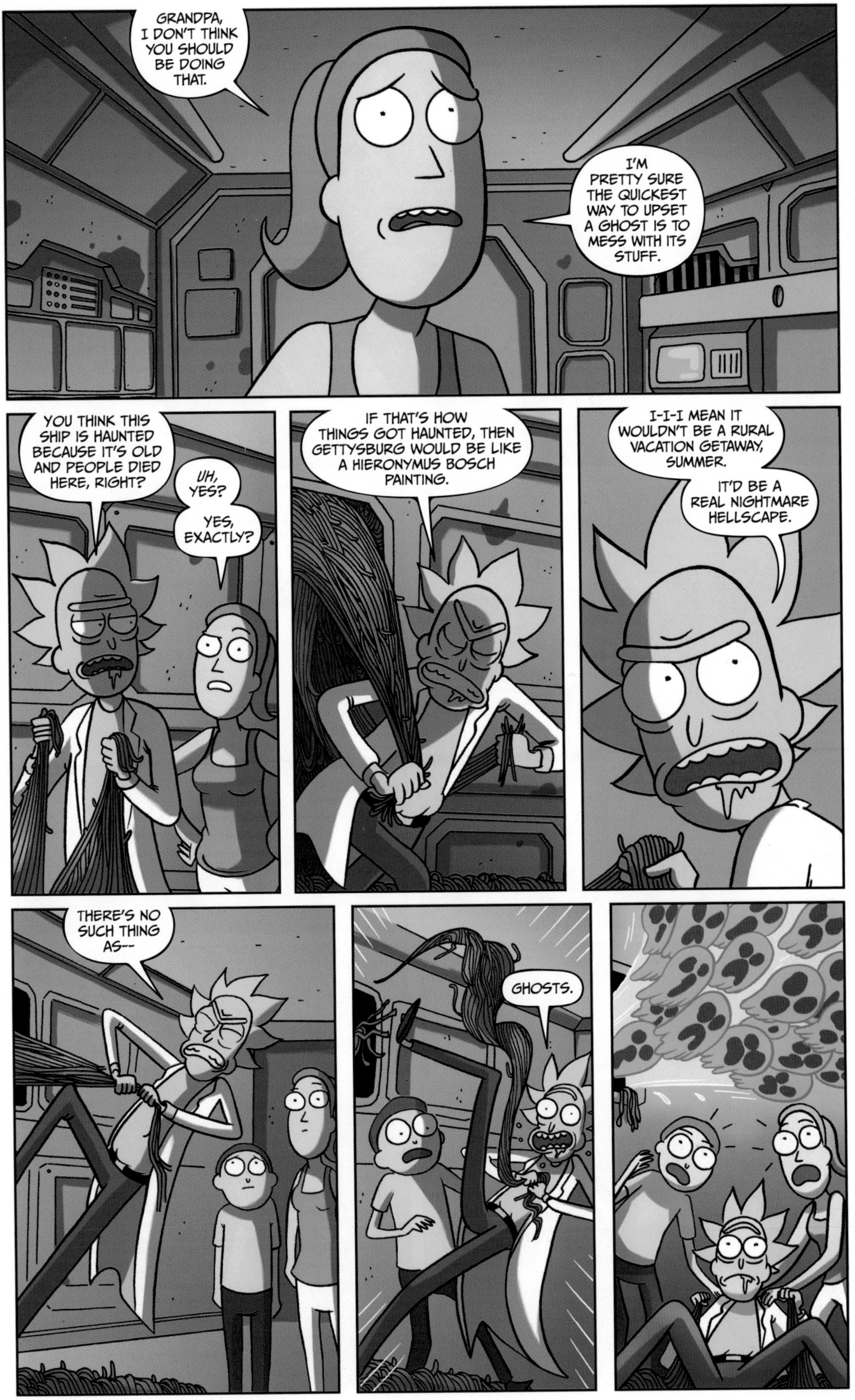
GRANDPA, I DON'T THINK YOU SHOULD BE DOING THAT.
I'M PRETTY SURE THE QUICKEST WAY TO UPSET A GHOST IS TO MESS WITH ITS STUFF.
YOU THINK THIS SHIP IS HAUNTED BECAUSE IT'S OLD AND PEOPLE DIED HERE, RIGHT?
UH, YES?
YES, EXACTLY?
IF THAT'S HOW THINGS GOT HAUNTED, THEN GETTYSBURG WOULD BE LIKE A HIERONYMUS BOSCH PAINTING.
I-I-I MEAN IT WOULDN'T BE A RURAL VACATION GETAWAY, SUMMER.
IT'D BE A REAL NIGHTMARE HELLSCAPE.
THERE'S NO SUCH THING AS--
GHOSTS.

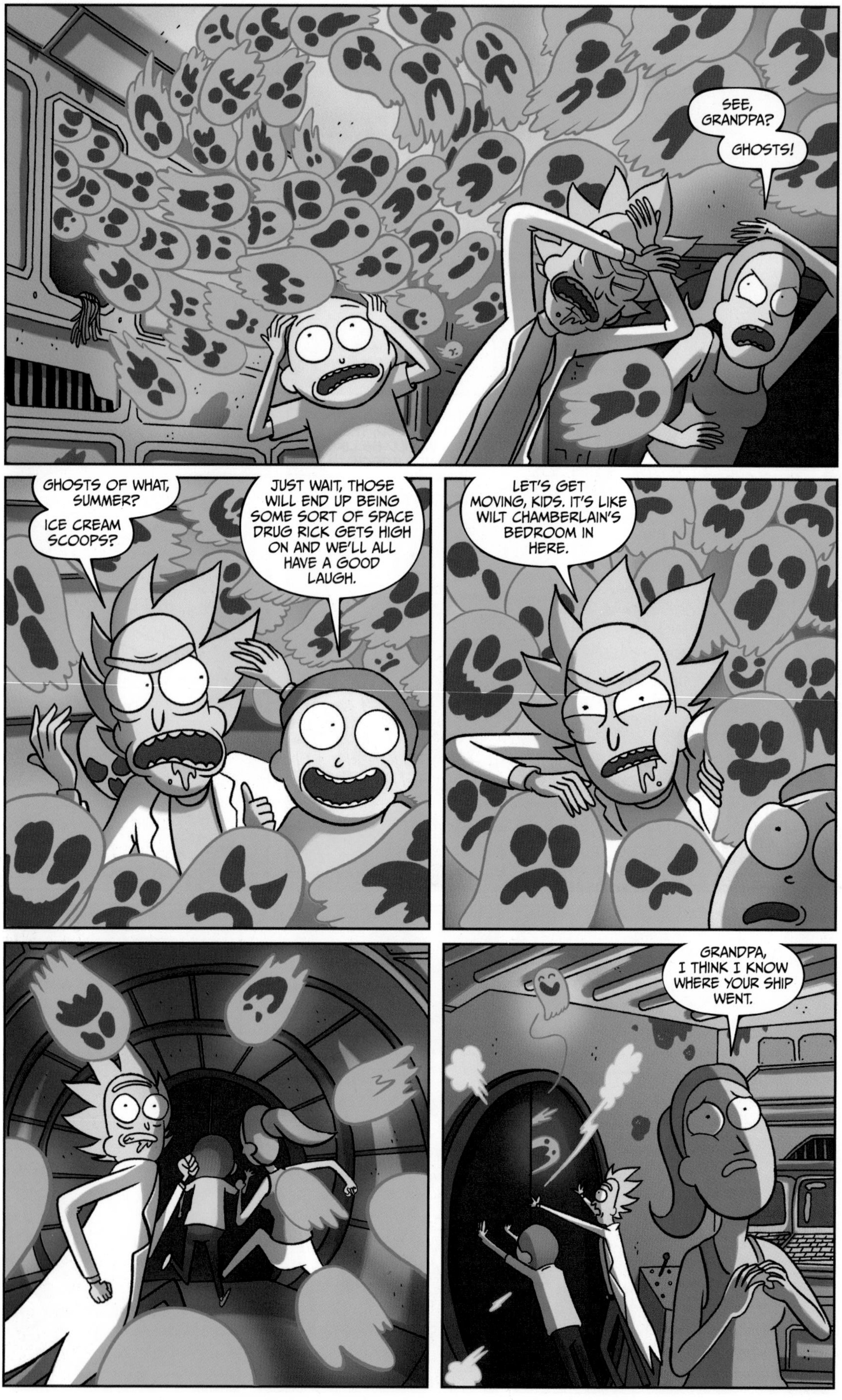
SEE, GRANDPA?
GHOSTS!
GHOSTS OF WHAT, SUMMER?
ICE CREAM SCOOPS?
JUST WAIT, THOSE WILL END UP BEING SOME SORT OF SPACE DRUG RICK GETS HIGH ON AND WE'LL ALL HAVE A GOOD LAUGH.
LET'S GET MOVING, KIDS. IT'S LIKE WILT CHAMBERLAIN'S BEDROOM IN HERE.
GRANDPA, I THINK I KNOW WHERE YOUR SHIP WENT.

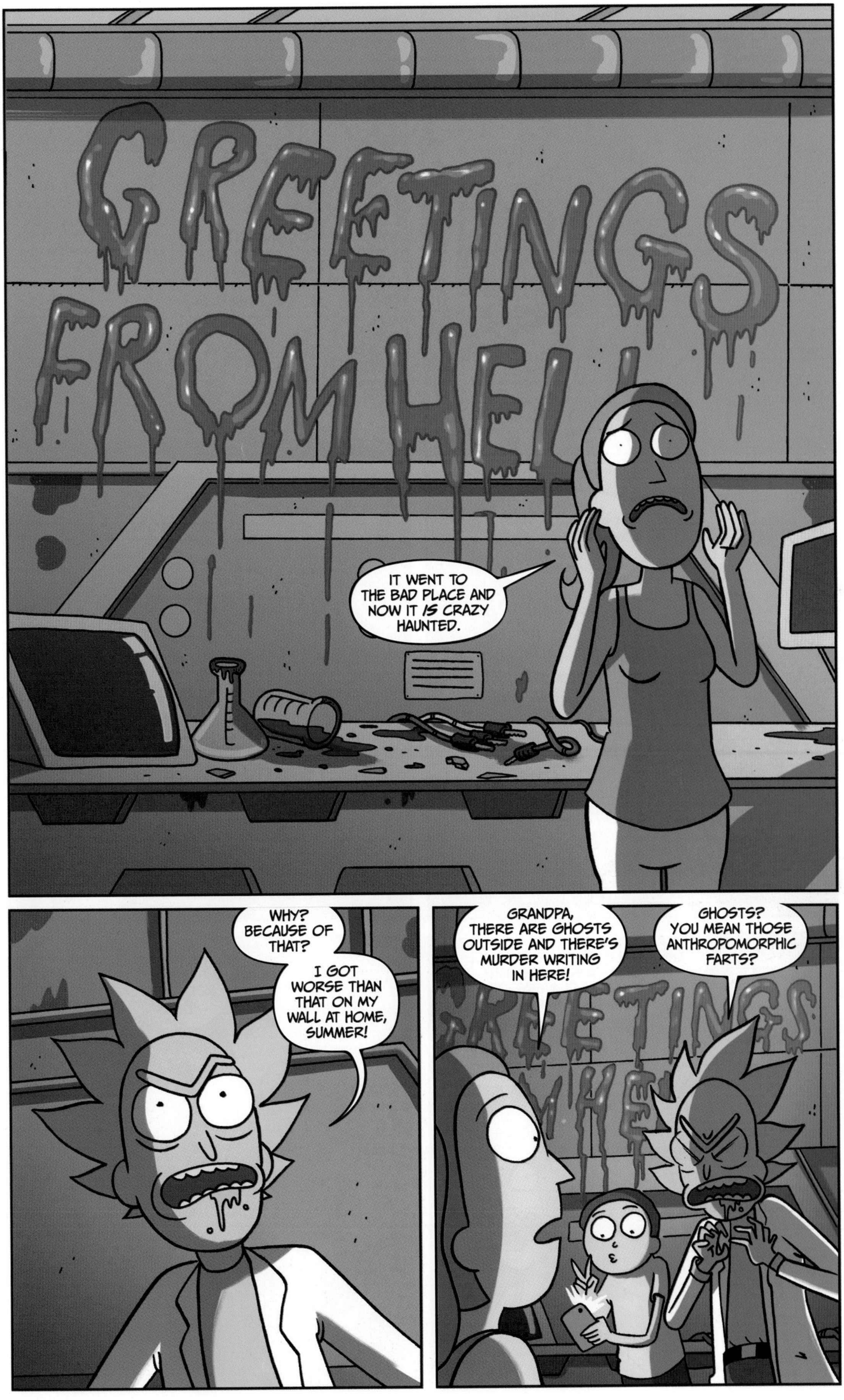
GREETINGS FROM HELL
IT WENT TO THE BAD PLACE AND NOW IT *IS* CRAZY HAUNTED.
WHY? BECAUSE OF THAT?
I GOT WORSE THAN THAT ON MY WALL AT HOME, SUMMER!
GRANDPA, THERE ARE GHOSTS OUTSIDE AND THERE'S MURDER WRITING IN HERE!
GHOSTS? YOU MEAN THOSE ANTHROPOMORPHIC FARTS?

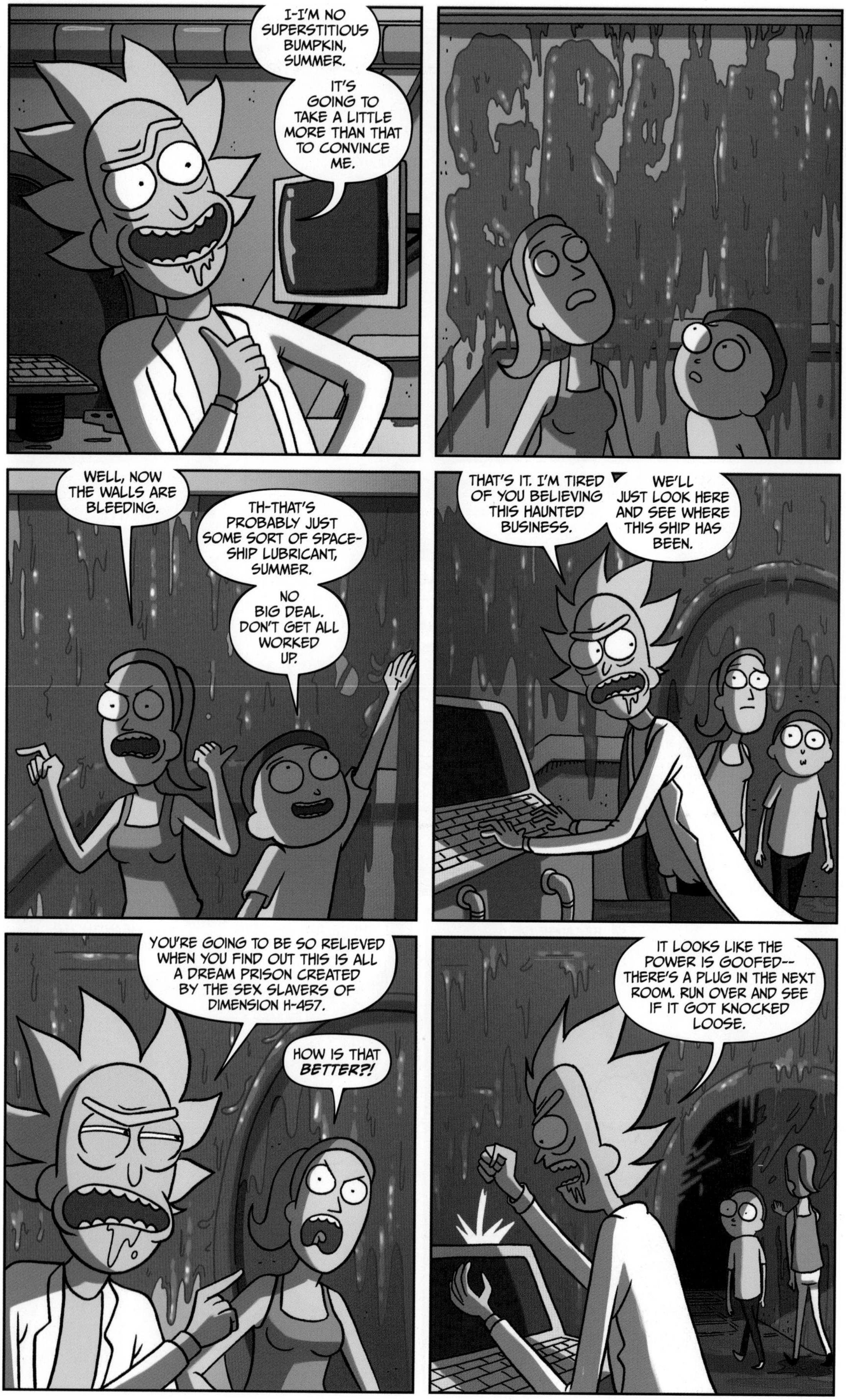
I-I'M NO SUPERSTITIOUS BUMPKIN, SUMMER.
IT'S GOING TO TAKE A LITTLE MORE THAN THAT TO CONVINCE ME.
WELL, NOW THE WALLS ARE BLEEDING.
TH-THAT'S PROBABLY JUST SOME SORT OF SPACE-SHIP LUBRICANT, SUMMER.
NO BIG DEAL. DON'T GET ALL WORKED UP.
THAT'S IT. I'M TIRED OF YOU BELIEVING THIS HAUNTED BUSINESS.
WE'LL JUST LOOK HERE AND SEE WHERE THIS SHIP HAS BEEN.
YOU'RE GOING TO BE SO RELIEVED WHEN YOU FIND OUT THIS IS ALL A DREAM PRISON CREATED BY THE SEX SLAVERS OF DIMENSION H-457.
HOW IS THAT *BETTER?!*
IT LOOKS LIKE THE POWER IS GOOFED-- THERE'S A PLUG IN THE NEXT ROOM. RUN OVER AND SEE IF IT GOT KNOCKED LOOSE.

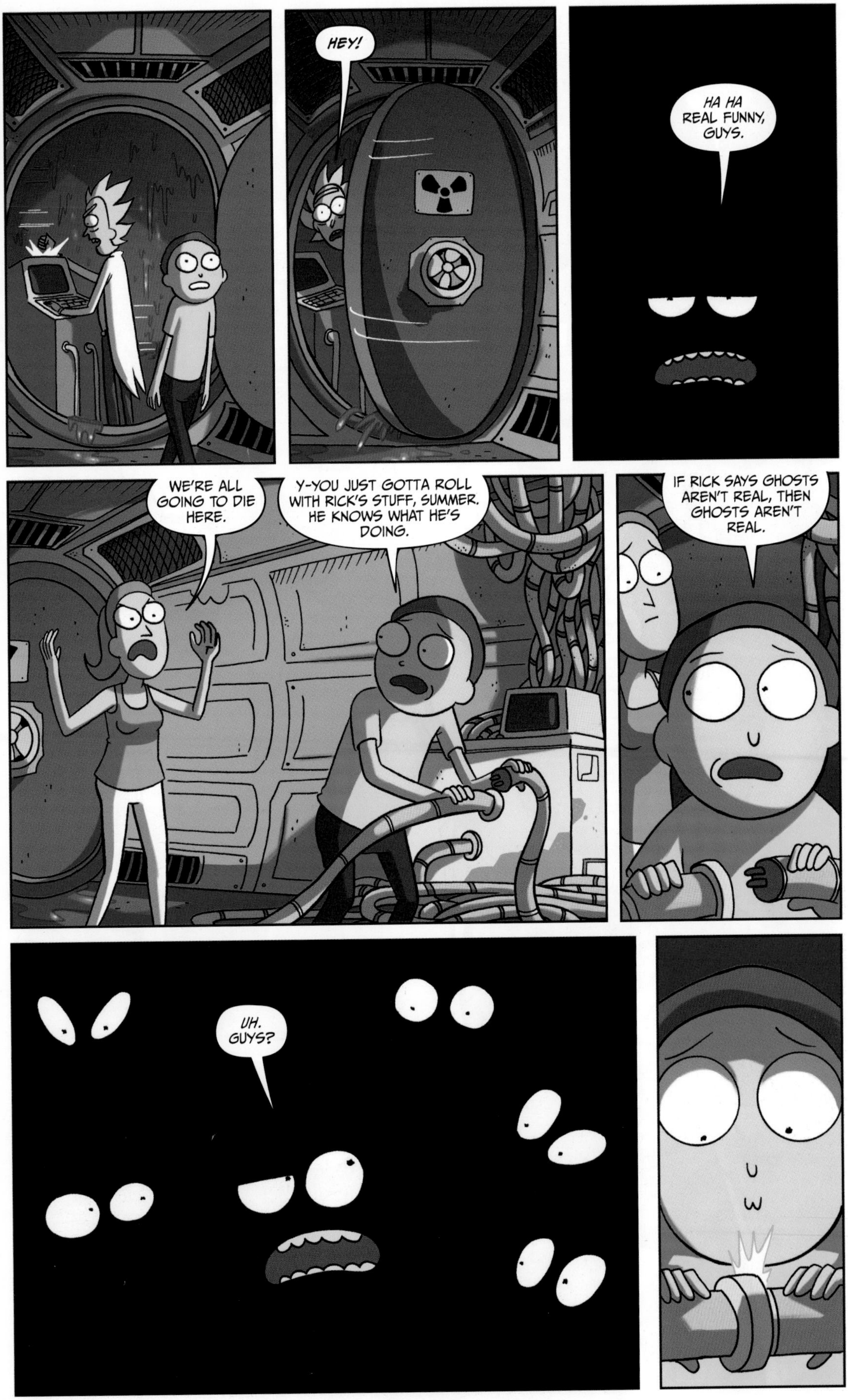
HEY!
HA HA
REAL FUNNY,
GUYS.
WE'RE ALL
GOING TO DIE
HERE.
Y-YOU JUST GOTTA ROLL
WITH RICK'S STUFF, SUMMER.
HE KNOWS WHAT HE'S
DOING.
IF RICK SAYS GHOSTS
AREN'T REAL, THEN
GHOSTS AREN'T
REAL.
UH.
GUYS?

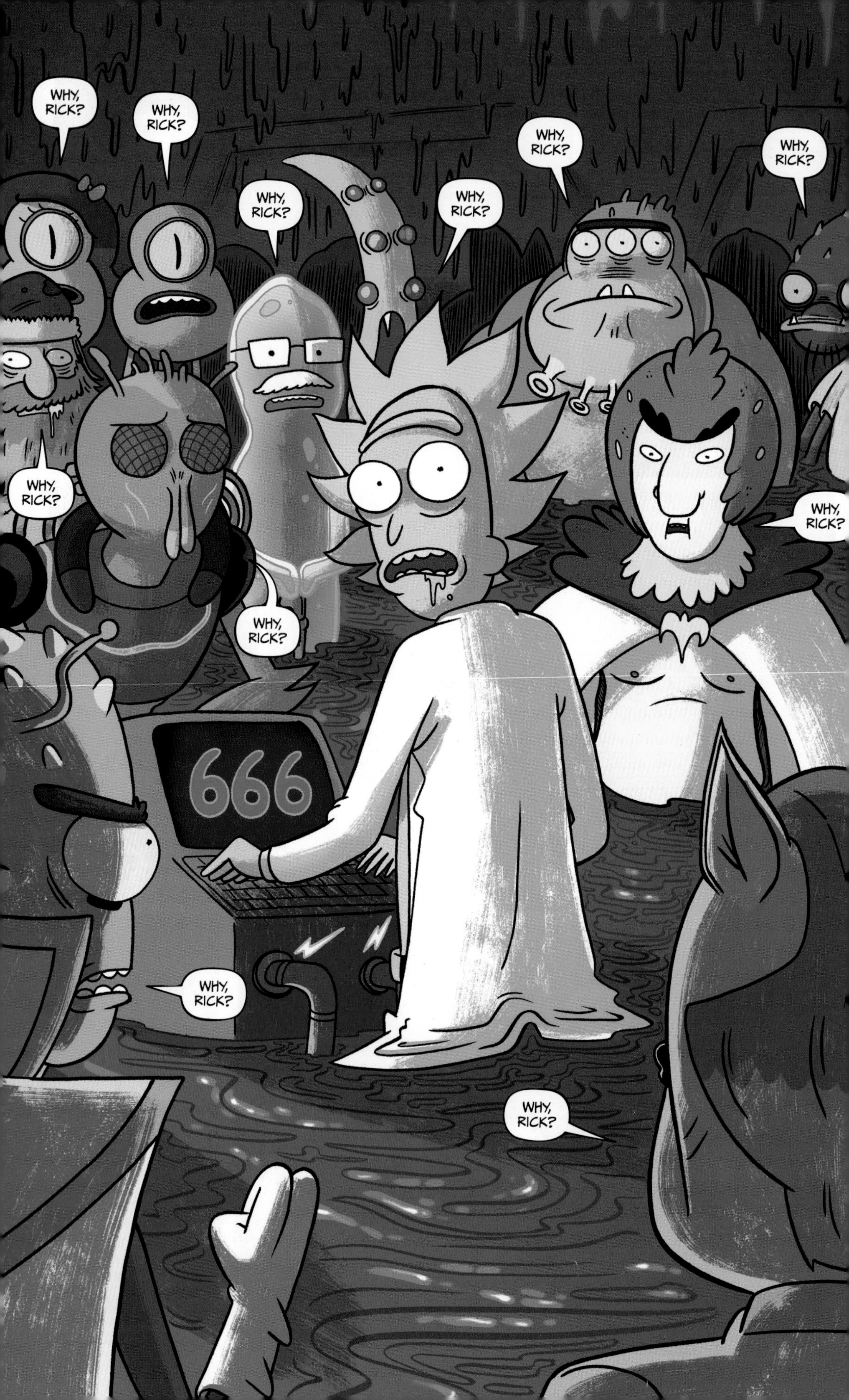
WHY, RICK?
WHY, RICK?
WHY, RICK?
WHY, RICK?
WHY, RICK?
WHY, RICK?
WHY, RICK?
WHY, RICK?
WHY, RICK?
666
WHY, RICK?
WHY, RICK?

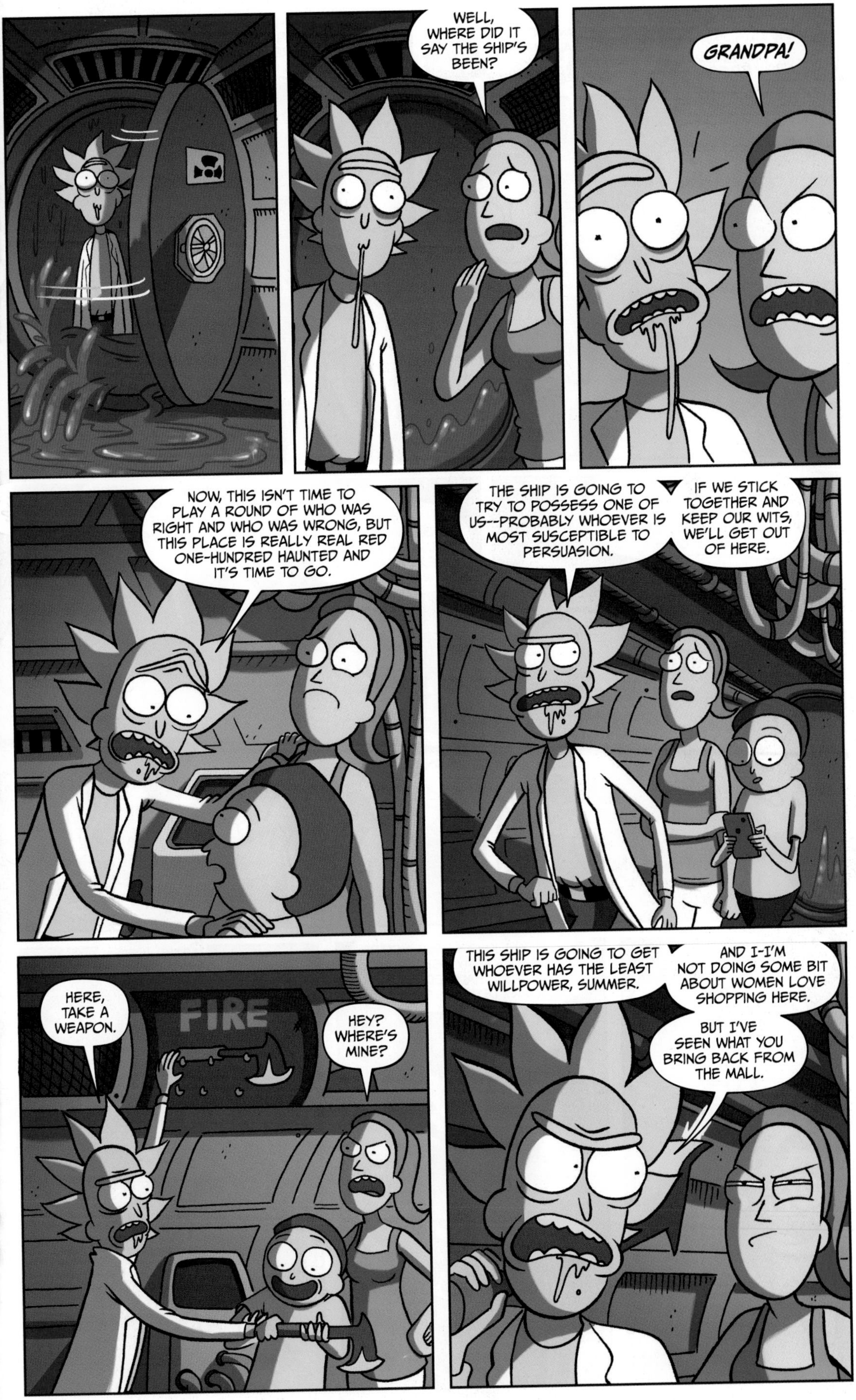

WELL, WHERE DID IT SAY THE SHIP'S BEEN?
GRANDPA!
NOW, THIS ISN'T TIME TO PLAY A ROUND OF WHO WAS RIGHT AND WHO WAS WRONG, BUT THIS PLACE IS REALLY REAL RED ONE-HUNDRED HAUNTED AND IT'S TIME TO GO.
THE SHIP IS GOING TO TRY TO POSSESS ONE OF US--PROBABLY WHOEVER IS MOST SUSCEPTIBLE TO PERSUASION.
IF WE STICK TOGETHER AND KEEP OUR WITS, WE'LL GET OUT OF HERE.
HERE, TAKE A WEAPON.
FIRE
HEY? WHERE'S MINE?
THIS SHIP IS GOING TO GET WHOEVER HAS THE LEAST WILLPOWER, SUMMER.
AND I-I'M NOT DOING SOME BIT ABOUT WOMEN LOVE SHOPPING HERE.
BUT I'VE SEEN WHAT YOU BRING BACK FROM THE MALL.

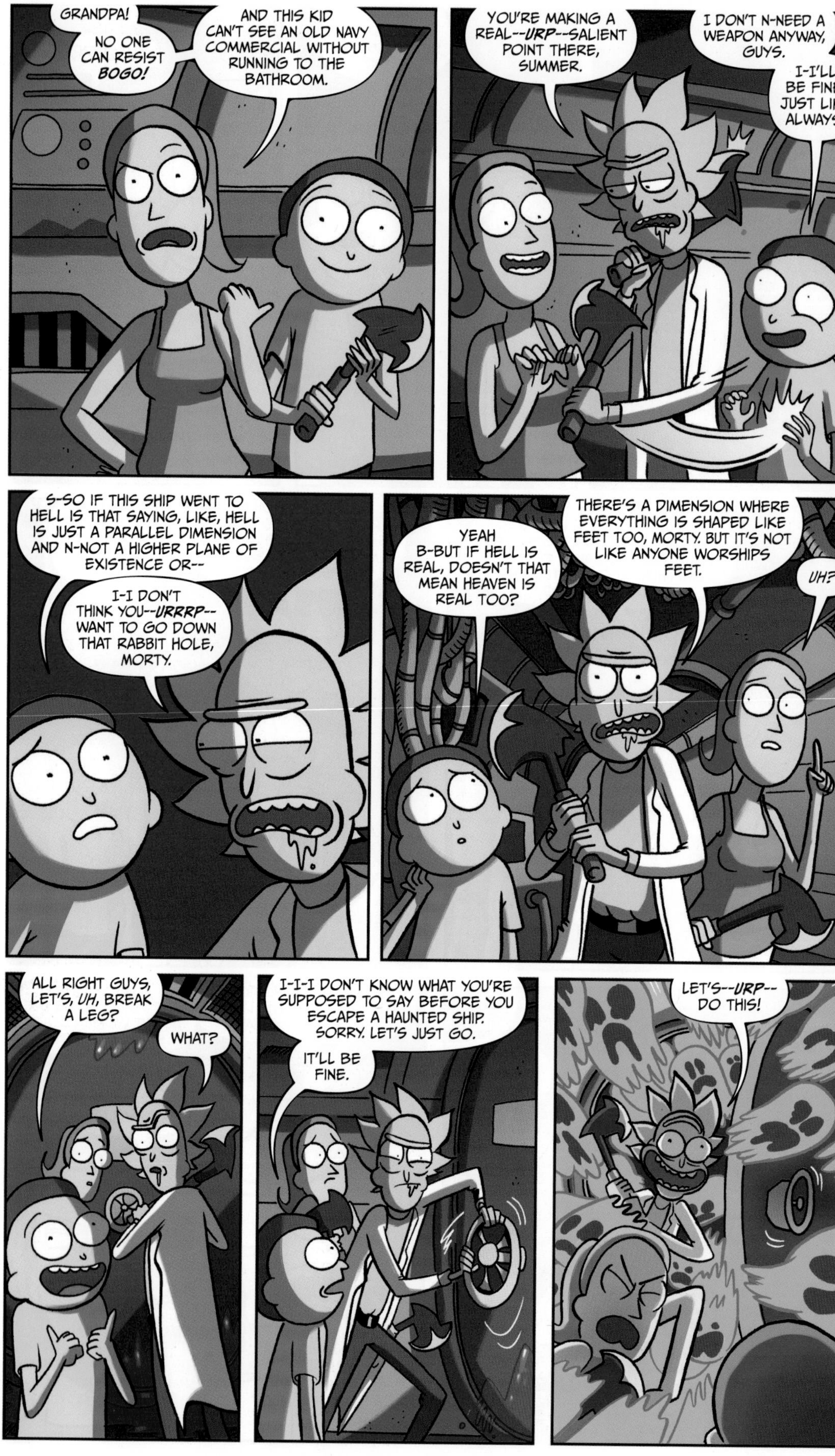
GRANDPA!
NO ONE CAN RESIST BOGO!
AND THIS KID CAN'T SEE AN OLD NAVY COMMERCIAL WITHOUT RUNNING TO THE BATHROOM.
YOU'RE MAKING A REAL--URP--SALIENT POINT THERE, SUMMER.
I DON'T N-NEED A WEAPON ANYWAY, GUYS.
I-I'LL BE FINE. JUST LIKE ALWAYS.
S-SO IF THIS SHIP WENT TO HELL IS THAT SAYING, LIKE, HELL IS JUST A PARALLEL DIMENSION AND N-NOT A HIGHER PLANE OF EXISTENCE OR--
I-I DON'T THINK YOU--URRRP--WANT TO GO DOWN THAT RABBIT HOLE, MORTY.
YEAH B-BUT IF HELL IS REAL, DOESN'T THAT MEAN HEAVEN IS REAL TOO?
THERE'S A DIMENSION WHERE EVERYTHING IS SHAPED LIKE FEET TOO, MORTY. BUT IT'S NOT LIKE ANYONE WORSHIPS FEET.
UH?
ALL RIGHT GUYS, LET'S, UH, BREAK A LEG?
WHAT?
I-I-I DON'T KNOW WHAT YOU'RE SUPPOSED TO SAY BEFORE YOU ESCAPE A HAUNTED SHIP. SORRY. LET'S JUST GO.
IT'LL BE FINE.
LET'S--URP--DO THIS!

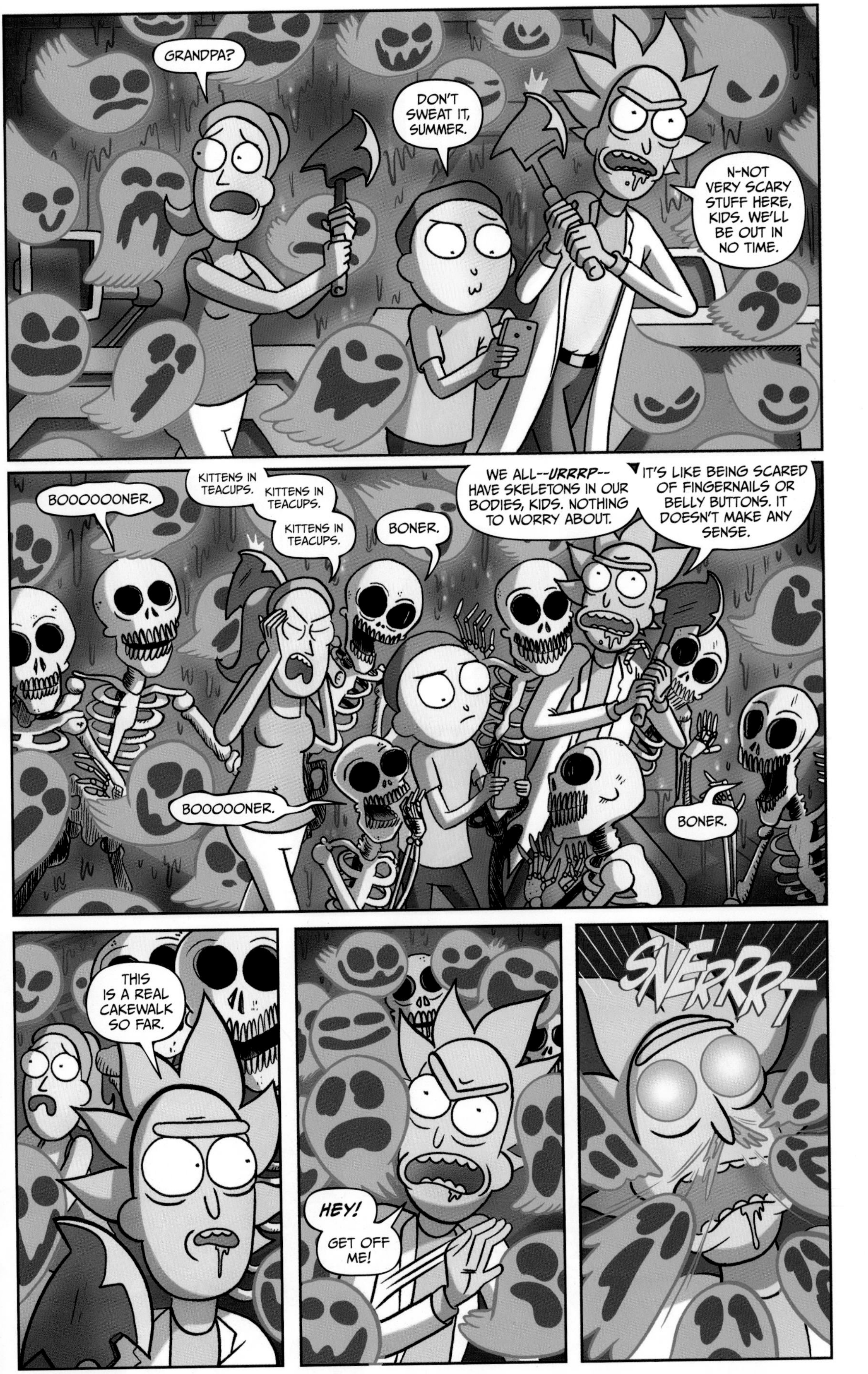
GRANDPA?
DON'T SWEAT IT, SUMMER.
N-NOT VERY SCARY STUFF HERE, KIDS. WE'LL BE OUT IN NO TIME.
BOOOOOONER.
KITTENS IN TEACUPS.
KITTENS IN TEACUPS.
KITTENS IN TEACUPS.
BONER.
WE ALL--*URRRP*-- HAVE SKELETONS IN OUR BODIES, KIDS. NOTHING TO WORRY ABOUT.
IT'S LIKE BEING SCARED OF FINGERNAILS OR BELLY BUTTONS. IT DOESN'T MAKE ANY SENSE.
BOOOOONER.
BONER.
THIS IS A REAL CAKEWALK SO FAR.
HEY!
GET OFF ME!
SNERRRT

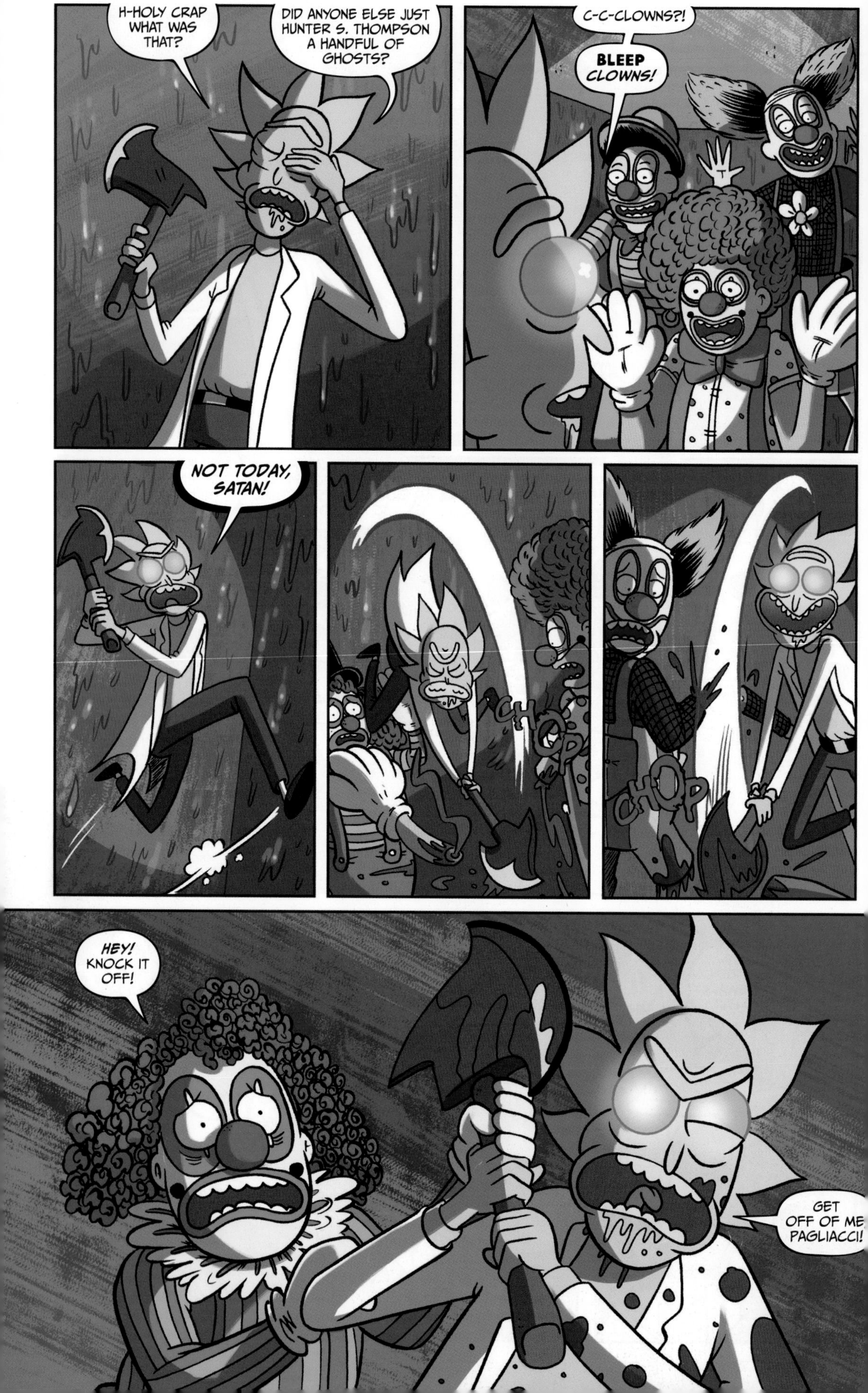
H-HOLY CRAP WHAT WAS THAT?
DID ANYONE ELSE JUST HUNTER S. THOMPSON A HANDFUL OF GHOSTS?
C-C-CLOWNS?!
BLEEP CLOWNS!
NOT TODAY, SATAN!
CHOP
CHOP
CHOP
HEY! KNOCK IT OFF!
GET OFF OF ME PAGLIACCI!

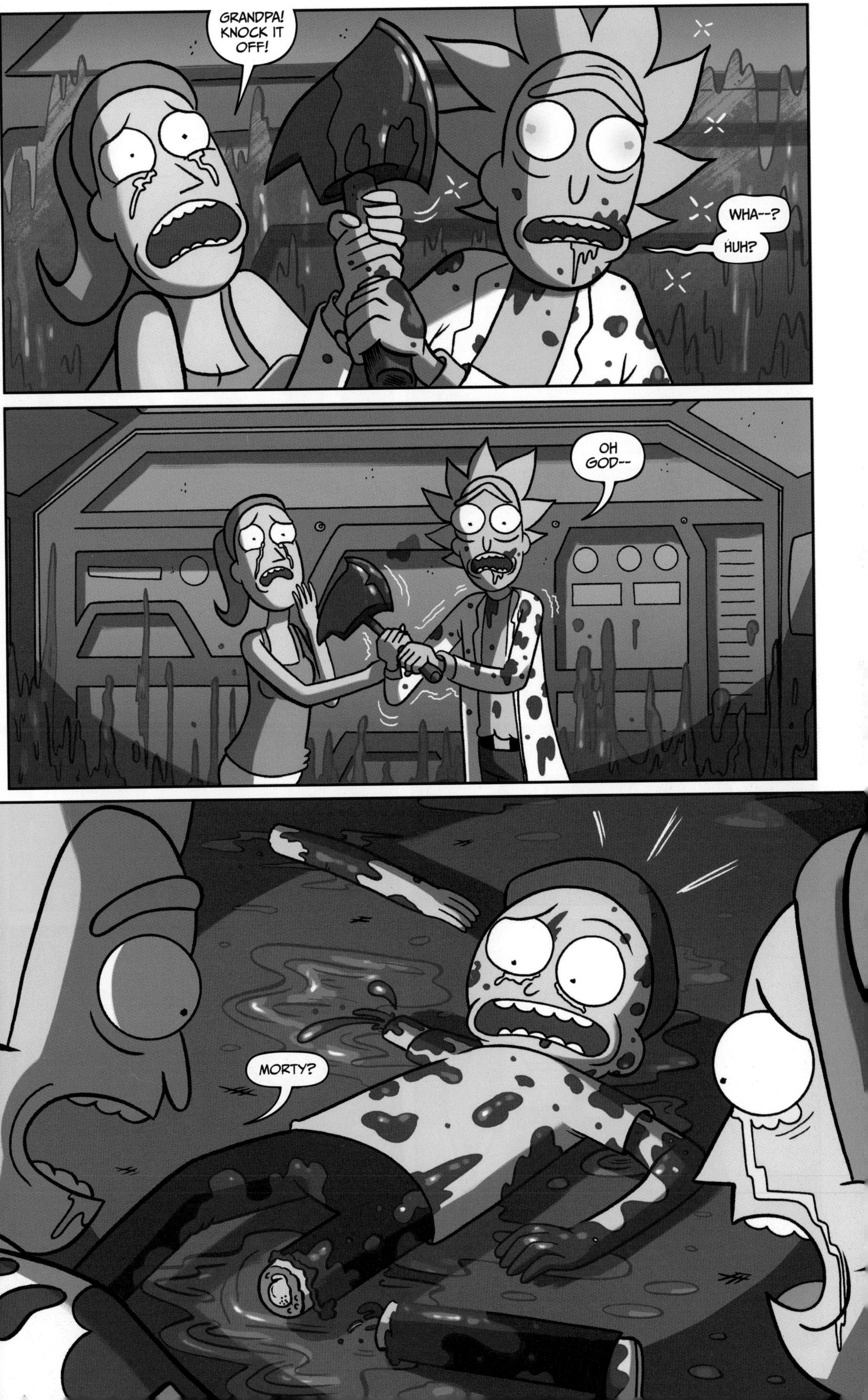
GRANDPA! KNOCK IT OFF!
WHA--?
HUH?
OH GOD--
MORTY?

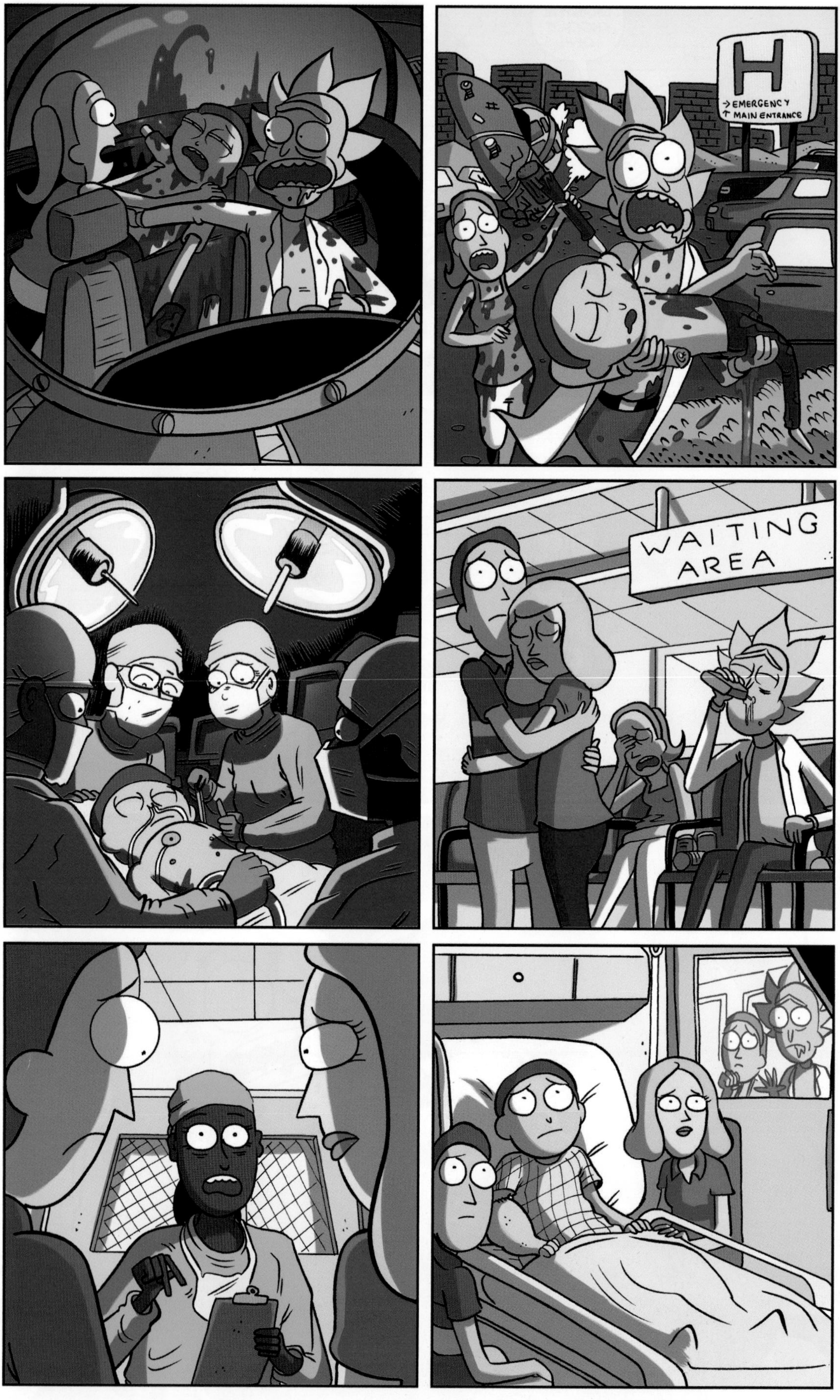
H
→ EMERGENCY
↑ MAIN ENTRANCE
WAITING AREA

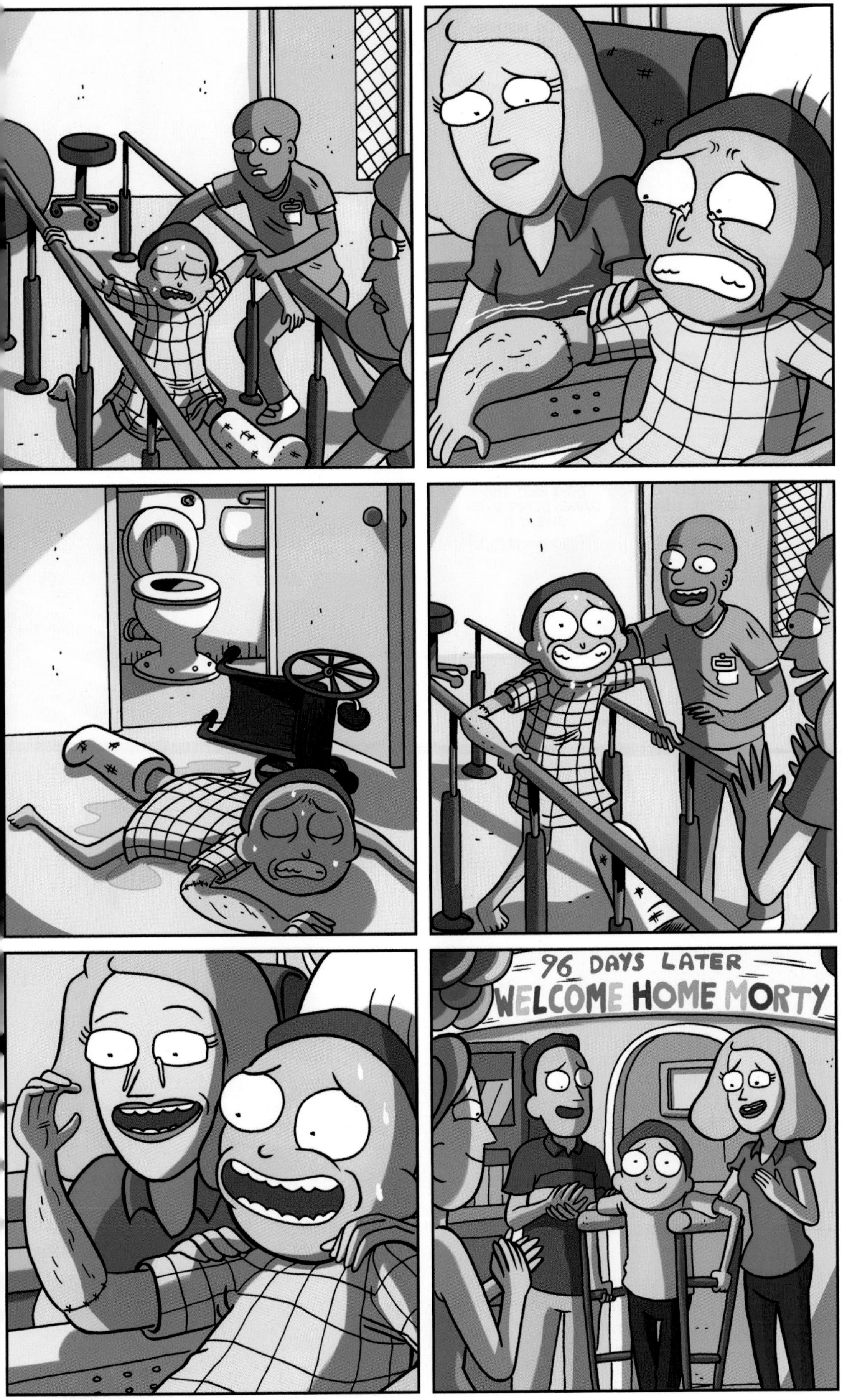
96 DAYS LATER
WELCOME HOME MORTY

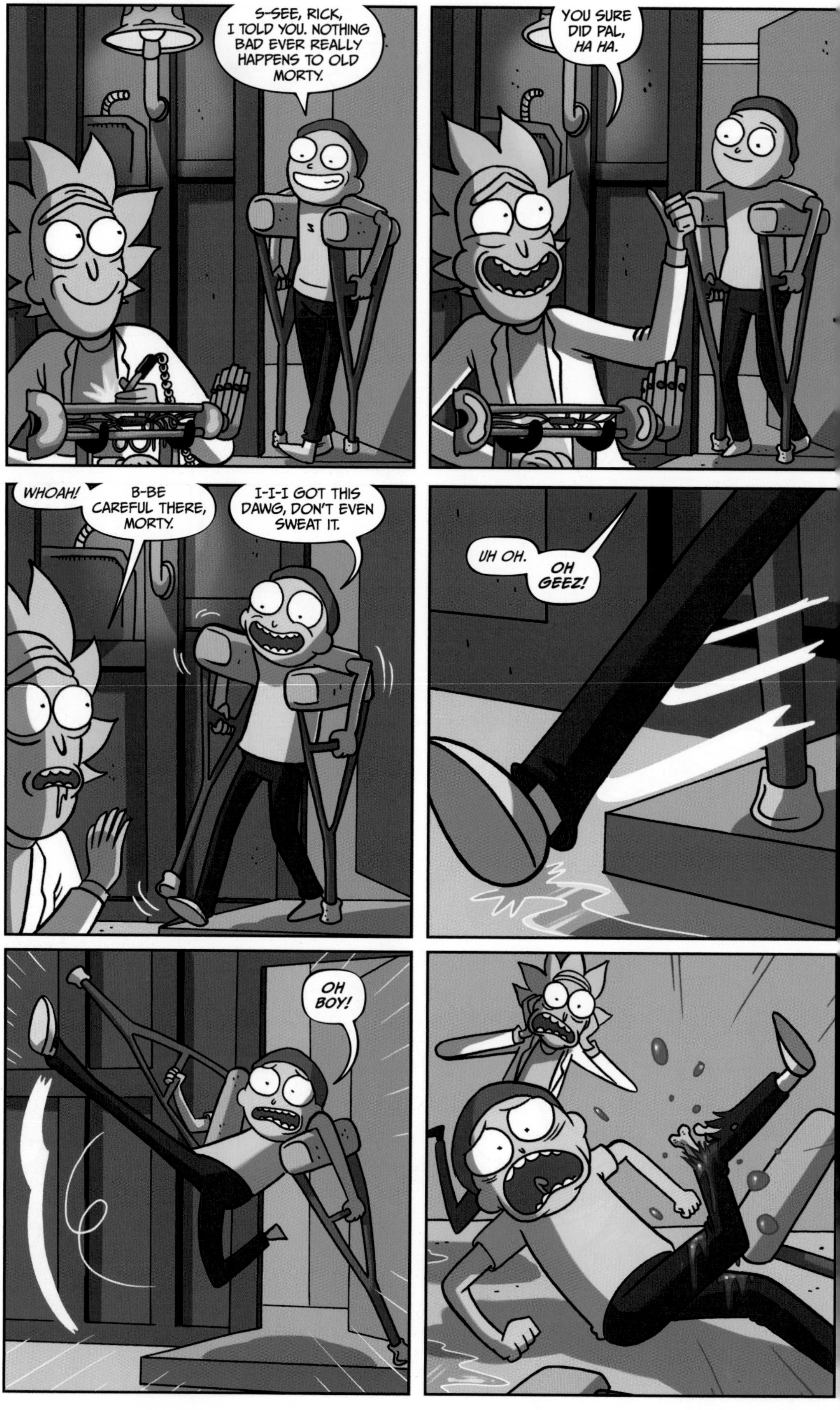
S-SEE, RICK, I TOLD YOU. NOTHING BAD EVER REALLY HAPPENS TO OLD MORTY.
YOU SURE DID PAL, HA HA.
WHOAH!
B-BE CAREFUL THERE, MORTY.
I-I-I GOT THIS DAWG, DON'T EVEN SWEAT IT.
UH OH.
OH GEEZ!
OH BOY!

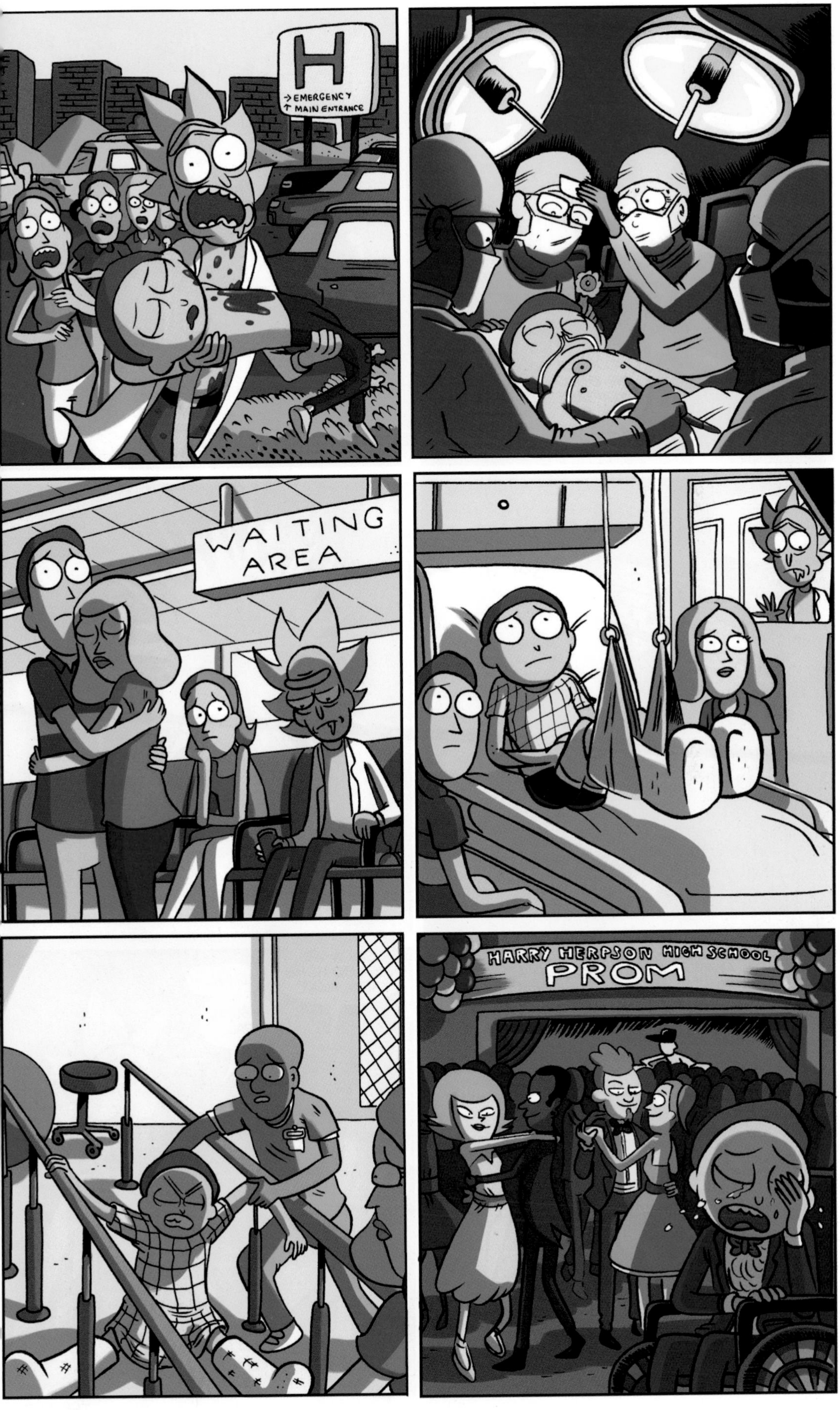
H
→ EMERGENCY
↑ MAIN ENTRANCE
WAITING AREA
HARRY HERPSON HIGH SCHOOL
PROM

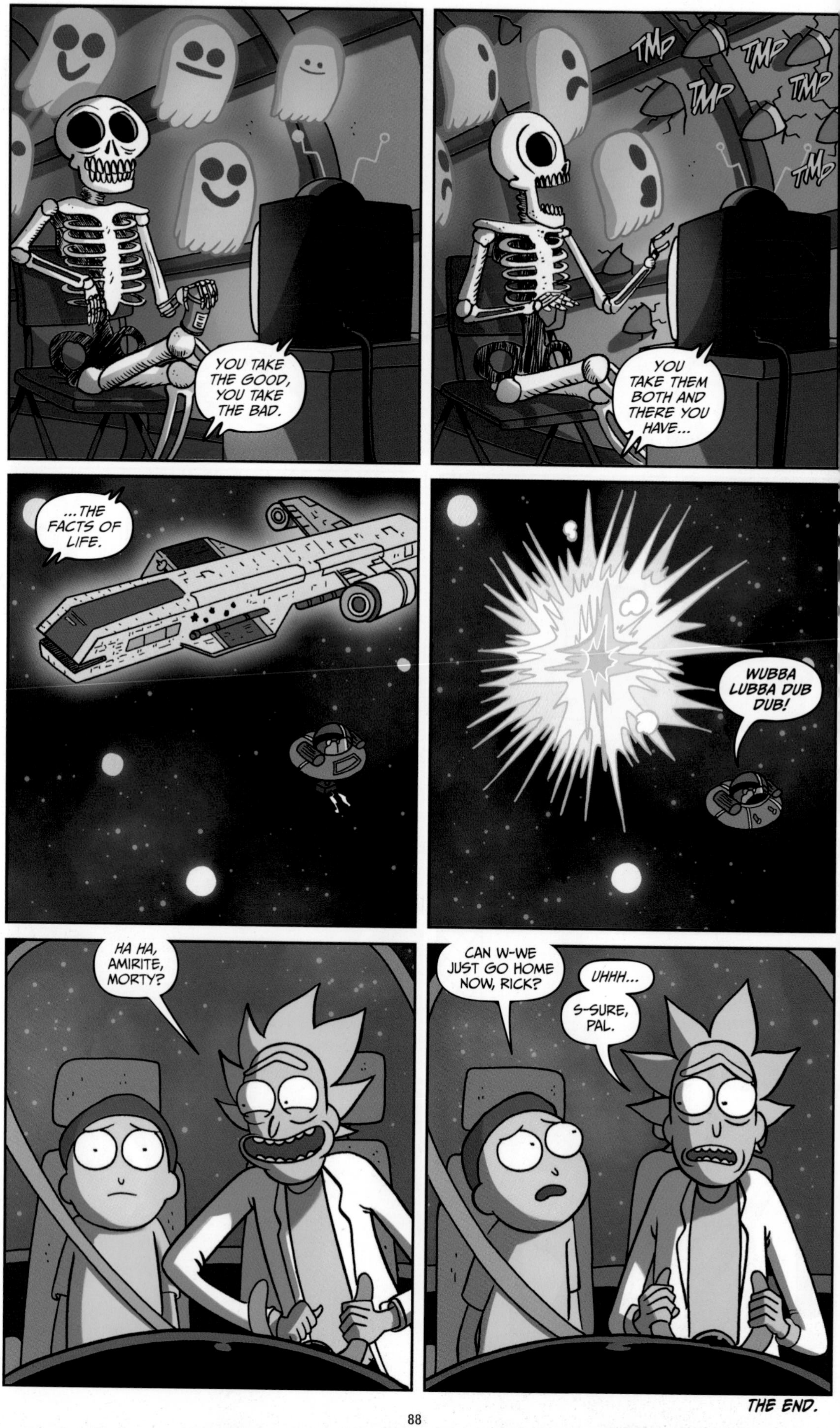
YOU TAKE THE GOOD, YOU TAKE THE BAD.
TMP TMP TMP TMP TMP
YOU TAKE THEM BOTH AND THERE YOU HAVE...
...THE FACTS OF LIFE.
WUBBA LUBBA DUB DUB!
HA HA, AMIRITE, MORTY?
CAN W-WE JUST GO HOME NOW, RICK?
UHHH...
S-SURE, PAL.
THE END.

Rick and Morty

"HONEY, I SHRUNK THE RICKS"

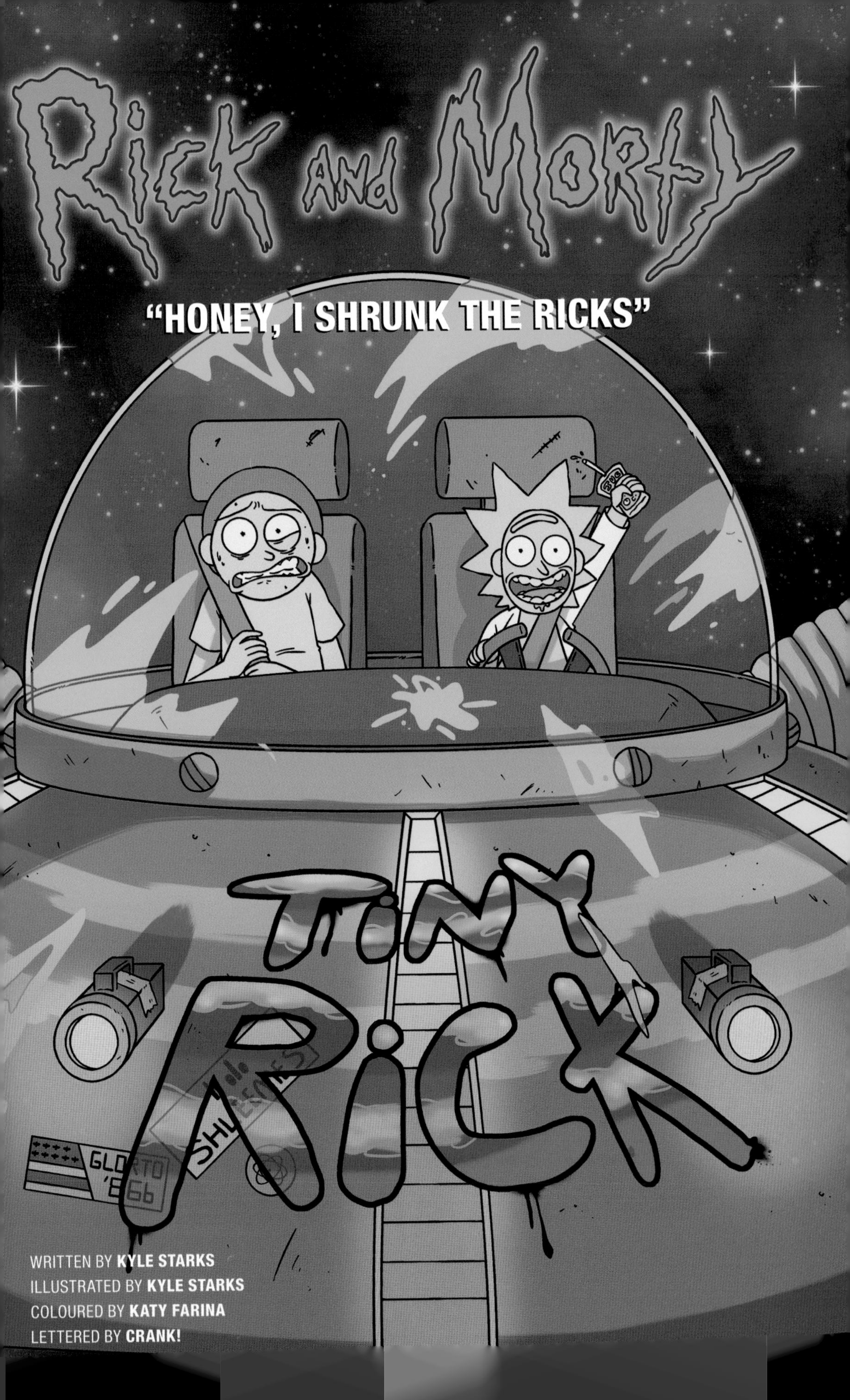

TINY RICK
GLORTO '86

WRITTEN BY **KYLE STARKS**
ILLUSTRATED BY **KYLE STARKS**
COLOURED BY **KATY FARINA**
LETTERED BY **CRANK!**

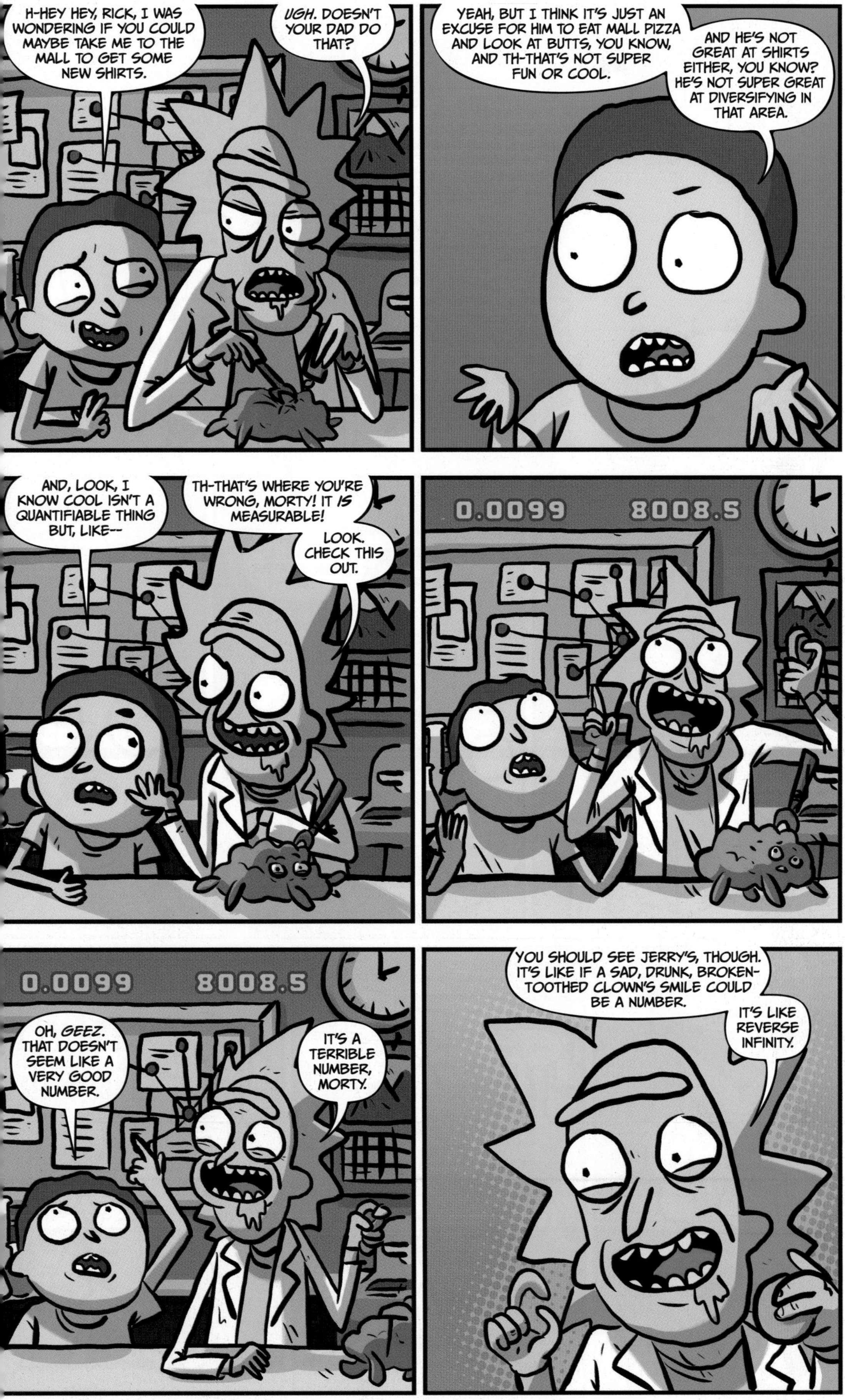
H-HEY HEY, RICK, I WAS WONDERING IF YOU COULD MAYBE TAKE ME TO THE MALL TO GET SOME NEW SHIRTS.
UGH. DOESN'T YOUR DAD DO THAT?
YEAH, BUT I THINK IT'S JUST AN EXCUSE FOR HIM TO EAT MALL PIZZA AND LOOK AT BUTTS, YOU KNOW, AND TH-THAT'S NOT SUPER FUN OR COOL.
AND HE'S NOT GREAT AT SHIRTS EITHER, YOU KNOW? HE'S NOT SUPER GREAT AT DIVERSIFYING IN THAT AREA.
AND, LOOK, I KNOW COOL ISN'T A QUANTIFIABLE THING BUT, LIKE--
TH-THAT'S WHERE YOU'RE WRONG, MORTY! IT *IS* MEASURABLE!
LOOK. CHECK THIS OUT.
0.0099
8008.5
0.0099
8008.5
OH, GEEZ. THAT DOESN'T SEEM LIKE A VERY GOOD NUMBER.
IT'S A TERRIBLE NUMBER, MORTY.
YOU SHOULD SEE JERRY'S, THOUGH. IT'S LIKE IF A SAD, DRUNK, BROKEN-TOOTHED CLOWN'S SMILE COULD BE A NUMBER.
IT'S LIKE REVERSE INFINITY.

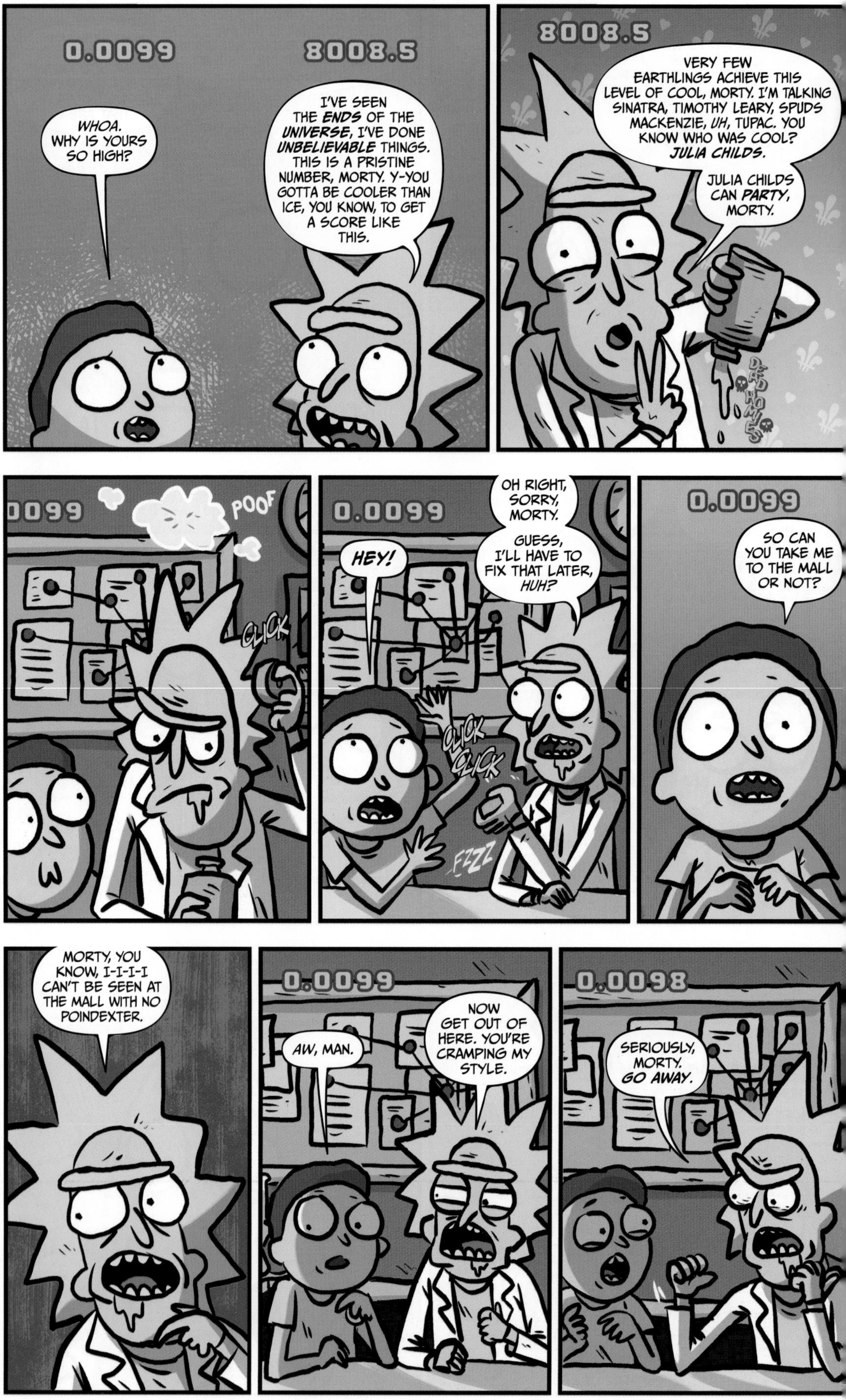
0.0099
WHOA. WHY IS YOURS SO HIGH?
8008.5
I'VE SEEN THE ENDS OF THE UNIVERSE, I'VE DONE UNBELIEVABLE THINGS. THIS IS A PRISTINE NUMBER, MORTY. Y-YOU GOTTA BE COOLER THAN ICE, YOU KNOW, TO GET A SCORE LIKE THIS.
8008.5
VERY FEW EARTHLINGS ACHIEVE THIS LEVEL OF COOL, MORTY. I'M TALKING SINATRA, TIMOTHY LEARY, SPUDS MACKENZIE, UH, TUPAC. YOU KNOW WHO WAS COOL? JULIA CHILDS.
JULIA CHILDS CAN PARTY, MORTY.
DEAD HOMIES
0099
POOF
CLICK
0.0099
HEY!
OH RIGHT, SORRY, MORTY.
GUESS, I'LL HAVE TO FIX THAT LATER, HUH?
CLICK CLICK
FZZZ
0.0099
SO CAN YOU TAKE ME TO THE MALL OR NOT?
MORTY, YOU KNOW, I-I-I-I CAN'T BE SEEN AT THE MALL WITH NO POINDEXTER.
0.0099
AW, MAN.
NOW GET OUT OF HERE. YOU'RE CRAMPING MY STYLE.
0.0098
SERIOUSLY, MORTY. GO AWAY.

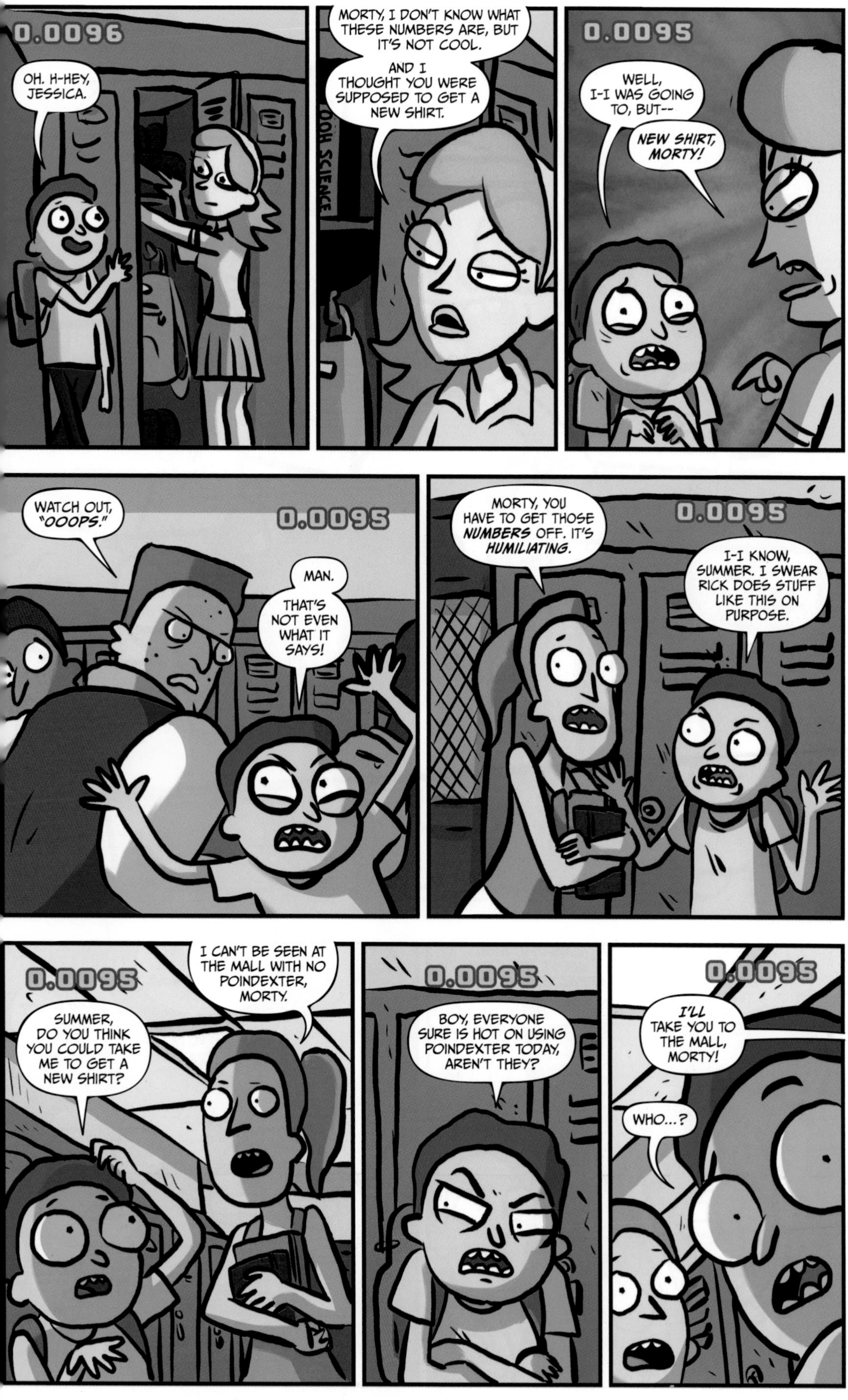
0.0096
OH. H-HEY, JESSICA.
MORTY, I DON'T KNOW WHAT THESE NUMBERS ARE, BUT IT'S NOT COOL.
AND I THOUGHT YOU WERE SUPPOSED TO GET A NEW SHIRT.
OOH SCIENCE
0.0095
WELL, I-I WAS GOING TO, BUT--
NEW SHIRT, MORTY!
WATCH OUT, "OOOPS."
0.0095
MAN.
THAT'S NOT EVEN WHAT IT SAYS!
MORTY, YOU HAVE TO GET THOSE NUMBERS OFF. IT'S HUMILIATING.
0.0095
I-I KNOW, SUMMER. I SWEAR RICK DOES STUFF LIKE THIS ON PURPOSE.
0.0095
SUMMER, DO YOU THINK YOU COULD TAKE ME TO GET A NEW SHIRT?
I CAN'T BE SEEN AT THE MALL WITH NO POINDEXTER, MORTY.
0.0095
BOY, EVERYONE SURE IS HOT ON USING POINDEXTER TODAY, AREN'T THEY?
0.0095
I'LL TAKE YOU TO THE MALL, MORTY!
WHO...?

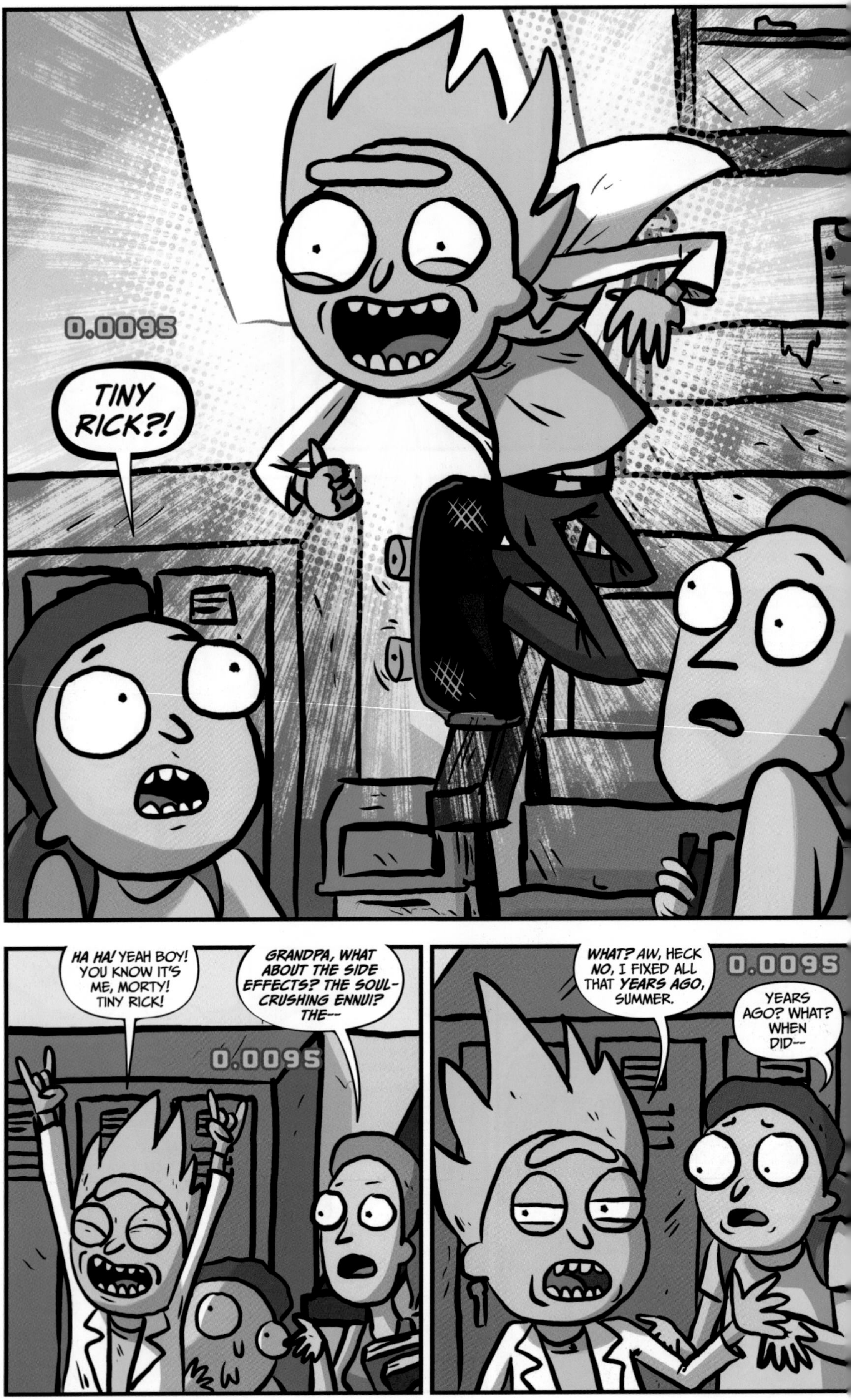
0.0095
TINY RICK?!
HA HA! YEAH BOY! YOU KNOW IT'S ME, MORTY! TINY RICK!
0.0095
GRANDPA, WHAT ABOUT THE SIDE EFFECTS? THE SOUL-CRUSHING ENNUI? THE--
WHAT? AW, HECK NO, I FIXED ALL THAT YEARS AGO, SUMMER.
0.0095
YEARS AGO? WHAT? WHEN DID--

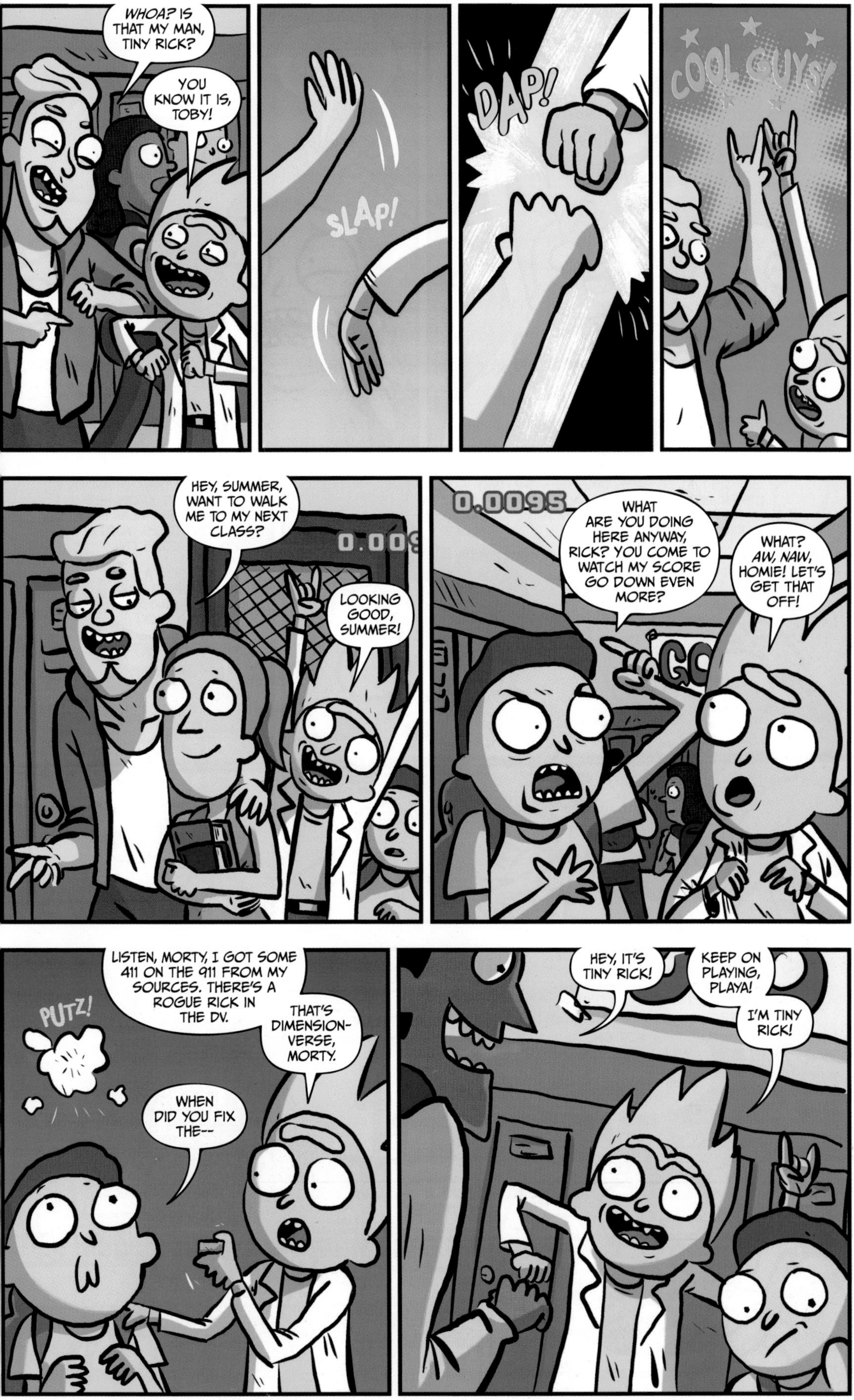
WHOA? IS THAT MY MAN, TINY RICK?
YOU KNOW IT IS, TOBY!
SLAP!
DAP!
COOL GUYS!
HEY, SUMMER, WANT TO WALK ME TO MY NEXT CLASS?
LOOKING GOOD, SUMMER!
0.0095
WHAT ARE YOU DOING HERE ANYWAY, RICK? YOU COME TO WATCH MY SCORE GO DOWN EVEN MORE?
WHAT? AW, NAW, HOMIE! LET'S GET THAT OFF!
LISTEN, MORTY, I GOT SOME 411 ON THE 911 FROM MY SOURCES. THERE'S A ROGUE RICK IN THE DV.
PUTZ!
THAT'S DIMENSION-VERSE, MORTY.
WHEN DID YOU FIX THE--
HEY, IT'S TINY RICK!
KEEP ON PLAYING, PLAYA!
I'M TINY RICK!

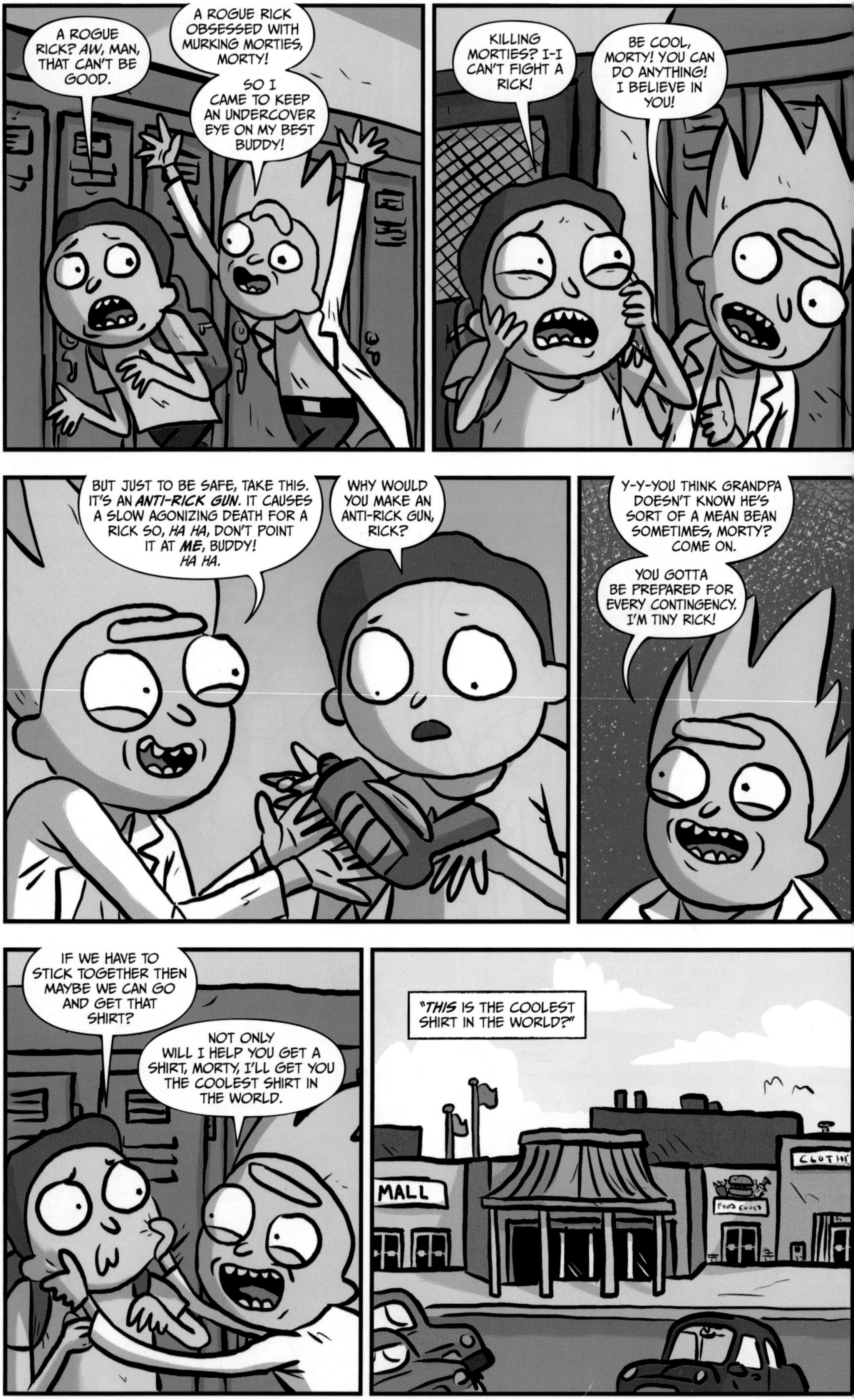
A ROGUE RICK? AW, MAN, THAT CAN'T BE GOOD.
A ROGUE RICK OBSESSED WITH MURKING MORTIES, MORTY!
SO I CAME TO KEEP AN UNDERCOVER EYE ON MY BEST BUDDY!
KILLING MORTIES? I-I CAN'T FIGHT A RICK!
BE COOL, MORTY! YOU CAN DO ANYTHING! I BELIEVE IN YOU!
BUT JUST TO BE SAFE, TAKE THIS. IT'S AN ANTI-RICK GUN. IT CAUSES A SLOW AGONIZING DEATH FOR A RICK SO, HA HA, DON'T POINT IT AT ME, BUDDY! HA HA.
WHY WOULD YOU MAKE AN ANTI-RICK GUN, RICK?
Y-Y-YOU THINK GRANDPA DOESN'T KNOW HE'S SORT OF A MEAN BEAN SOMETIMES, MORTY? COME ON.
YOU GOTTA BE PREPARED FOR EVERY CONTINGENCY. I'M TINY RICK!
IF WE HAVE TO STICK TOGETHER THEN MAYBE WE CAN GO AND GET THAT SHIRT?
NOT ONLY WILL I HELP YOU GET A SHIRT, MORTY, I'LL GET YOU THE COOLEST SHIRT IN THE WORLD.
"THIS IS THE COOLEST SHIRT IN THE WORLD?"
MALL

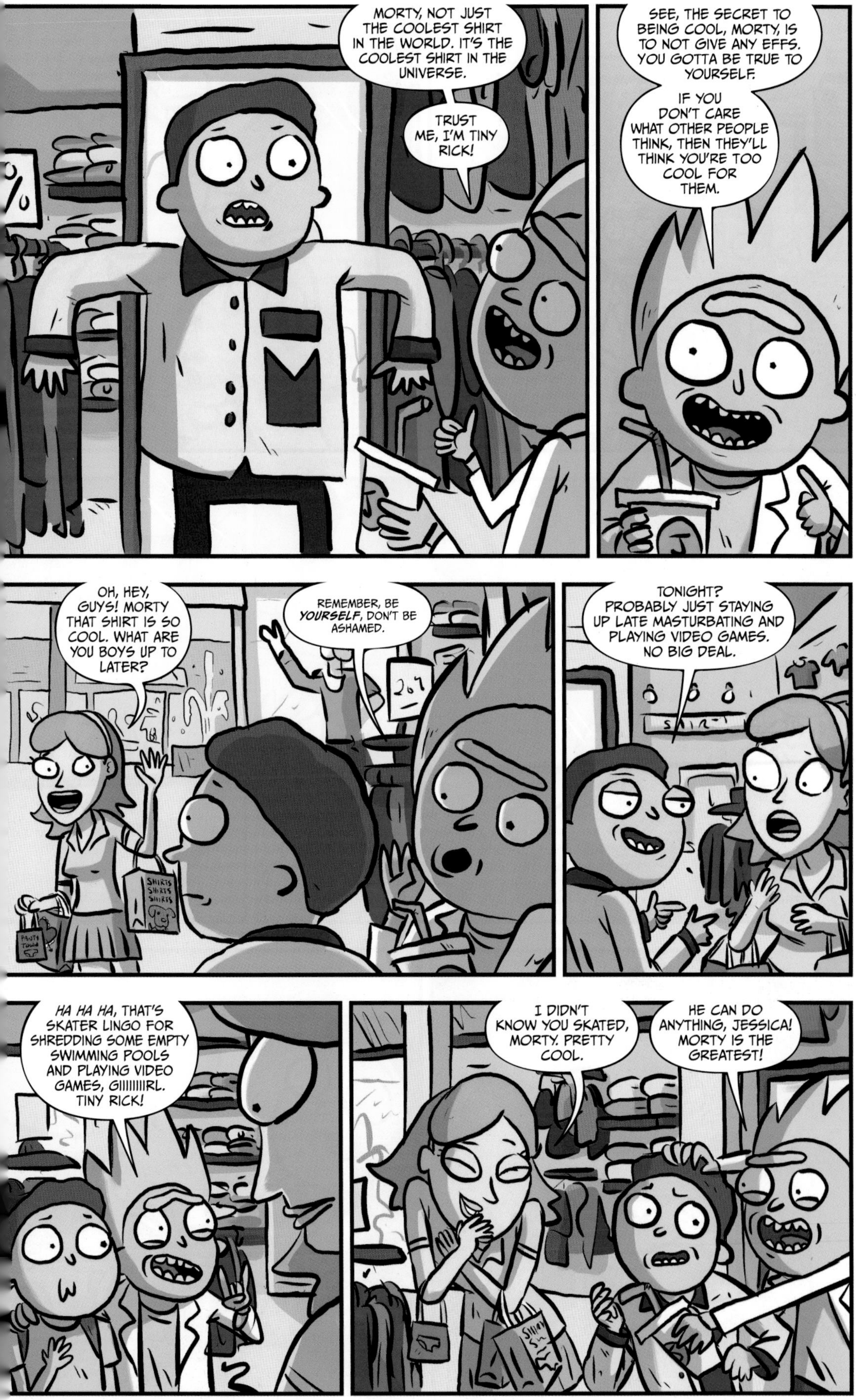
MORTY, NOT JUST THE COOLEST SHIRT IN THE WORLD. IT'S THE COOLEST SHIRT IN THE UNIVERSE.
TRUST ME, I'M TINY RICK!
SEE, THE SECRET TO BEING COOL, MORTY, IS TO NOT GIVE ANY EFFS. YOU GOTTA BE TRUE TO YOURSELF.
IF YOU DON'T CARE WHAT OTHER PEOPLE THINK, THEN THEY'LL THINK YOU'RE TOO COOL FOR THEM.
OH, HEY, GUYS! MORTY THAT SHIRT IS SO COOL. WHAT ARE YOU BOYS UP TO LATER?
REMEMBER, BE *YOURSELF*, DON'T BE ASHAMED.
TONIGHT? PROBABLY JUST STAYING UP LATE MASTURBATING AND PLAYING VIDEO GAMES. NO BIG DEAL.
HA HA HA, THAT'S SKATER LINGO FOR SHREDDING SOME EMPTY SWIMMING POOLS AND PLAYING VIDEO GAMES, GIIIIIIIRL. TINY RICK!
I DIDN'T KNOW YOU SKATED, MORTY. PRETTY COOL.
HE CAN DO ANYTHING, JESSICA! MORTY IS THE GREATEST!

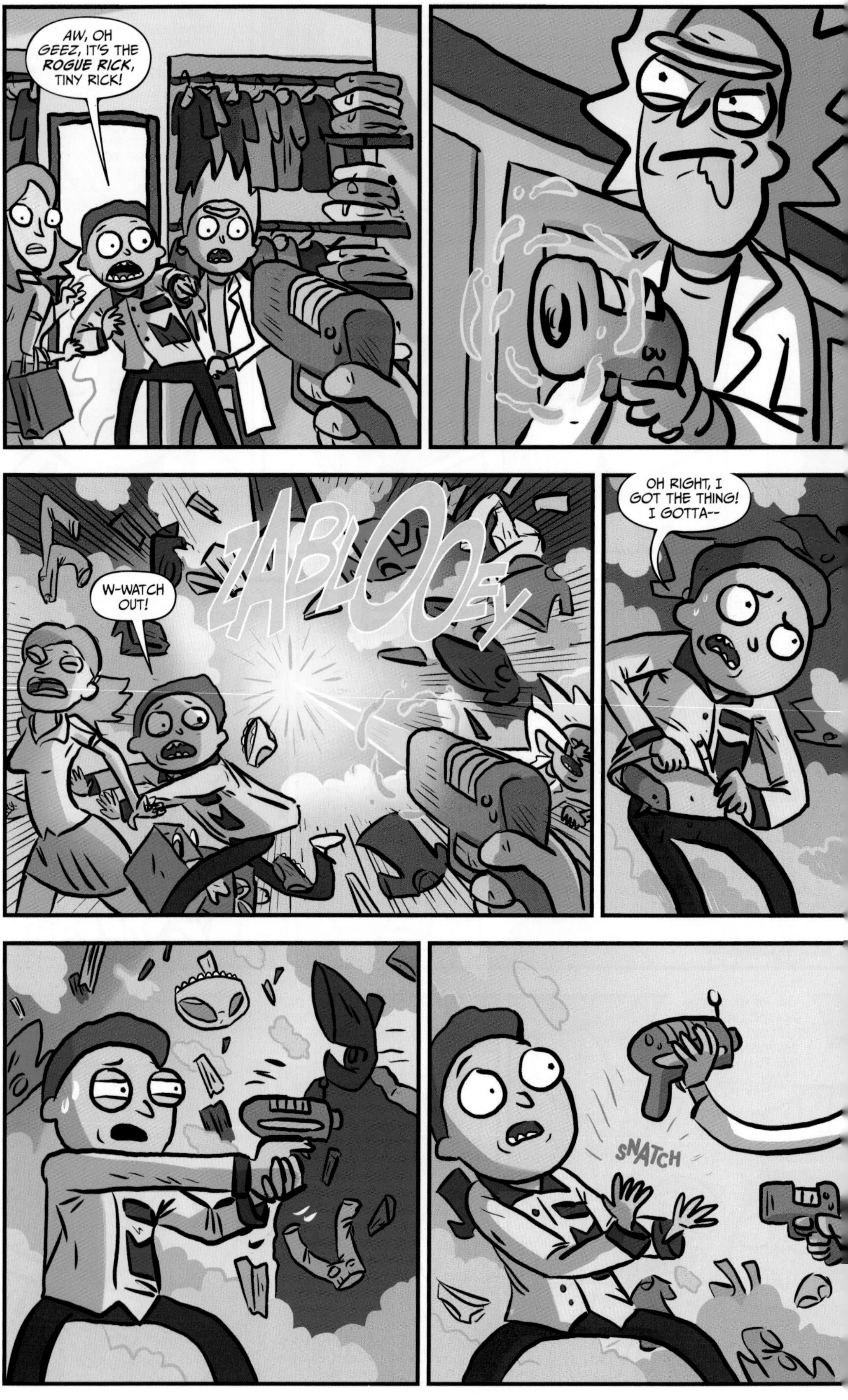
AW, OH GEEZ, IT'S THE ROGUE RICK, TINY RICK!
W-WATCH OUT!
ZABLOOEY
OH RIGHT, I GOT THE THING! I GOTTA--
SNATCH

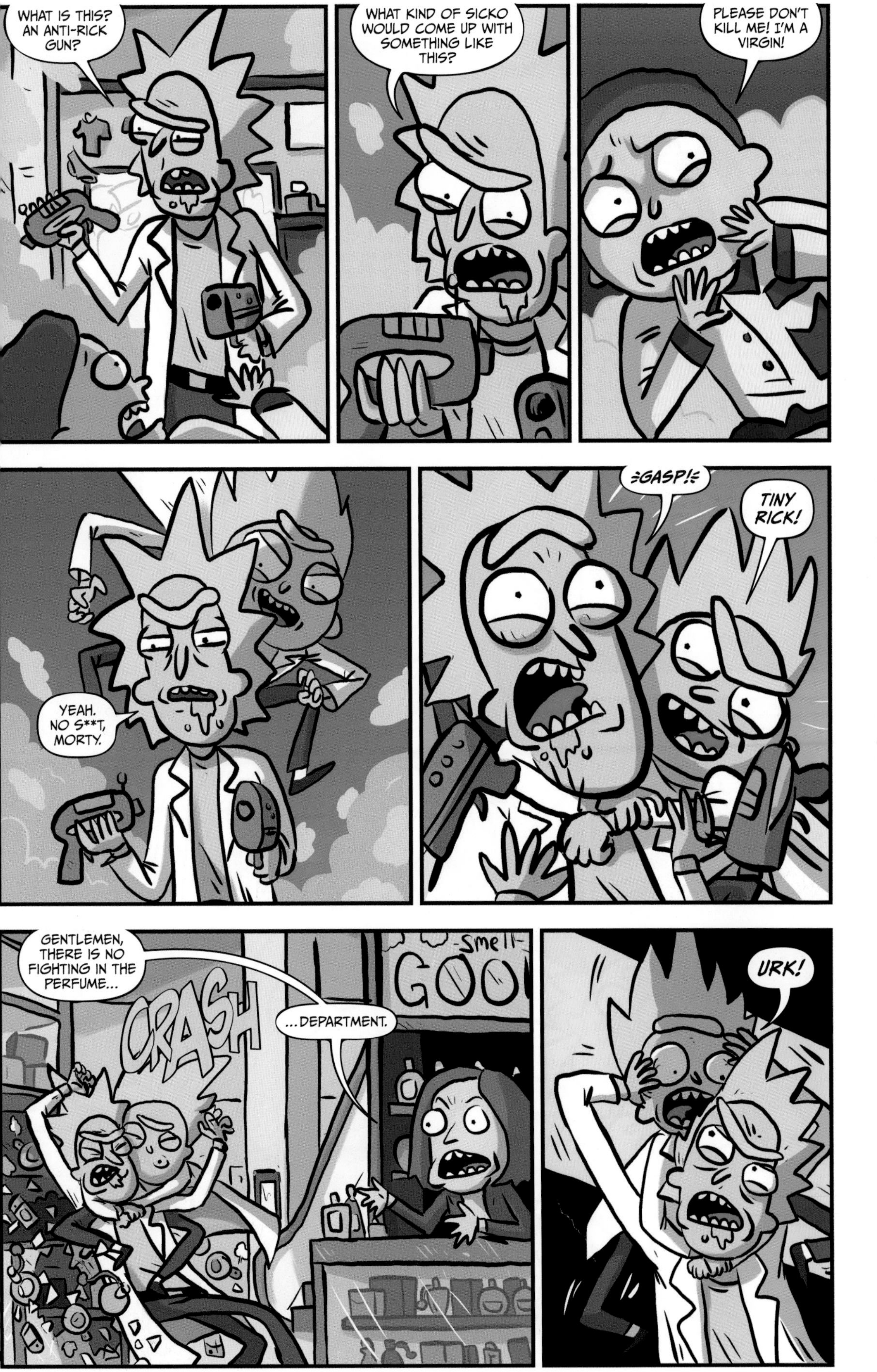
WHAT IS THIS? AN ANTI-RICK GUN?
WHAT KIND OF SICKO WOULD COME UP WITH SOMETHING LIKE THIS?
PLEASE DON'T KILL ME! I'M A VIRGIN!
YEAH. NO S**T, MORTY.
GASP!
TINY RICK!
GENTLEMEN, THERE IS NO FIGHTING IN THE PERFUME...
CRASH
...DEPARTMENT.
-Smell-
GOO
URK!

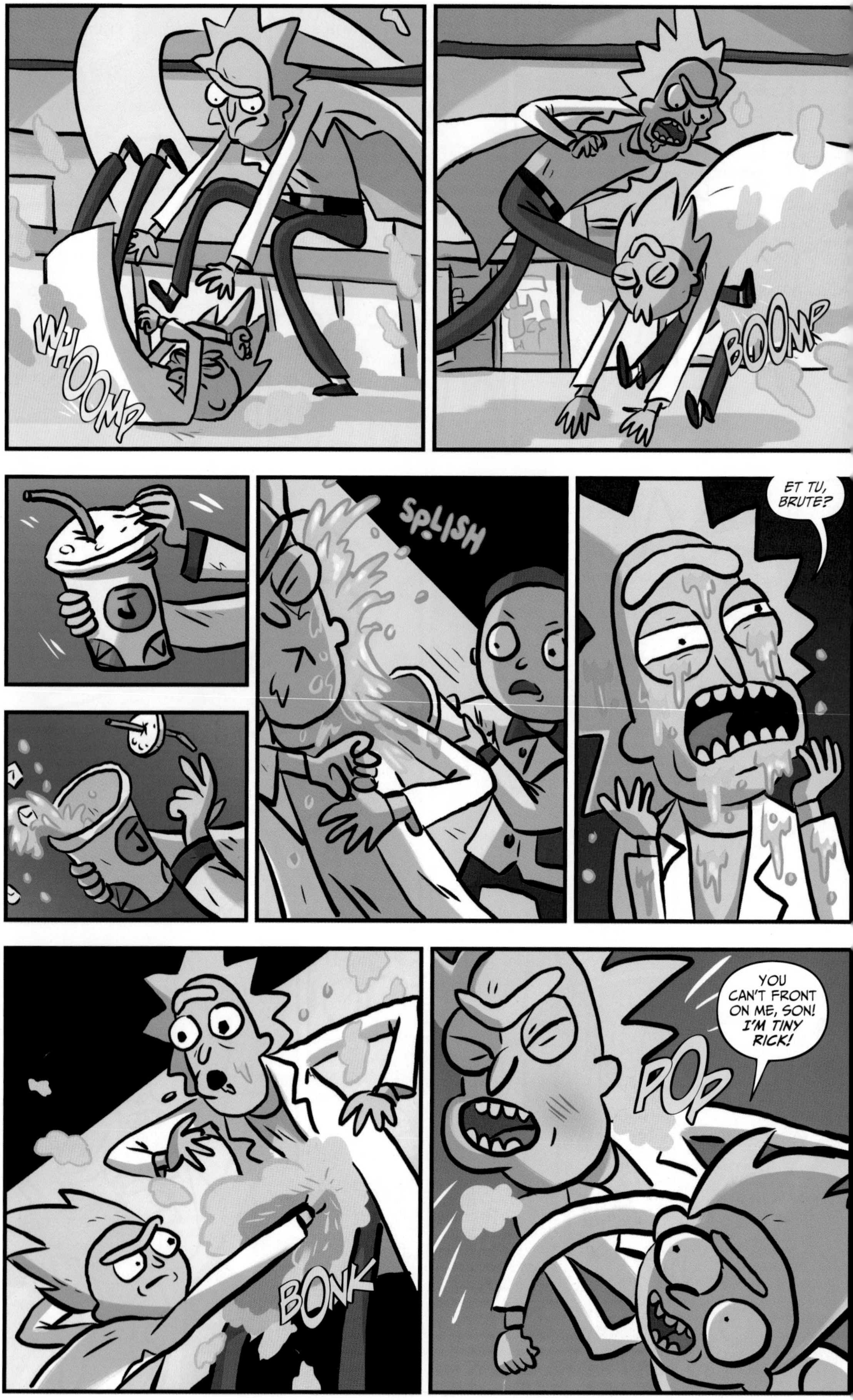
WHOOMP
BOOMP
SPLISH
ET TU, BRUTE?
BONK
POP
YOU CAN'T FRONT ON ME, SON! I'M TINY RICK!

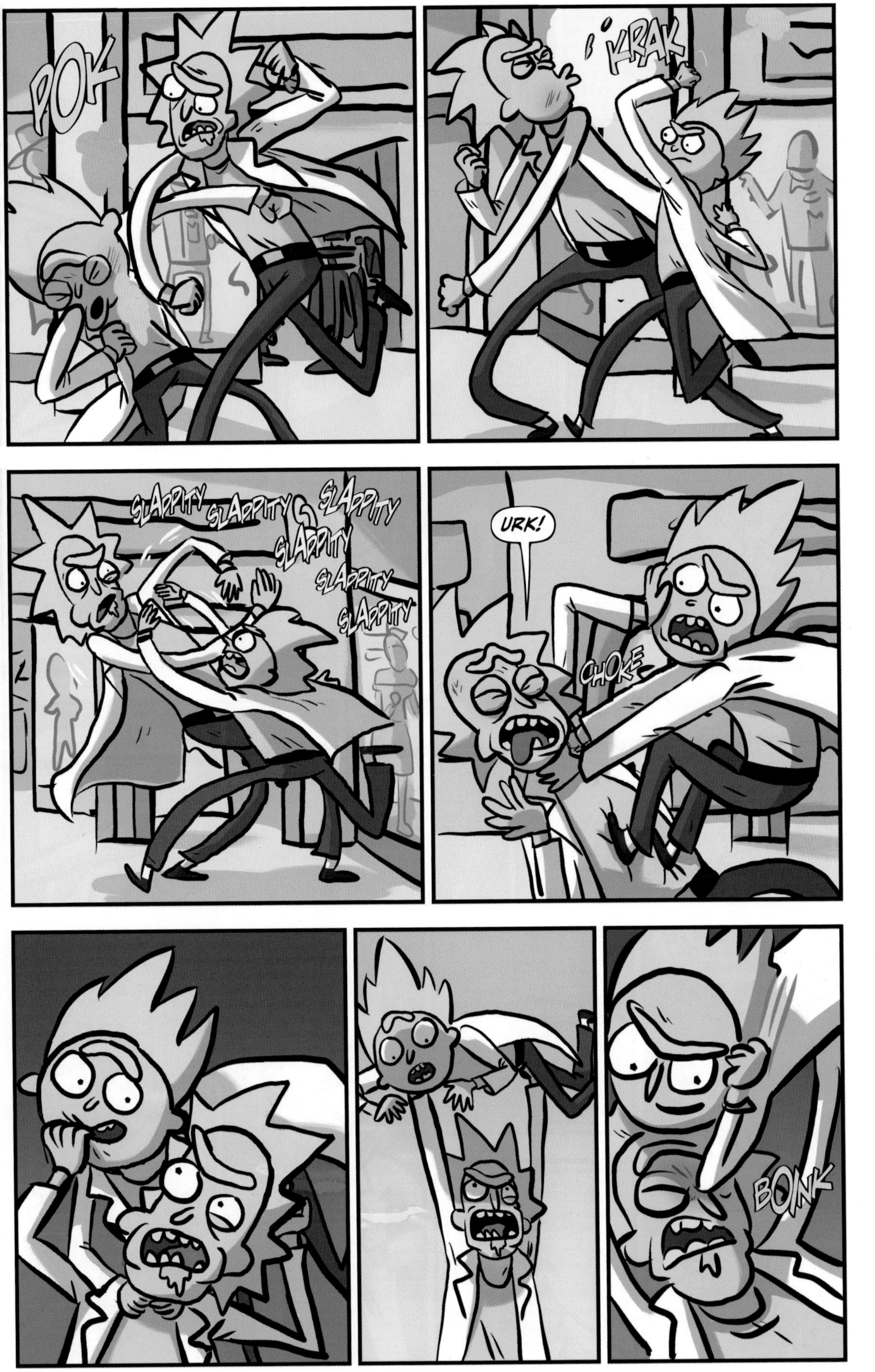
POK
KRAK
SLAPPITY SLAPPITY SLAPPITY
SLAPPITY
SLAPPITY
SLAPPITY
URK!
CHOKE
BOINK

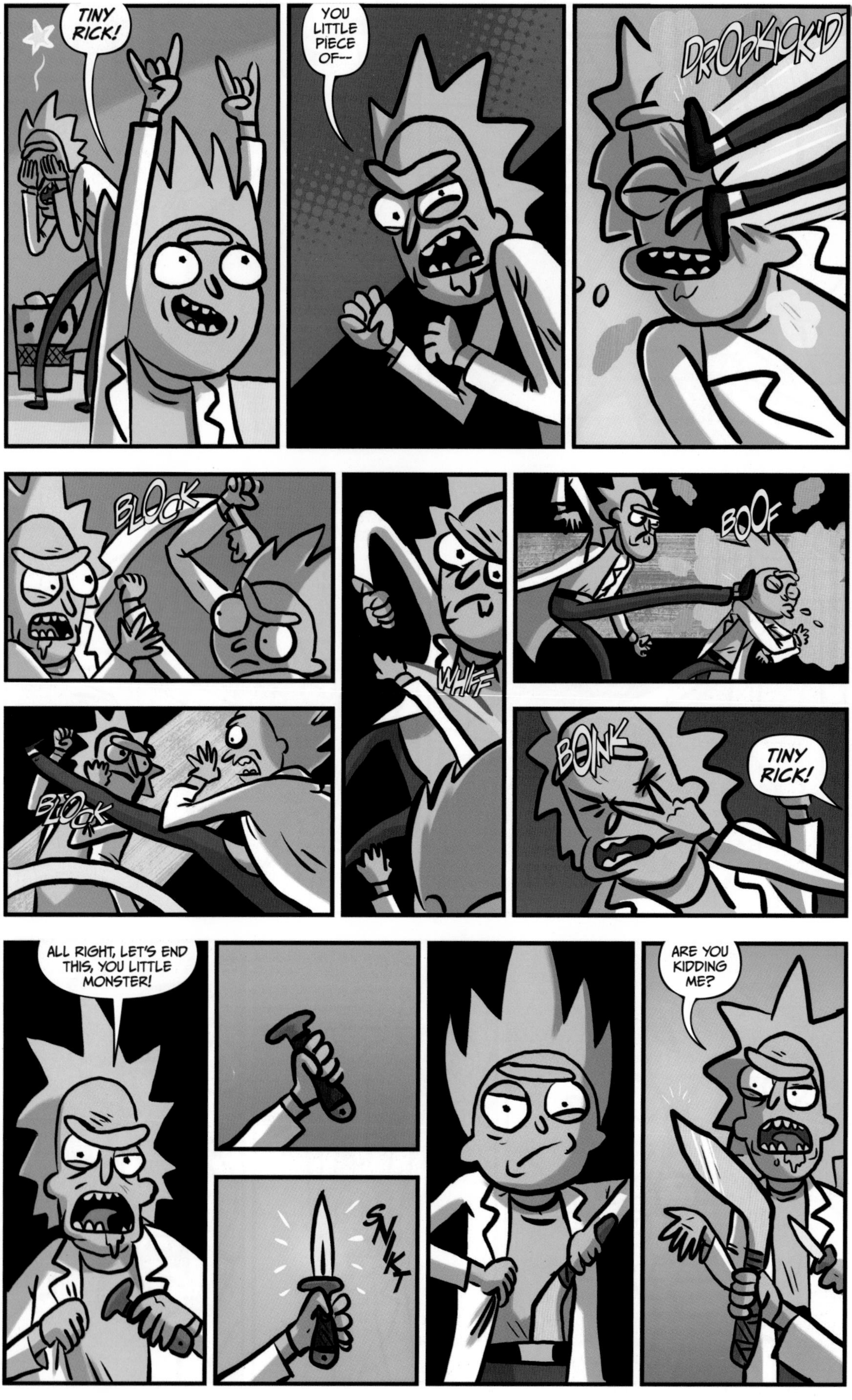
TINY RICK!
YOU LITTLE PIECE OF--
DROPKICK'D
BLOCK
WHIFF
BOOF
BLOCK
BONK
TINY RICK!
ALL RIGHT, LET'S END THIS, YOU LITTLE MONSTER!
SNIKT
ARE YOU KIDDING ME?

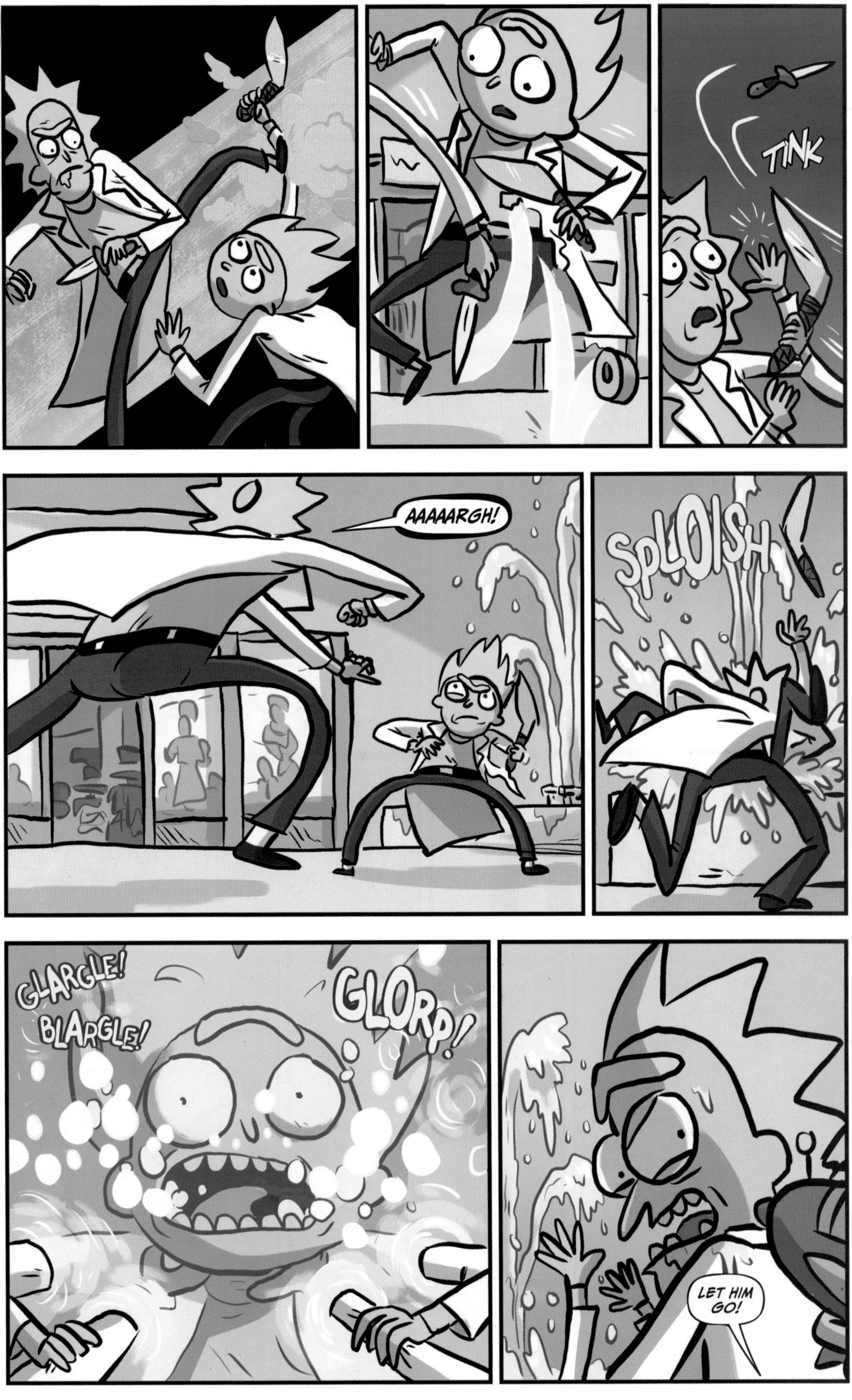
TINK
AAAAARGH!
SPLOISH
GLARGLE!
BLARGLE!
GLORP!
LET HIM GO!

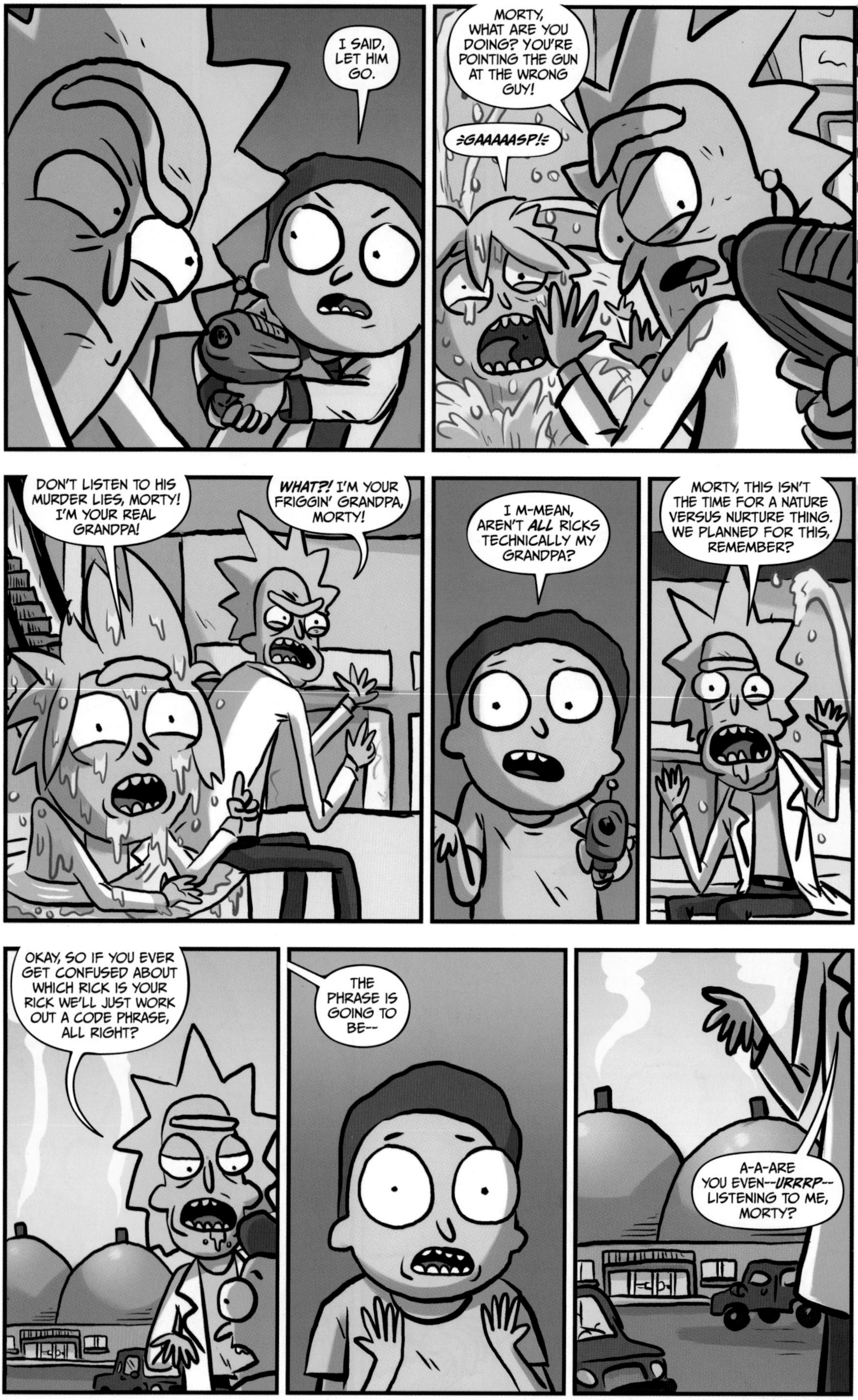
I SAID, LET HIM GO.
MORTY, WHAT ARE YOU DOING? YOU'RE POINTING THE GUN AT THE WRONG GUY!
GAAAAASP!
DON'T LISTEN TO HIS MURDER LIES, MORTY! I'M YOUR REAL GRANDPA!
WHAT?! I'M YOUR FRIGGIN' GRANDPA, MORTY!
I M-MEAN, AREN'T ALL RICKS TECHNICALLY MY GRANDPA?
MORTY, THIS ISN'T THE TIME FOR A NATURE VERSUS NURTURE THING. WE PLANNED FOR THIS, REMEMBER?
OKAY, SO IF YOU EVER GET CONFUSED ABOUT WHICH RICK IS YOUR RICK WE'LL JUST WORK OUT A CODE PHRASE, ALL RIGHT?
THE PHRASE IS GOING TO BE--
A-A-ARE YOU EVEN--URRRP-- LISTENING TO ME, MORTY?

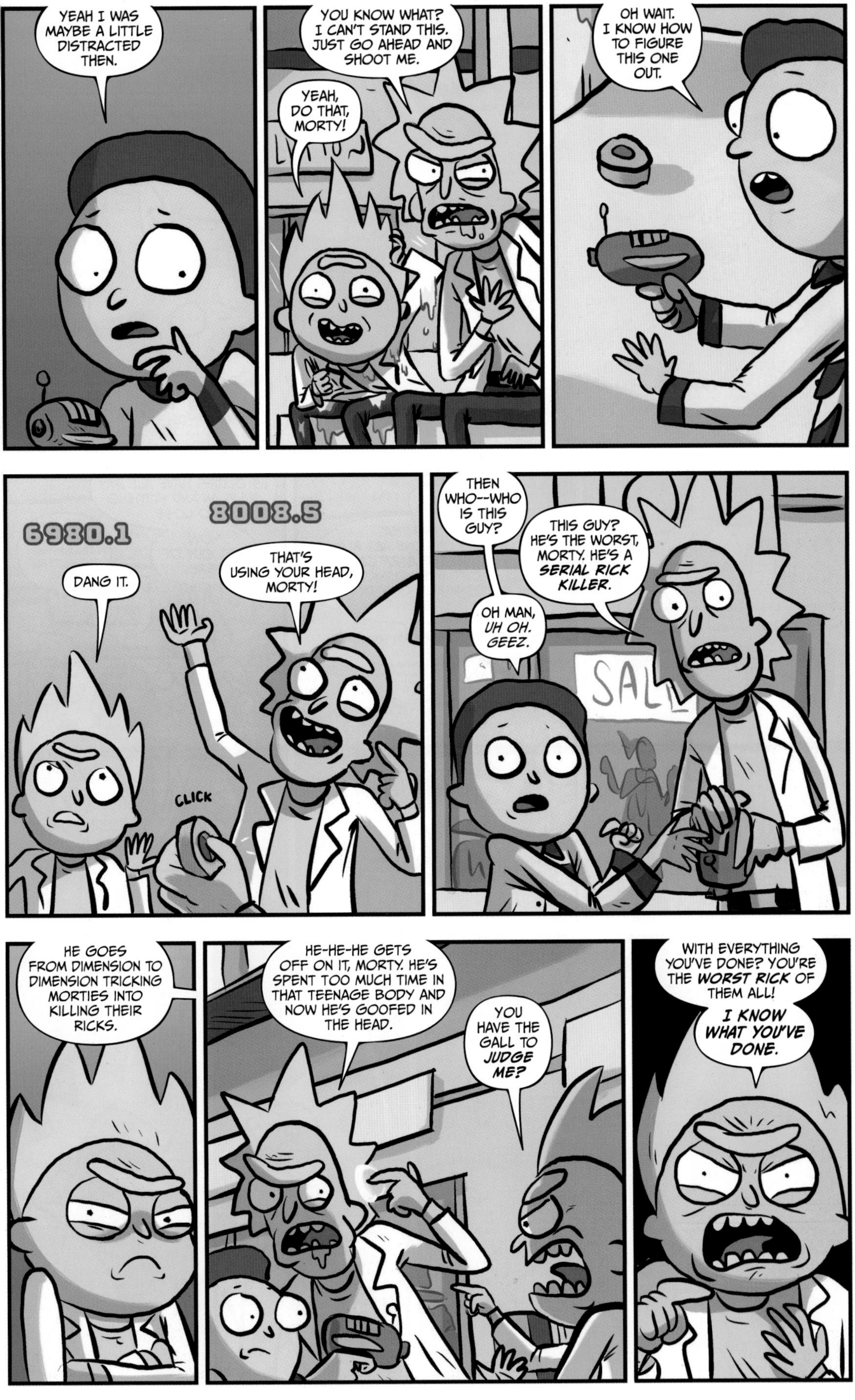
YEAH I WAS MAYBE A LITTLE DISTRACTED THEN.
YOU KNOW WHAT? I CAN'T STAND THIS. JUST GO AHEAD AND SHOOT ME.
YEAH, DO THAT, MORTY!
OH WAIT. I KNOW HOW TO FIGURE THIS ONE OUT.
6980.1
8008.5
DANG IT.
THAT'S USING YOUR HEAD, MORTY!
CLICK
THEN WHO--WHO IS THIS GUY?
THIS GUY? HE'S THE WORST, MORTY. HE'S A SERIAL RICK KILLER.
OH MAN, UH OH. GEEZ.
SALE
HE GOES FROM DIMENSION TO DIMENSION TRICKING MORTIES INTO KILLING THEIR RICKS.
HE-HE-HE GETS OFF ON IT, MORTY. HE'S SPENT TOO MUCH TIME IN THAT TEENAGE BODY AND NOW HE'S GOOFED IN THE HEAD.
YOU HAVE THE GALL TO JUDGE ME?
WITH EVERYTHING YOU'VE DONE? YOU'RE THE WORST RICK OF THEM ALL!
I KNOW WHAT YOU'VE DONE.

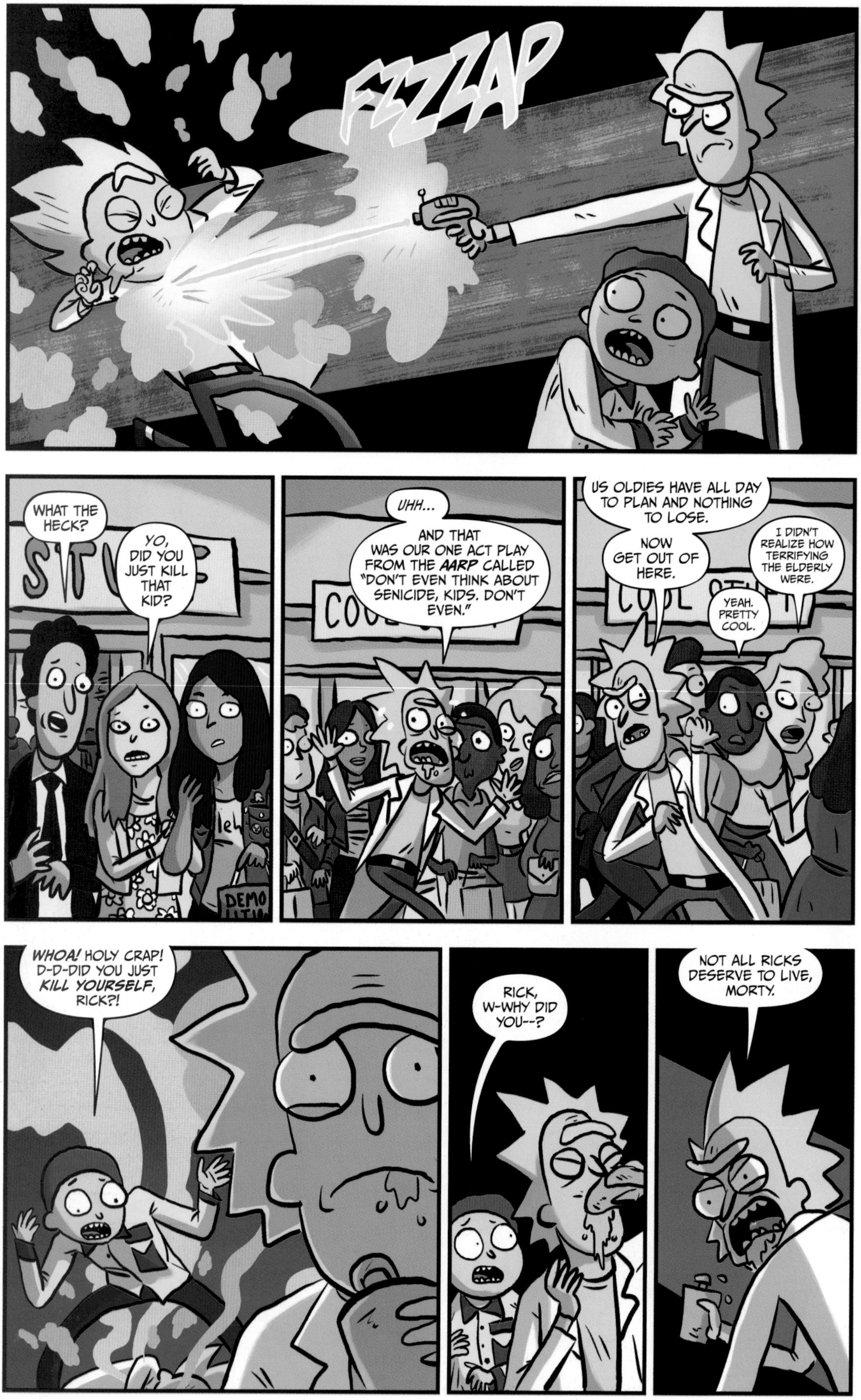
FZZZAP
WHAT THE HECK?
YO, DID YOU JUST KILL THAT KID?
UHH...
AND THAT WAS OUR ONE ACT PLAY FROM THE AARP CALLED "DON'T EVEN THINK ABOUT SENICIDE, KIDS. DON'T EVEN."
US OLDIES HAVE ALL DAY TO PLAN AND NOTHING TO LOSE.
NOW GET OUT OF HERE.
I DIDN'T REALIZE HOW TERRIFYING THE ELDERLY WERE.
YEAH. PRETTY COOL.
WHOA! HOLY CRAP! D-D-DID YOU JUST KILL YOURSELF, RICK?!
RICK, W-WHY DID YOU--?
NOT ALL RICKS DESERVE TO LIVE, MORTY.

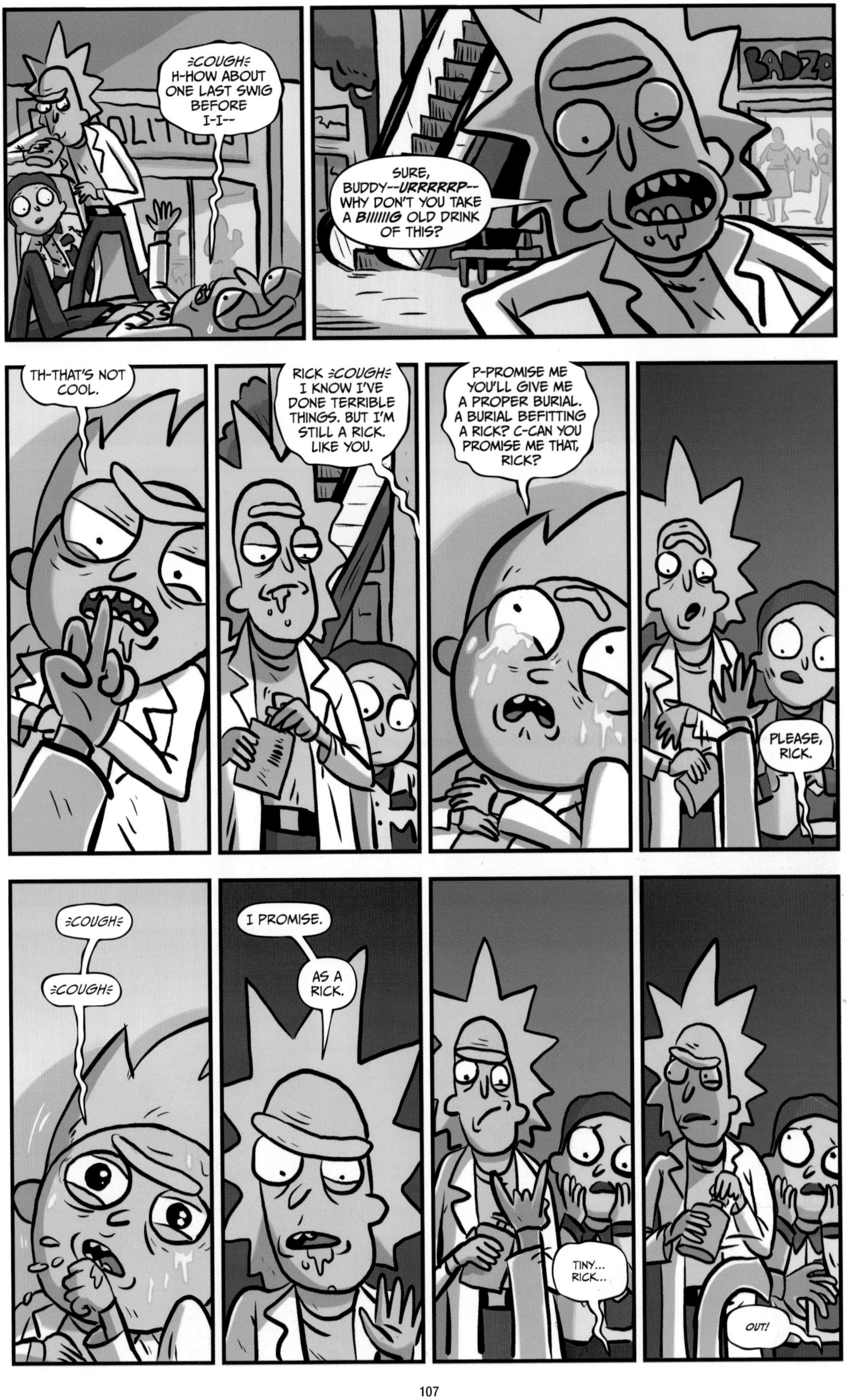

≋COUGH≋ H-HOW ABOUT ONE LAST SWIG BEFORE I-I--
SURE, BUDDY--URRRRRP-- WHY DON'T YOU TAKE A BIIIIIG OLD DRINK OF THIS?
TH-THAT'S NOT COOL.
RICK ≋COUGH≋ I KNOW I'VE DONE TERRIBLE THINGS. BUT I'M STILL A RICK. LIKE YOU.
P-PROMISE ME YOU'LL GIVE ME A PROPER BURIAL. A BURIAL BEFITTING A RICK? C-CAN YOU PROMISE ME THAT, RICK?
PLEASE, RICK.
≋COUGH≋
≋COUGH≋
I PROMISE.
AS A RICK.
TINY... RICK...
OUT!

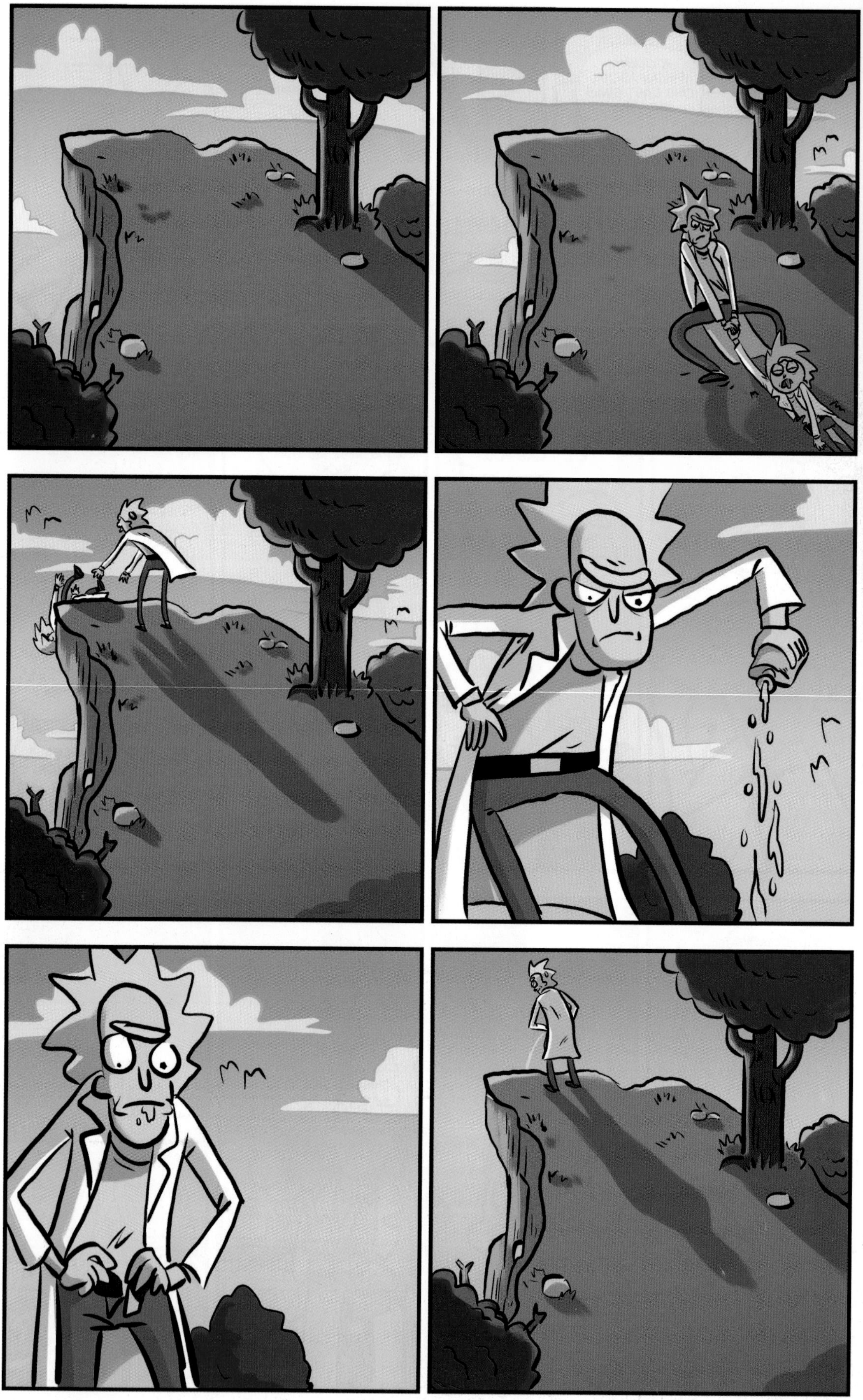

BONUS SHORTS

WRITTEN, ILLUSTRATED, AND COLOURED BY **MARC ELLERBY**
LETTERED BY **CRANK!**

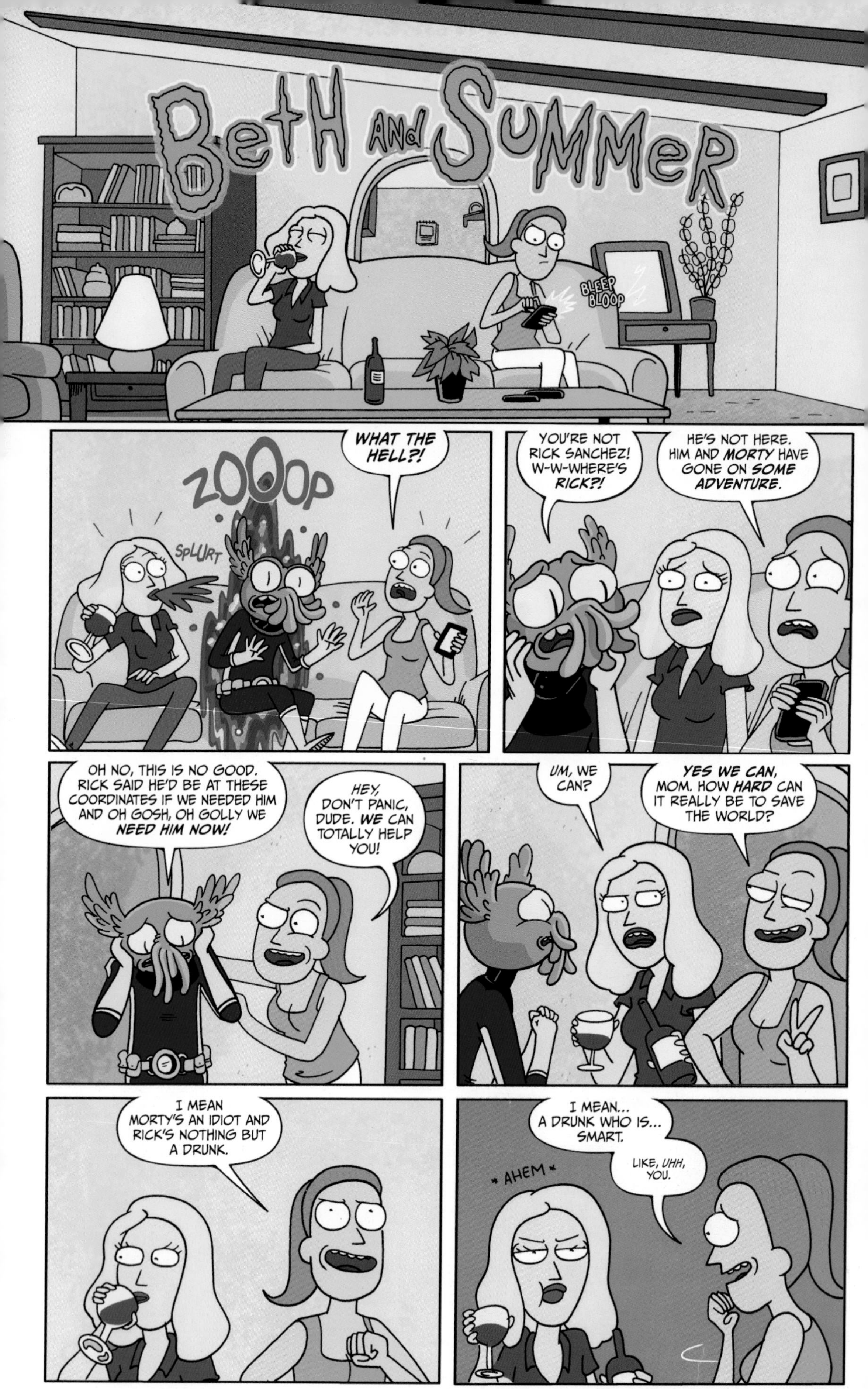
BETH AND SUMMER
BLEEP BLOOP
ZOOOP
SPLURT
WHAT THE HELL?!
YOU'RE NOT RICK SANCHEZ! W-W-WHERE'S RICK?!
HE'S NOT HERE. HIM AND MORTY HAVE GONE ON SOME ADVENTURE.
OH NO, THIS IS NO GOOD. RICK SAID HE'D BE AT THESE COORDINATES IF WE NEEDED HIM AND OH GOSH, OH GOLLY WE NEED HIM NOW!
HEY, DON'T PANIC, DUDE. WE CAN TOTALLY HELP YOU!
UM, WE CAN?
YES WE CAN, MOM. HOW HARD CAN IT REALLY BE TO SAVE THE WORLD?
I MEAN MORTY'S AN IDIOT AND RICK'S NOTHING BUT A DRUNK.
I MEAN... A DRUNK WHO IS... SMART.
AHEM
LIKE, UHH, YOU.

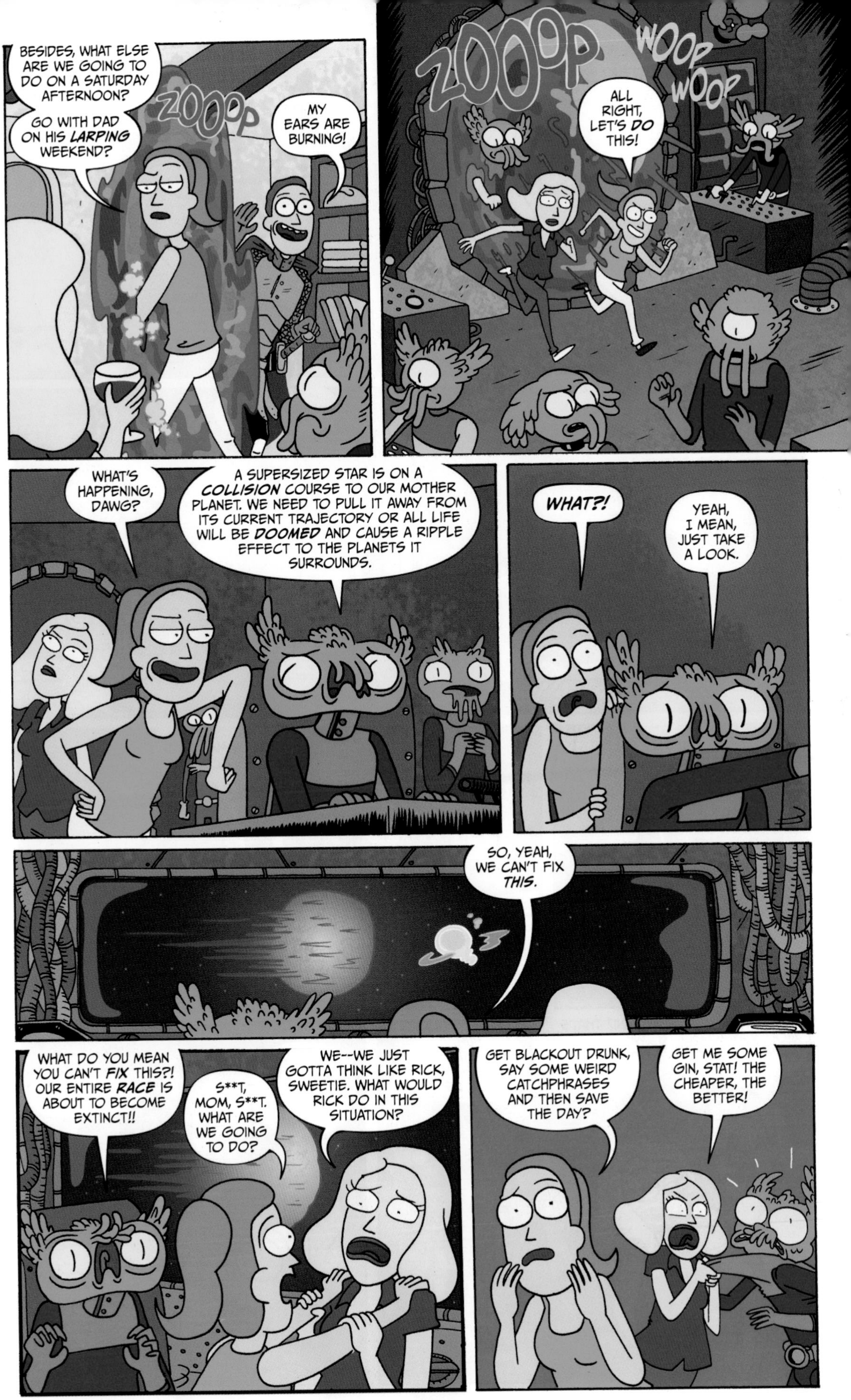

BESIDES, WHAT ELSE ARE WE GOING TO DO ON A SATURDAY AFTERNOON?
GO WITH DAD ON HIS *LARPING* WEEKEND?
ZOOOP
MY EARS ARE BURNING!
ZOOOOP
WOOP WOOP
ALL RIGHT, LET'S *DO* THIS!
WHAT'S HAPPENING, DAWG?
A SUPERSIZED STAR IS ON A *COLLISION* COURSE TO OUR MOTHER PLANET. WE NEED TO PULL IT AWAY FROM ITS CURRENT TRAJECTORY OR ALL LIFE WILL BE *DOOMED* AND CAUSE A RIPPLE EFFECT TO THE PLANETS IT SURROUNDS.
WHAT?!
YEAH, I MEAN, JUST TAKE A LOOK.
SO, YEAH, WE CAN'T FIX *THIS*.
WHAT DO YOU MEAN YOU CAN'T *FIX* THIS?! OUR ENTIRE *RACE* IS ABOUT TO BECOME EXTINCT!!
S**T, MOM, S**T. WHAT ARE WE GOING TO DO?
WE--WE JUST GOTTA THINK LIKE RICK, SWEETIE. WHAT WOULD RICK DO IN THIS SITUATION?
GET BLACKOUT DRUNK, SAY SOME WEIRD CATCHPHRASES AND THEN SAVE THE DAY?
GET ME SOME GIN, STAT! THE CHEAPER, THE BETTER!

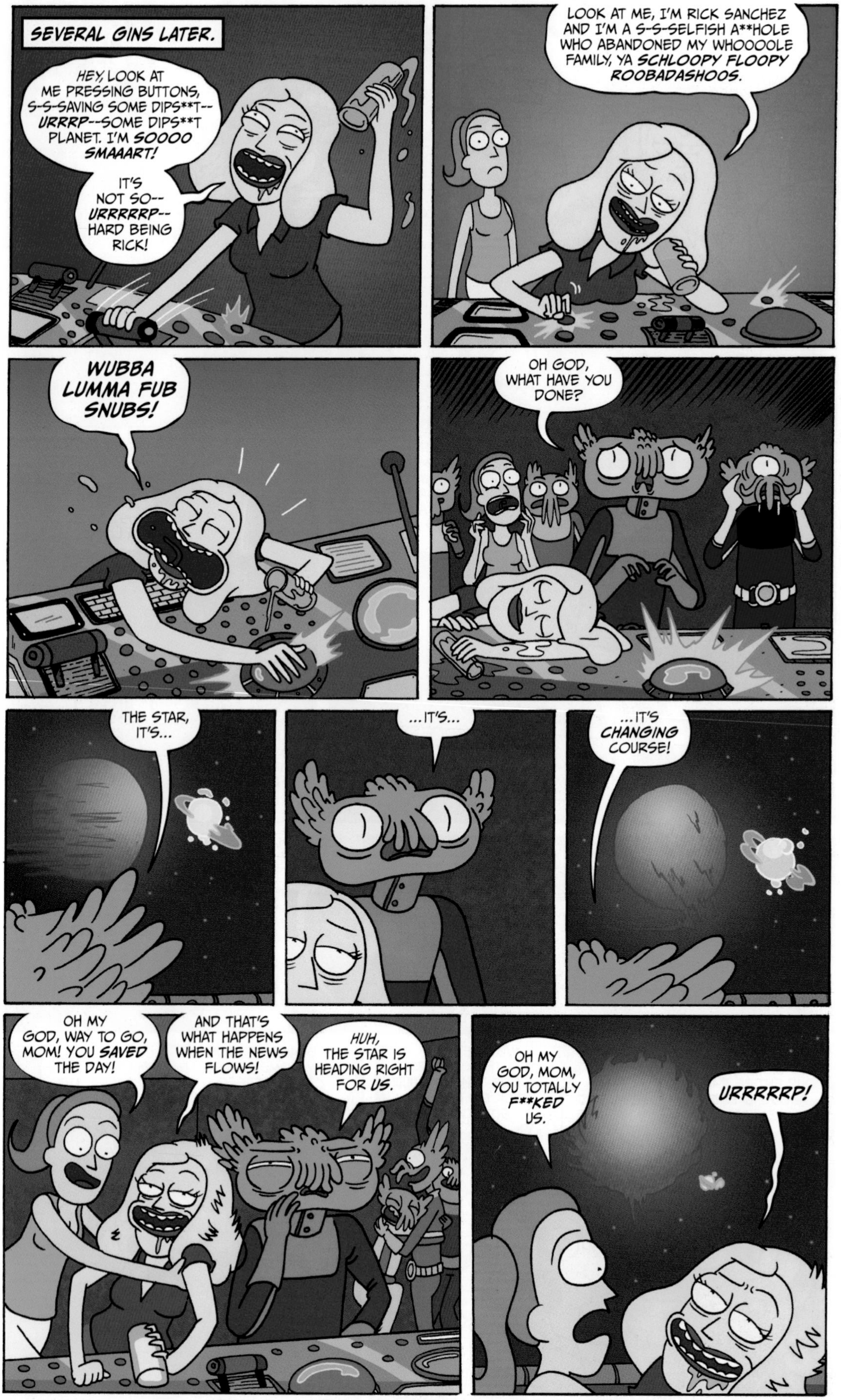
SEVERAL GINS LATER.
HEY, LOOK AT ME PRESSING BUTTONS, S-S-SAVING SOME DIPS**T-- URRRP--SOME DIPS**T PLANET. I'M SOOOO SMAAART!
IT'S NOT SO-- URRRRRP-- HARD BEING RICK!
LOOK AT ME, I'M RICK SANCHEZ AND I'M A S-S-SELFISH A**HOLE WHO ABANDONED MY WHOOOOLE FAMILY, YA SCHLOOPY FLOOPY ROOBADASHOOS.
WUBBA LUMMA FUB SNUBS!
OH GOD, WHAT HAVE YOU DONE?
THE STAR, IT'S...
...IT'S...
...IT'S CHANGING COURSE!
OH MY GOD, WAY TO GO, MOM! YOU SAVED THE DAY!
AND THAT'S WHAT HAPPENS WHEN THE NEWS FLOWS!
HUH, THE STAR IS HEADING RIGHT FOR US.
OH MY GOD, MOM, YOU TOTALLY F**KED US.
URRRRRP!

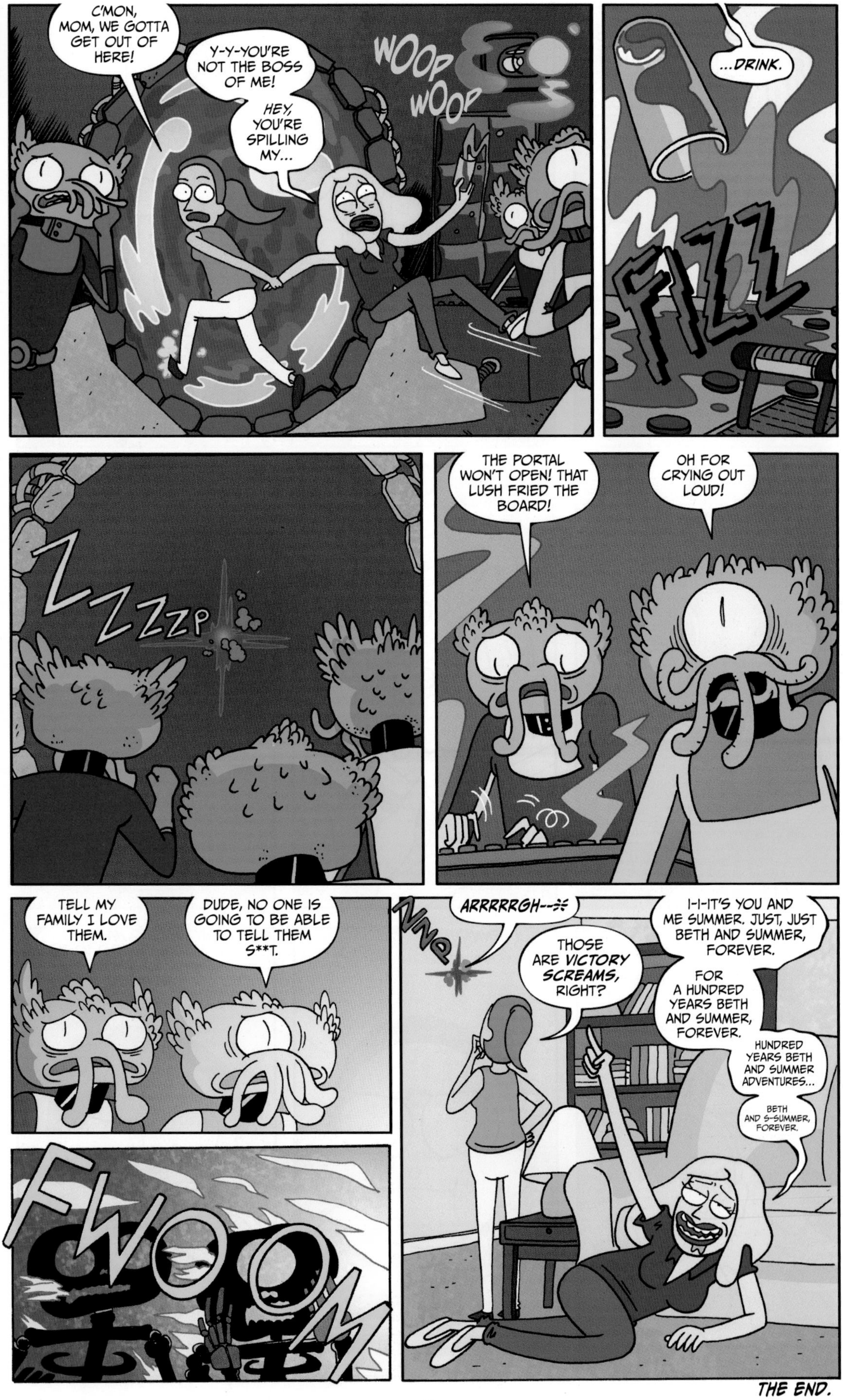
C'MON, MOM, WE GOTTA GET OUT OF HERE!
Y-Y-YOU'RE NOT THE BOSS OF ME!
HEY, YOU'RE SPILLING MY...
WOOP WOOP
...DRINK.
FIZZ
ZZZZP
THE PORTAL WON'T OPEN! THAT LUSH FRIED THE BOARD!
OH FOR CRYING OUT LOUD!
TELL MY FAMILY I LOVE THEM.
DUDE, NO ONE IS GOING TO BE ABLE TO TELL THEM S**T.
FWOOM
ARRRRRGH--
THOSE ARE VICTORY SCREAMS, RIGHT?
I-I-IT'S YOU AND ME SUMMER. JUST, JUST BETH AND SUMMER, FOREVER.
FOR A HUNDRED YEARS BETH AND SUMMER, FOREVER.
HUNDRED YEARS BETH AND SUMMER ADVENTURES...
BETH AND S-SUMMER, FOREVER.

THE END.

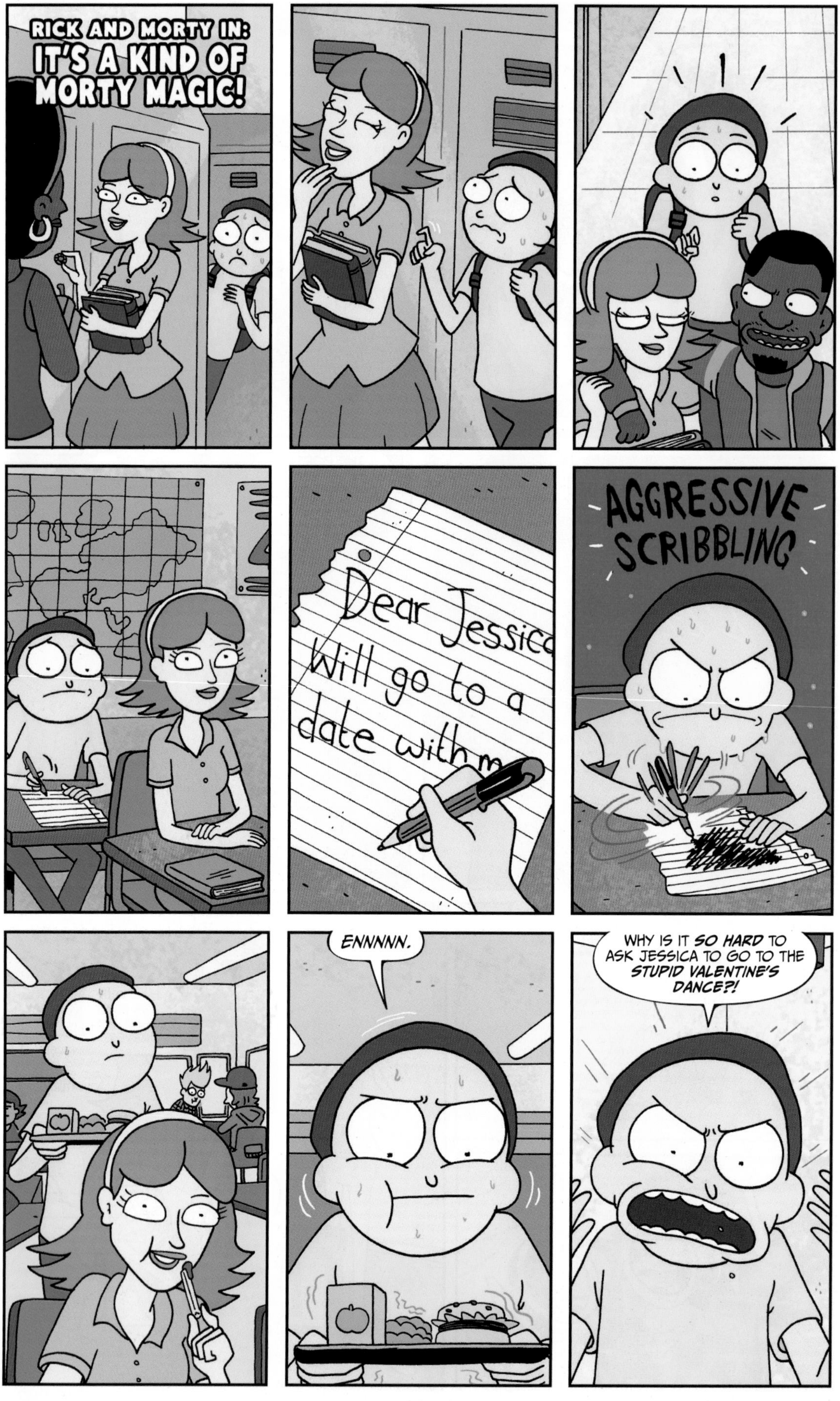
RICK AND MORTY IN:
IT'S A KIND OF MORTY MAGIC!
Dear Jessica
Will go to a
date with m
AGGRESSIVE SCRIBBLING
ENNNNN.
WHY IS IT SO HARD TO ASK JESSICA TO GO TO THE STUPID VALENTINE'S DANCE?!

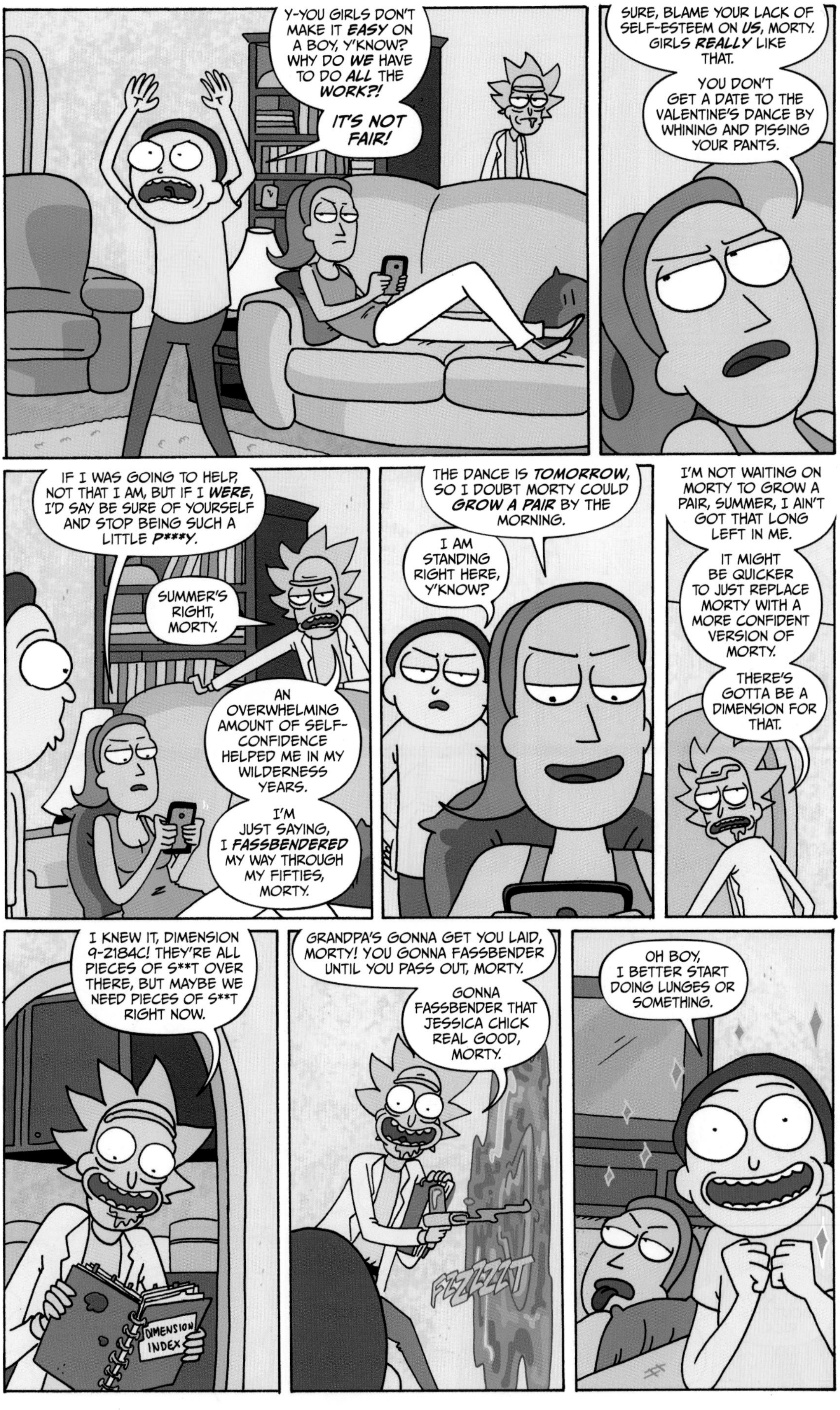

Y-YOU GIRLS DON'T MAKE IT EASY ON A BOY, Y'KNOW? WHY DO WE HAVE TO DO ALL THE WORK?!
IT'S NOT FAIR!
SURE, BLAME YOUR LACK OF SELF-ESTEEM ON US, MORTY. GIRLS REALLY LIKE THAT.
YOU DON'T GET A DATE TO THE VALENTINE'S DANCE BY WHINING AND PISSING YOUR PANTS.
IF I WAS GOING TO HELP, NOT THAT I AM, BUT IF I WERE, I'D SAY BE SURE OF YOURSELF AND STOP BEING SUCH A LITTLE P***Y.
SUMMER'S RIGHT, MORTY.
AN OVERWHELMING AMOUNT OF SELF-CONFIDENCE HELPED ME IN MY WILDERNESS YEARS.
I'M JUST SAYING, I FASSBENDERED MY WAY THROUGH MY FIFTIES, MORTY.
THE DANCE IS TOMORROW, SO I DOUBT MORTY COULD GROW A PAIR BY THE MORNING.
I AM STANDING RIGHT HERE, Y'KNOW?
I'M NOT WAITING ON MORTY TO GROW A PAIR, SUMMER, I AIN'T GOT THAT LONG LEFT IN ME.
IT MIGHT BE QUICKER TO JUST REPLACE MORTY WITH A MORE CONFIDENT VERSION OF MORTY.
THERE'S GOTTA BE A DIMENSION FOR THAT.
I KNEW IT, DIMENSION 9-2184C! THEY'RE ALL PIECES OF S**T OVER THERE, BUT MAYBE WE NEED PIECES OF S**T RIGHT NOW.
DIMENSION INDEX
GRANDPA'S GONNA GET YOU LAID, MORTY! YOU GONNA FASSBENDER UNTIL YOU PASS OUT, MORTY.
GONNA FASSBENDER THAT JESSICA CHICK REAL GOOD, MORTY.
FZZZZZT
OH BOY, I BETTER START DOING LUNGES OR SOMETHING.

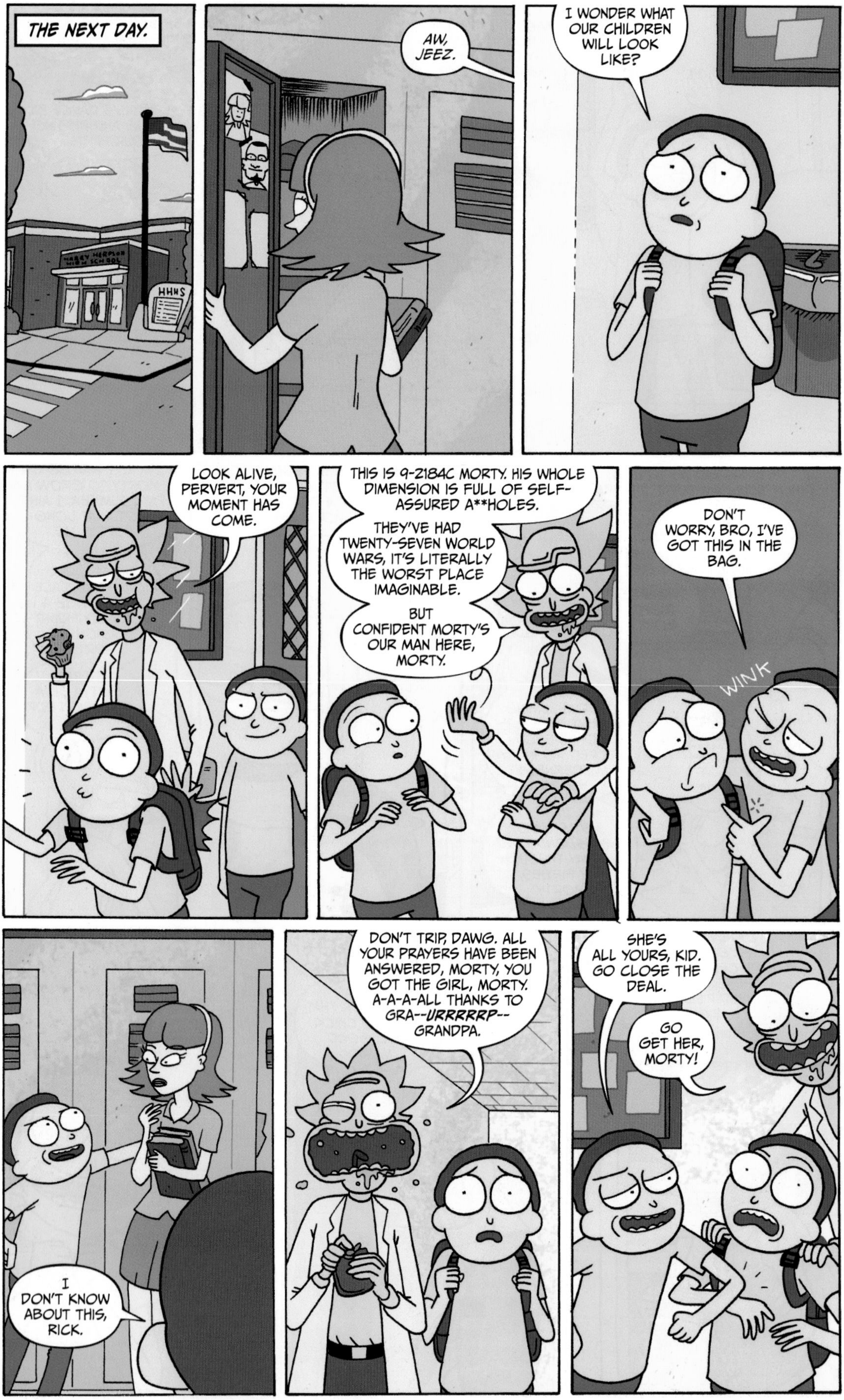
THE NEXT DAY.
HHHS
AW, JEEZ.
I WONDER WHAT OUR CHILDREN WILL LOOK LIKE?
LOOK ALIVE, PERVERT, YOUR MOMENT HAS COME.
THIS IS 9-2184C MORTY. HIS WHOLE DIMENSION IS FULL OF SELF-ASSURED A**HOLES.
THEY'VE HAD TWENTY-SEVEN WORLD WARS, IT'S LITERALLY THE WORST PLACE IMAGINABLE.
BUT CONFIDENT MORTY'S OUR MAN HERE, MORTY.
DON'T WORRY, BRO, I'VE GOT THIS IN THE BAG.
WINK
I DON'T KNOW ABOUT THIS, RICK.
DON'T TRIP, DAWG. ALL YOUR PRAYERS HAVE BEEN ANSWERED, MORTY, YOU GOT THE GIRL, MORTY. A-A-A-ALL THANKS TO GRA--URRRRRP--GRANDPA.
SHE'S ALL YOURS, KID. GO CLOSE THE DEAL.
GO GET HER, MORTY!

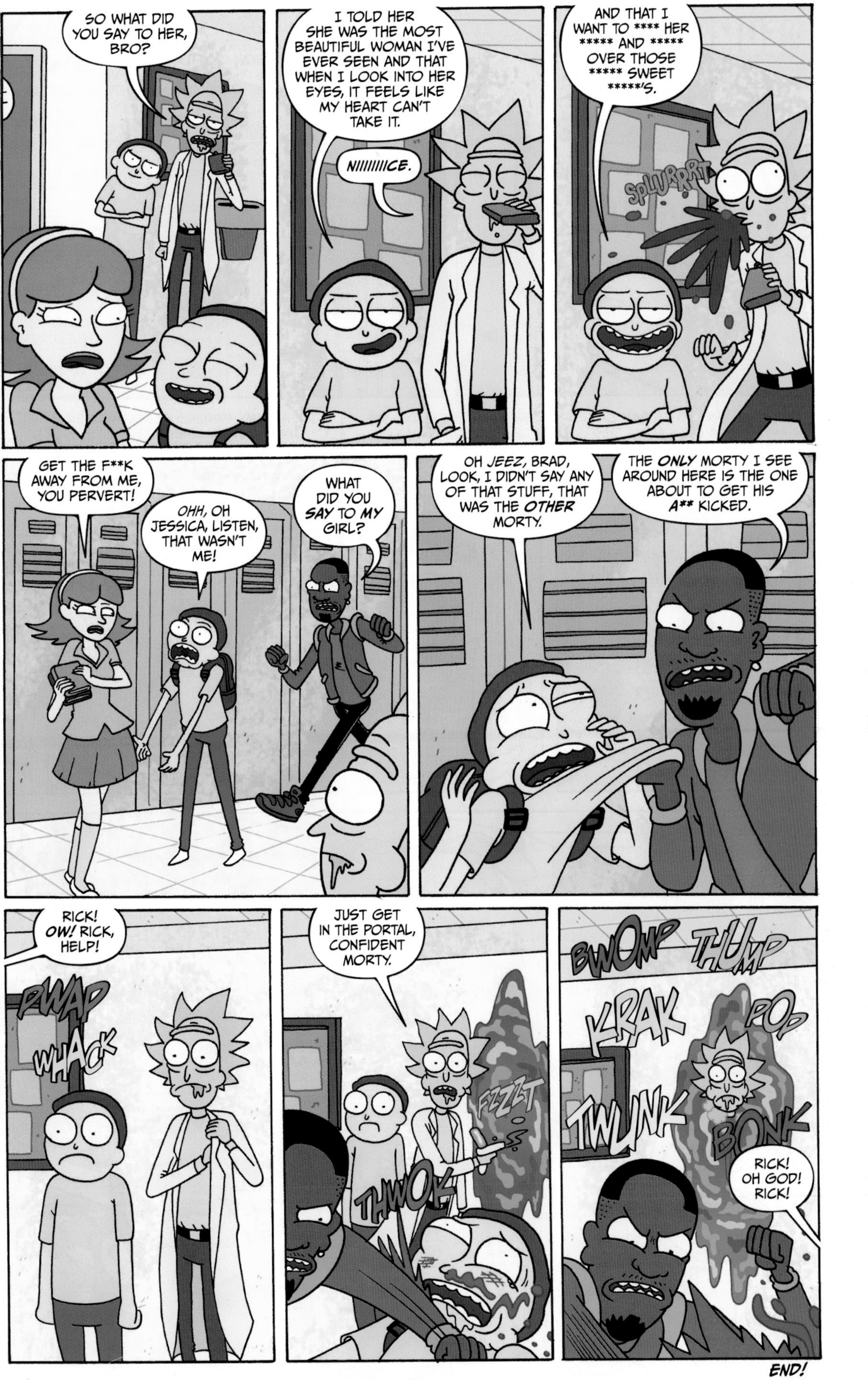

SO WHAT DID YOU SAY TO HER, BRO?
I TOLD HER SHE WAS THE MOST BEAUTIFUL WOMAN I'VE EVER SEEN AND THAT WHEN I LOOK INTO HER EYES, IT FEELS LIKE MY HEART CAN'T TAKE IT.
NIIIIIIIICE.
AND THAT I WANT TO **** HER ***** AND ***** OVER THOSE ***** SWEET *****'S.
SPLURRRT
GET THE F**K AWAY FROM ME, YOU PERVERT!
OHH, OH JESSICA, LISTEN, THAT WASN'T ME!
WHAT DID YOU SAY TO MY GIRL?
OH JEEZ, BRAD, LOOK, I DIDN'T SAY ANY OF THAT STUFF, THAT WAS THE OTHER MORTY.
THE ONLY MORTY I SEE AROUND HERE IS THE ONE ABOUT TO GET HIS A** KICKED.
RICK! OW! RICK, HELP!
PWAP
WHACK
JUST GET IN THE PORTAL, CONFIDENT MORTY.
FZZZT
THWOK
BWOMP
THUMP
KRAK
POP
TWUNK
BONK
RICK! OH GOD! RICK!

END!

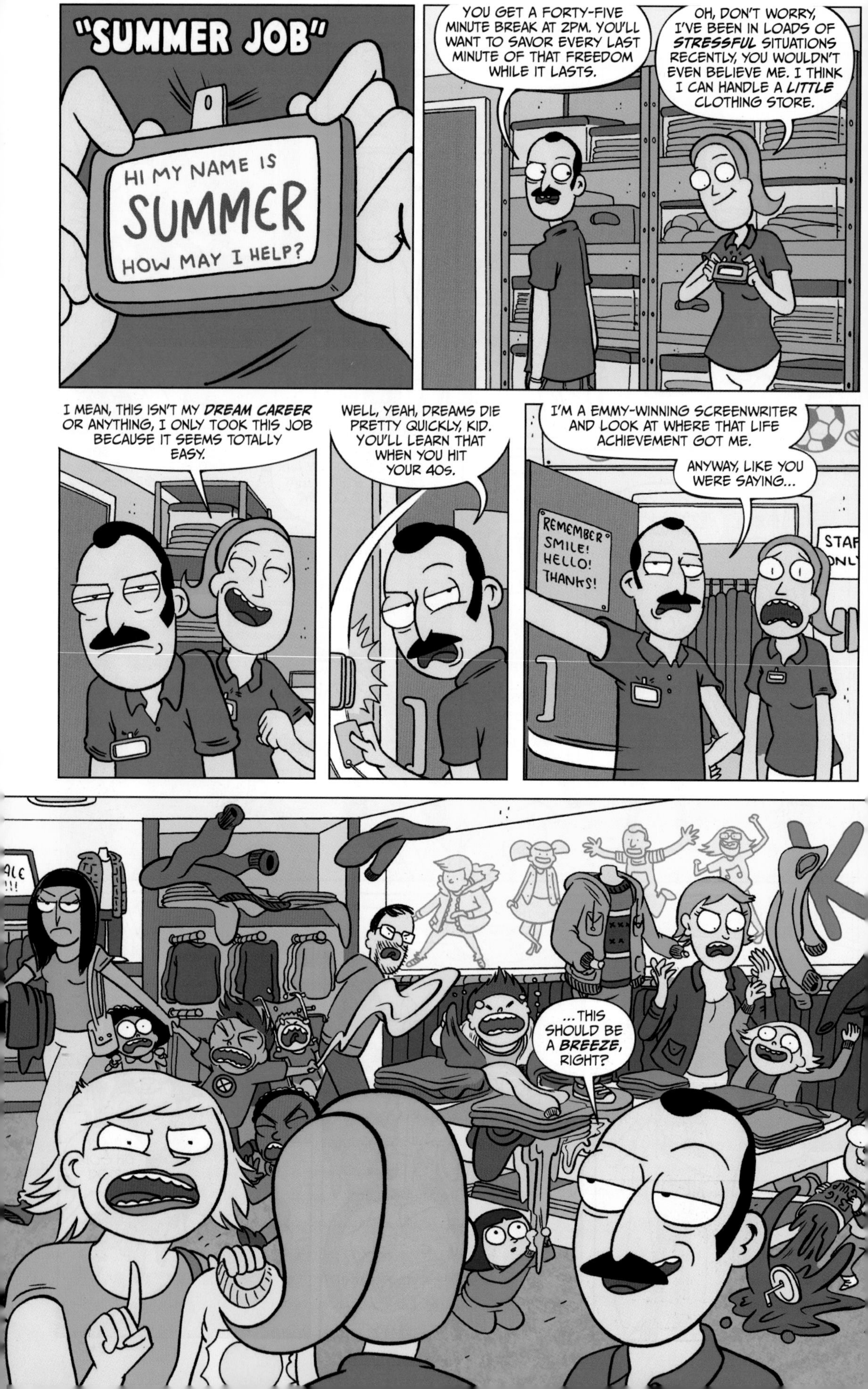
"SUMMER JOB"
HI MY NAME IS SUMMER HOW MAY I HELP?
YOU GET A FORTY-FIVE MINUTE BREAK AT 2PM. YOU'LL WANT TO SAVOR EVERY LAST MINUTE OF THAT FREEDOM WHILE IT LASTS.
OH, DON'T WORRY, I'VE BEEN IN LOADS OF STRESSFUL SITUATIONS RECENTLY, YOU WOULDN'T EVEN BELIEVE ME. I THINK I CAN HANDLE A LITTLE CLOTHING STORE.
I MEAN, THIS ISN'T MY DREAM CAREER OR ANYTHING, I ONLY TOOK THIS JOB BECAUSE IT SEEMS TOTALLY EASY.
WELL, YEAH, DREAMS DIE PRETTY QUICKLY, KID. YOU'LL LEARN THAT WHEN YOU HIT YOUR 40S.
I'M A EMMY-WINNING SCREENWRITER AND LOOK AT WHERE THAT LIFE ACHIEVEMENT GOT ME.
ANYWAY, LIKE YOU WERE SAYING...
REMEMBER SMILE! HELLO! THANKS!
...THIS SHOULD BE A BREEZE, RIGHT?

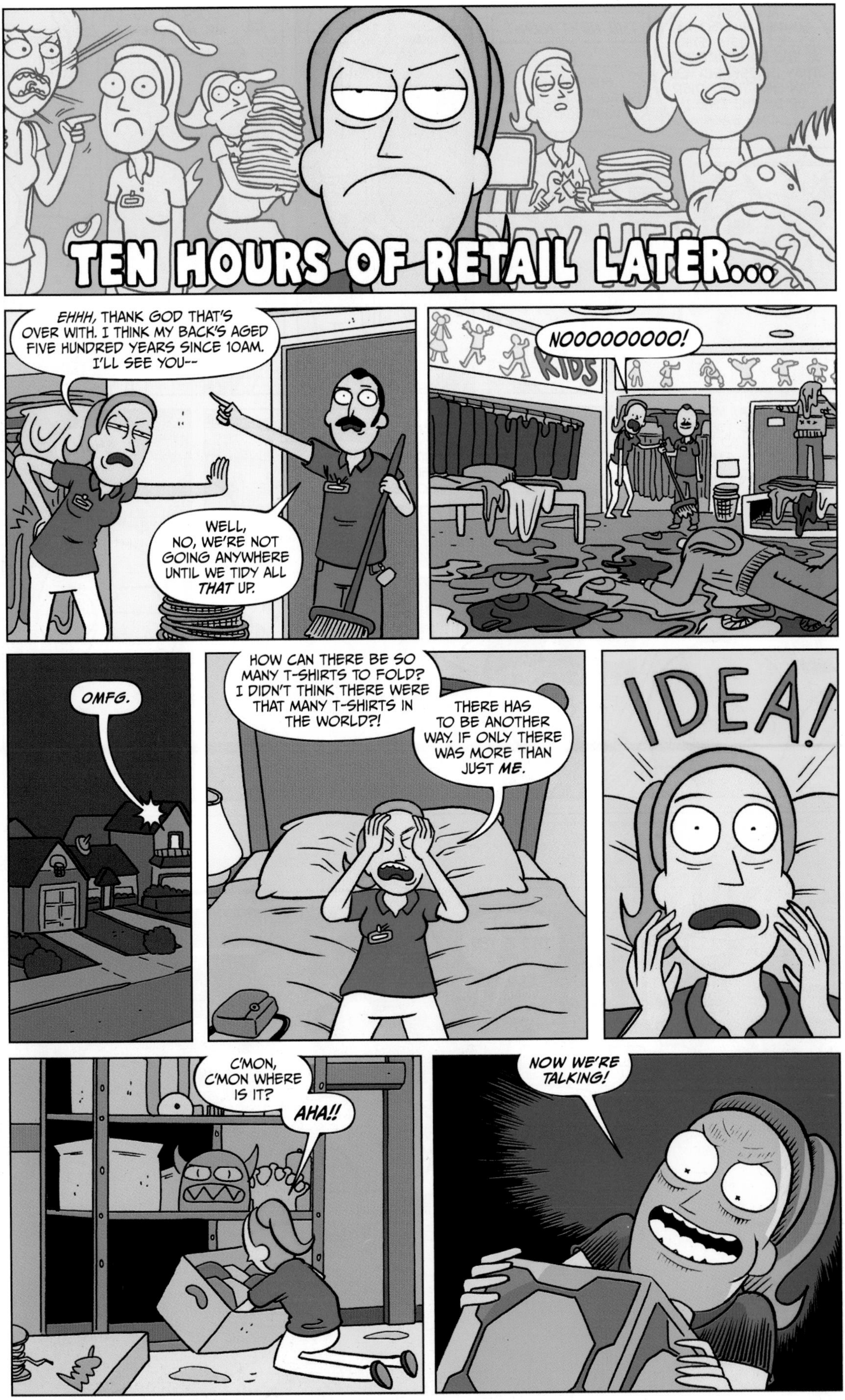
TEN HOURS OF RETAIL LATER...
EHHH, THANK GOD THAT'S OVER WITH. I THINK MY BACK'S AGED FIVE HUNDRED YEARS SINCE 10AM. I'LL SEE YOU--
WELL, NO, WE'RE NOT GOING ANYWHERE UNTIL WE TIDY ALL THAT UP.
NOOOOOOOOO!
KIDS
OMFG.
HOW CAN THERE BE SO MANY T-SHIRTS TO FOLD? I DIDN'T THINK THERE WERE THAT MANY T-SHIRTS IN THE WORLD?!
THERE HAS TO BE ANOTHER WAY. IF ONLY THERE WAS MORE THAN JUST ME.
IDEA!
C'MON, C'MON WHERE IS IT?
AHA!!
NOW WE'RE TALKING!

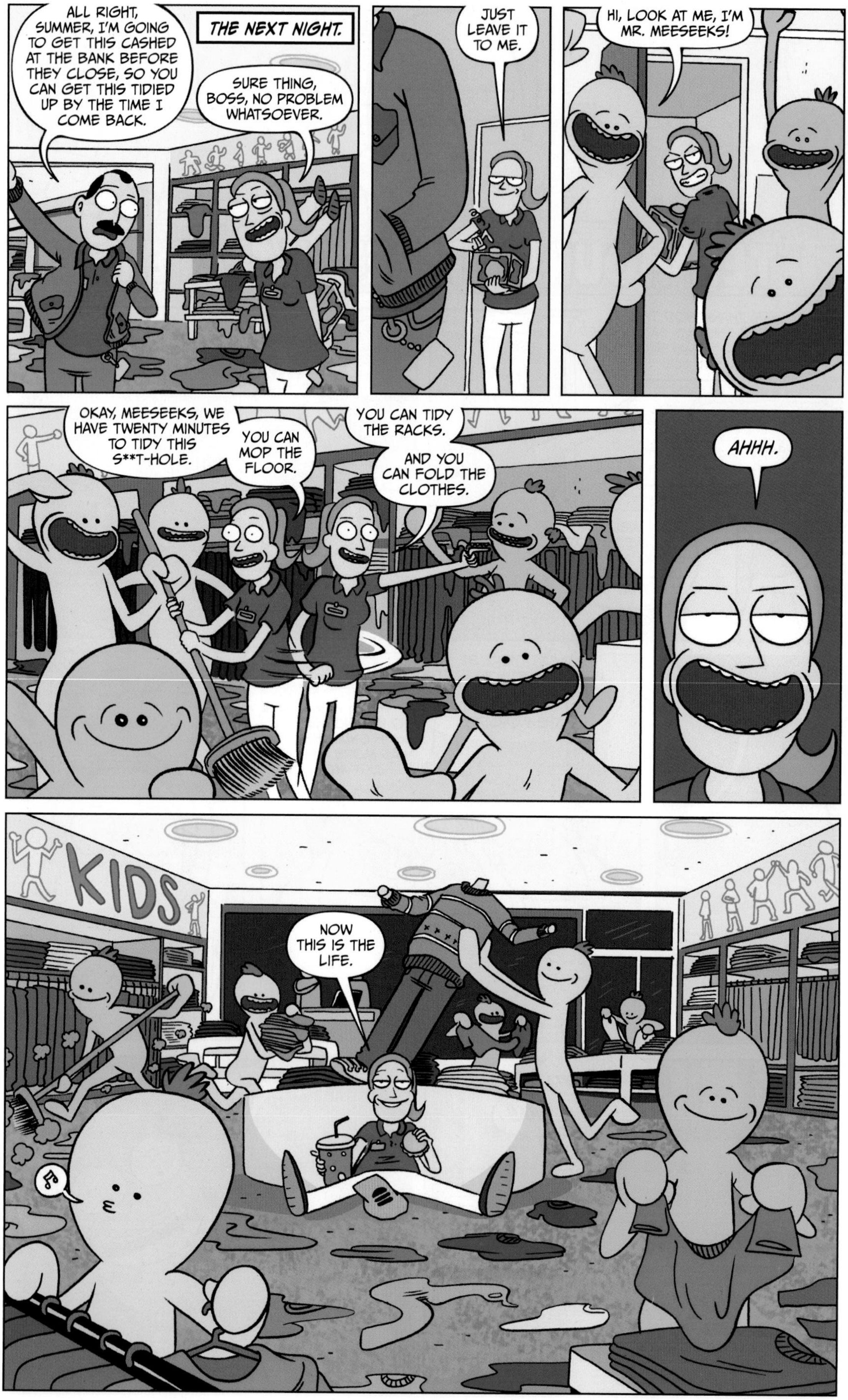
ALL RIGHT, SUMMER, I'M GOING TO GET THIS CASHED AT THE BANK BEFORE THEY CLOSE, SO YOU CAN GET THIS TIDIED UP BY THE TIME I COME BACK.
THE NEXT NIGHT.
SURE THING, BOSS, NO PROBLEM WHATSOEVER.
JUST LEAVE IT TO ME.
HI, LOOK AT ME, I'M MR. MEESEEKS!
OKAY, MEESEEKS, WE HAVE TWENTY MINUTES TO TIDY THIS S**T-HOLE.
YOU CAN MOP THE FLOOR.
YOU CAN TIDY THE RACKS.
AND YOU CAN FOLD THE CLOTHES.
AHHH.
KIDS
NOW THIS IS THE LIFE.
♫

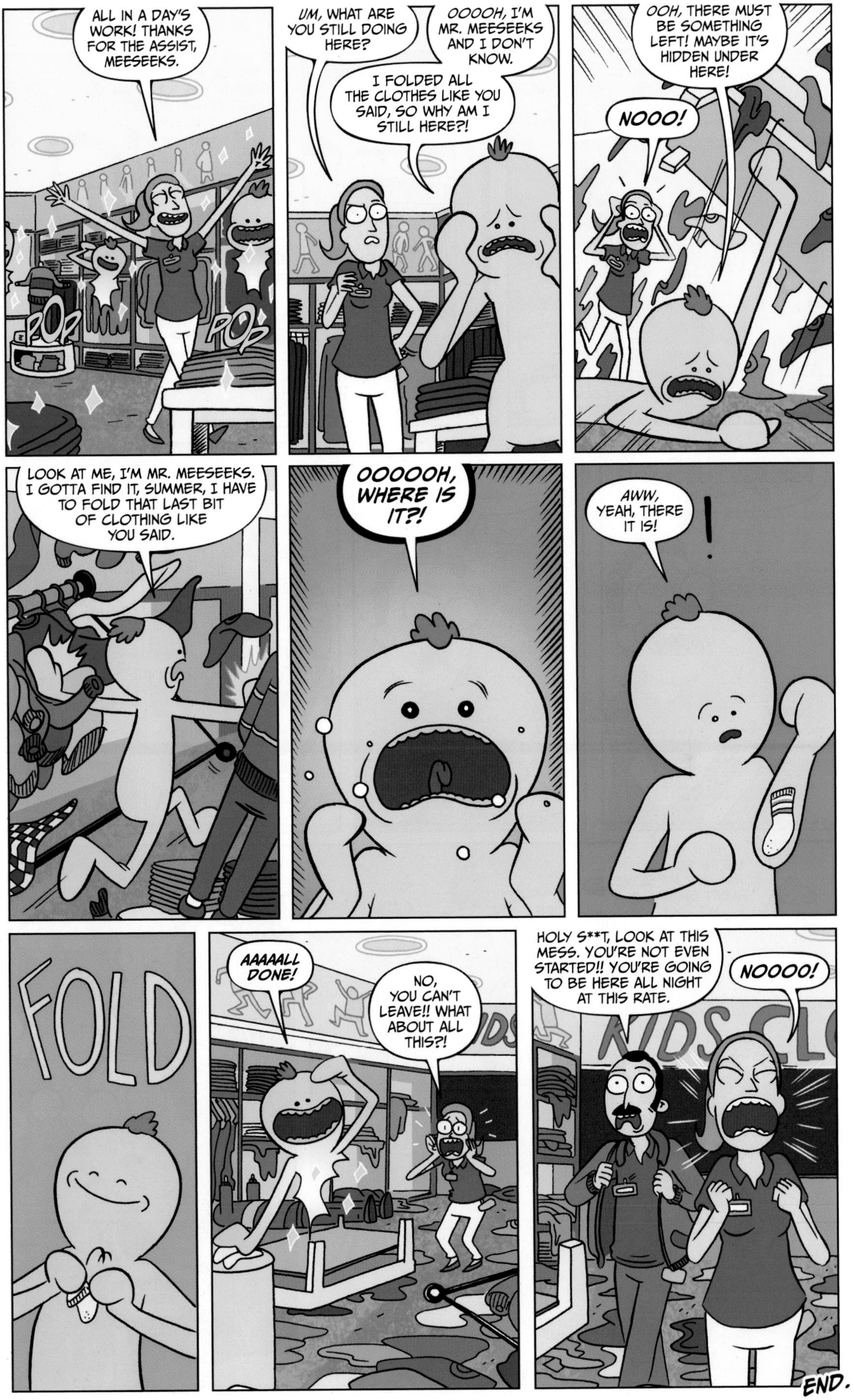
ALL IN A DAY'S WORK! THANKS FOR THE ASSIST, MEESEEKS.
POP
POP
UM, WHAT ARE YOU STILL DOING HERE?
OOOOH, I'M MR. MEESEEKS AND I DON'T KNOW.
I FOLDED ALL THE CLOTHES LIKE YOU SAID, SO WHY AM I STILL HERE?!
OOH, THERE MUST BE SOMETHING LEFT! MAYBE IT'S HIDDEN UNDER HERE!
NOOO!
LOOK AT ME, I'M MR. MEESEEKS. I GOTTA FIND IT, SUMMER, I HAVE TO FOLD THAT LAST BIT OF CLOTHING LIKE YOU SAID.
OOOOOH, WHERE IS IT?!
AWW, YEAH, THERE IT IS!
!
FOLD
AAAAALL DONE!
NO, YOU CAN'T LEAVE!! WHAT ABOUT ALL THIS?!
HOLY S**T, LOOK AT THIS MESS. YOU'RE NOT EVEN STARTED!! YOU'RE GOING TO BE HERE ALL NIGHT AT THIS RATE.
NOOOO!
END.

RICK AND JERRY IN: "SUPERIOR POSTERIOR"

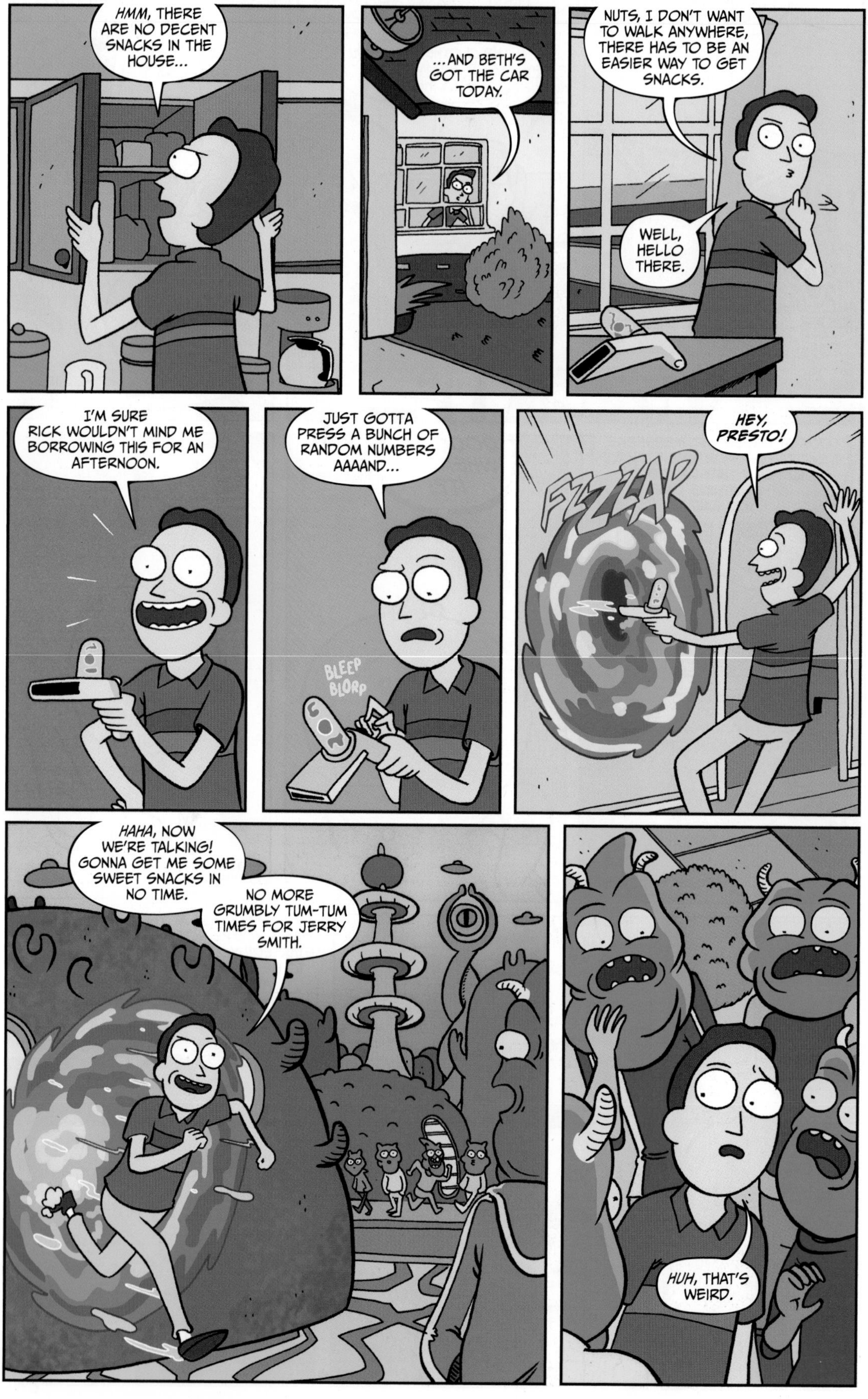
HMM, THERE ARE NO DECENT SNACKS IN THE HOUSE...
...AND BETH'S GOT THE CAR TODAY.
NUTS, I DON'T WANT TO WALK ANYWHERE, THERE HAS TO BE AN EASIER WAY TO GET SNACKS.
WELL, HELLO THERE.
I'M SURE RICK WOULDN'T MIND ME BORROWING THIS FOR AN AFTERNOON.
JUST GOTTA PRESS A BUNCH OF RANDOM NUMBERS AAAAND...
BLEEP BLORP
HEY, PRESTO!
FZZZAP
HAHA, NOW WE'RE TALKING! GONNA GET ME SOME SWEET SNACKS IN NO TIME.
NO MORE GRUMBLY TUM-TUM TIMES FOR JERRY SMITH.
HUH, THAT'S WEIRD.

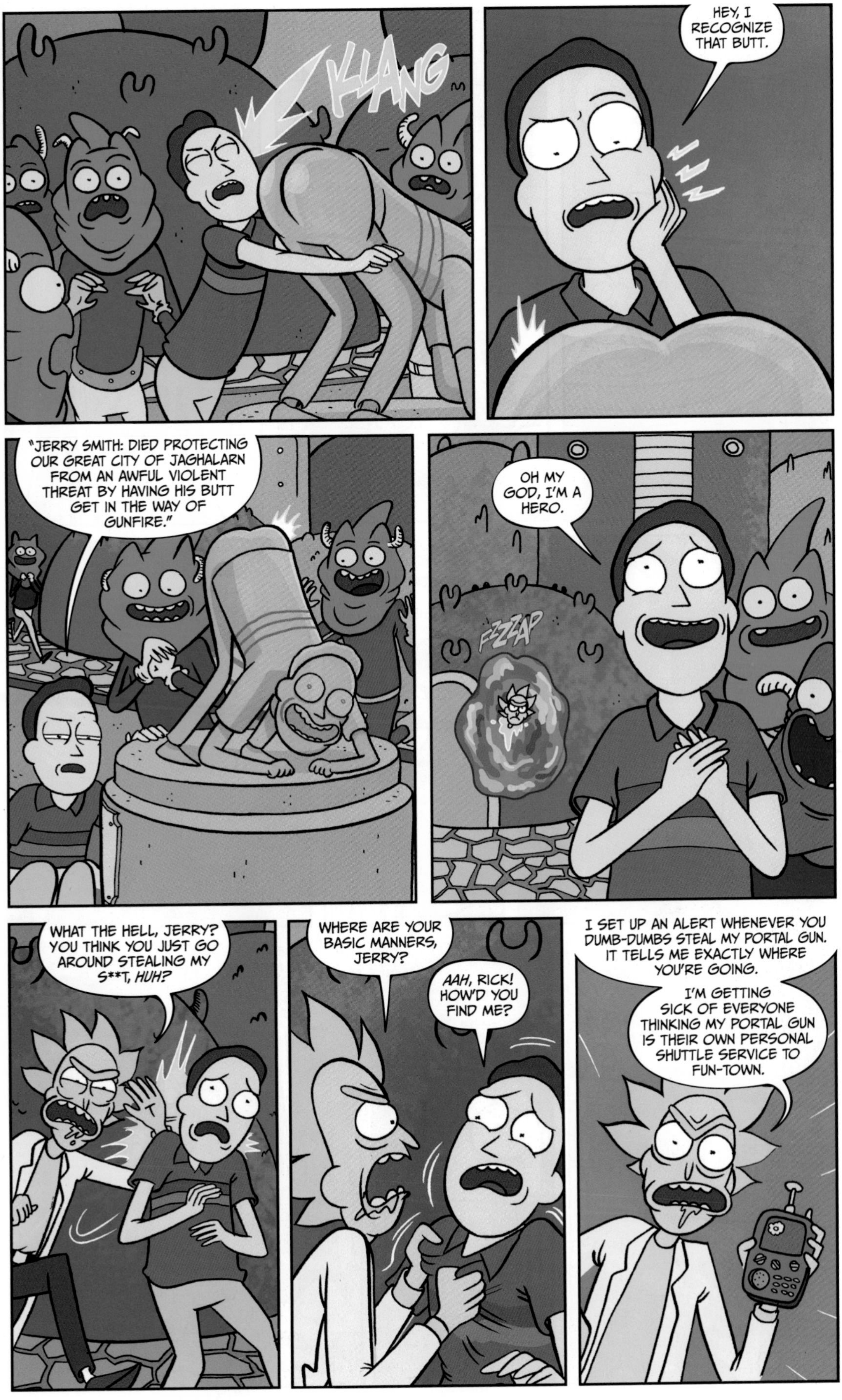
KLANG
HEY, I RECOGNIZE THAT BUTT.
"JERRY SMITH: DIED PROTECTING OUR GREAT CITY OF JAGHALARN FROM AN AWFUL VIOLENT THREAT BY HAVING HIS BUTT GET IN THE WAY OF GUNFIRE."
OH MY GOD, I'M A HERO.
FZZZAP
WHAT THE HELL, JERRY? YOU THINK YOU JUST GO AROUND STEALING MY S**T, *HUH?*
WHERE ARE YOUR BASIC MANNERS, JERRY?
AAH, RICK! HOW'D YOU FIND ME?
I SET UP AN ALERT WHENEVER YOU DUMB-DUMBS STEAL MY PORTAL GUN. IT TELLS ME EXACTLY WHERE YOU'RE GOING.
I'M GETTING SICK OF EVERYONE THINKING MY PORTAL GUN IS THEIR OWN PERSONAL SHUTTLE SERVICE TO FUN-TOWN.

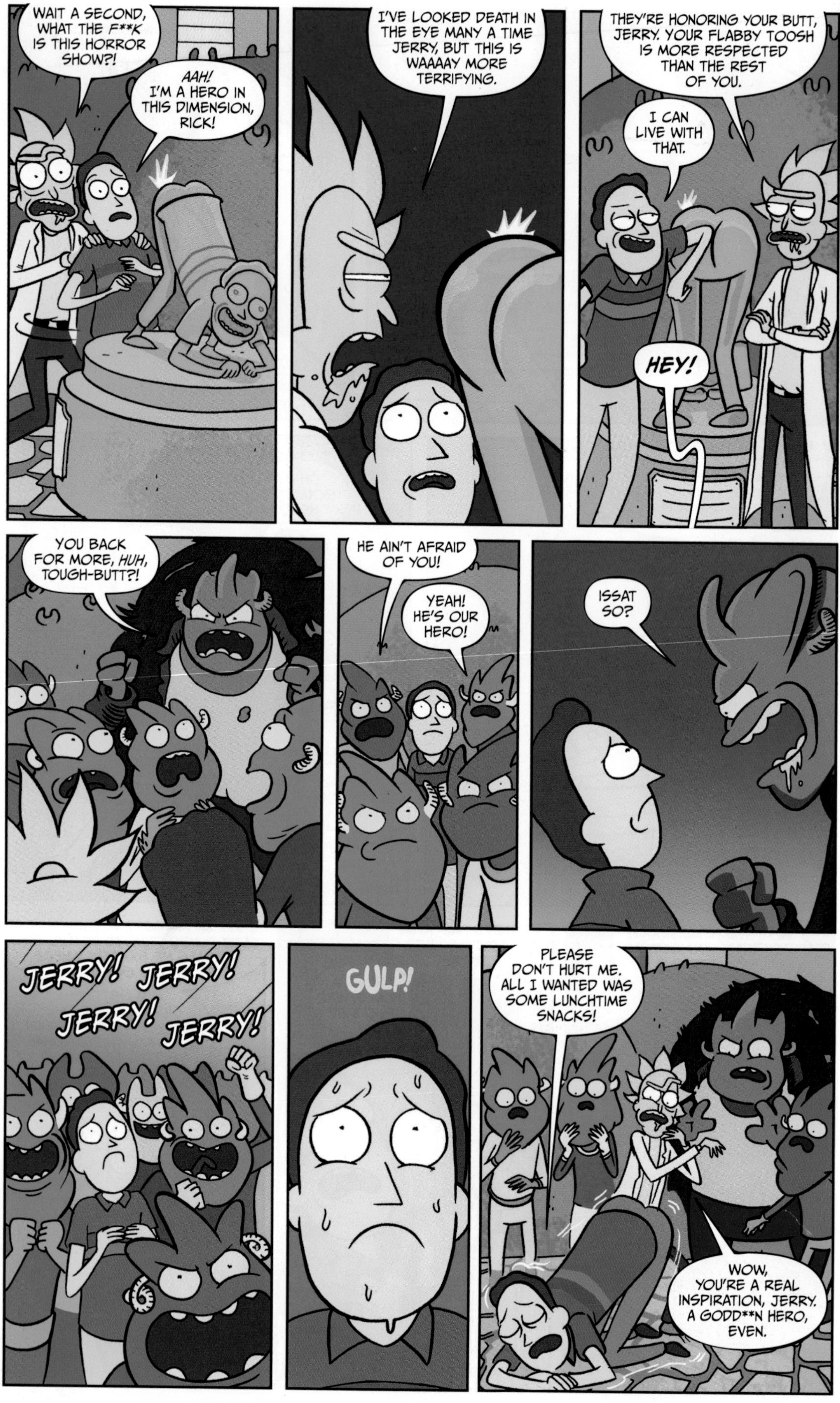
WAIT A SECOND, WHAT THE F**K IS THIS HORROR SHOW?!
AAH! I'M A HERO IN THIS DIMENSION, RICK!
I'VE LOOKED DEATH IN THE EYE MANY A TIME JERRY, BUT THIS IS WAAAAY MORE TERRIFYING.
THEY'RE HONORING YOUR BUTT, JERRY. YOUR FLABBY TOOSH IS MORE RESPECTED THAN THE REST OF YOU.
I CAN LIVE WITH THAT.
HEY!
YOU BACK FOR MORE, HUH, TOUGH-BUTT?!
HE AIN'T AFRAID OF YOU!
YEAH! HE'S OUR HERO!
ISSAT SO?
JERRY! JERRY! JERRY! JERRY!
GULP!
PLEASE DON'T HURT ME. ALL I WANTED WAS SOME LUNCHTIME SNACKS!
WOW, YOU'RE A REAL INSPIRATION, JERRY. A GODD**N HERO, EVEN.

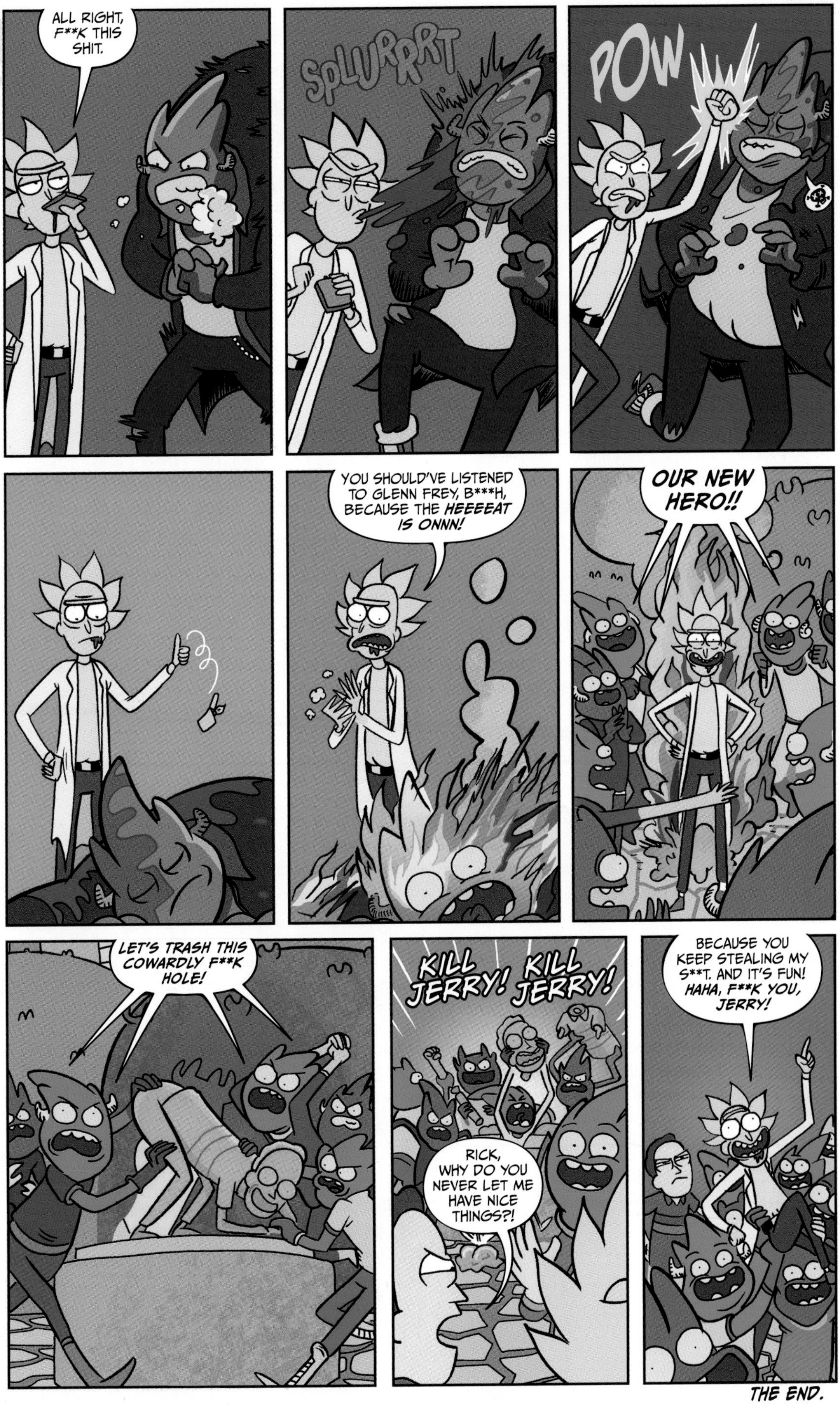
ALL RIGHT, F**K THIS SHIT.
SPLURRRT
POW
YOU SHOULD'VE LISTENED TO GLENN FREY, B***H, BECAUSE THE HEEEEAT IS ONNN!
OUR NEW HERO!!
LET'S TRASH THIS COWARDLY F**K HOLE!
KILL JERRY! KILL JERRY!
RICK, WHY DO YOU NEVER LET ME HAVE NICE THINGS?!
BECAUSE YOU KEEP STEALING MY S**T. AND IT'S FUN! HAHA, F**K YOU, JERRY!
THE END.

DAN HARMON is the Emmy® winning creator/executive producer of the comedy series *Community* as well as the co-creator/executive producer of Adult Swim's *Rick and Morty*.

Harmon's pursuit of minimal work for maximum reward took him from stand-up to improv to sketch comedy, then finally to Los Angeles, where he began writing feature screenplays with fellow Milwaukeean Rob Schrab. As part of his deal with Robert Zemeckis at Imagemovers, Harmon co-wrote the feature film *Monster House*. Following this, Harmon co-wrote the Ben Stiller-directed pilot *Heat Vision and Jack*, starring Jack Black and Owen Wilson.

Disillusioned by the legitimate industry, Harmon began attending classes at nearby Glendale Community College. At the same time, Harmon and Schrab founded Channel 101, an untelevised non-profit audience-controlled network for undiscovered filmmakers, many of whom used it to launch mainstream careers, including the boys behind SNL's Digital Shorts. Harmon, along with Schrab, partnered with Sarah Silverman to create her Comedy Central series, *The Sarah Silverman Program*, where he served as head writer for the first season.

Harmon went on to create, write, and perform in the short-lived VH1 sketch series *Acceptable TV* before eventually creating the critically acclaimed and fan-favorite comedy *Community*. The show originally aired on NBC for five seasons before being acquired by Yahoo, which premiered season six of the show in March 2015. In 2009, he won an Emmy for Outstanding Music and Lyrics for the opening number of the 81st Annual Academy Awards.

Along with Justin Roiland, Harmon created the breakout Adult Swim animated series *Rick and Morty*. The show premiered in December 2013 and quickly became a ratings hit. Harmon and Roiland have wrapped up season three, which premiered in 2017.

In 2014, Harmon was the star of the documentary *Harmontown*, which premiered at the SXSW Film Festival and chronicled his 20-city stand-up/podcast tour of the same name. The documentary was released theatrically in October 2014.

JUSTIN ROILAND grew up in Manteca, California, where he did the basic stuff children do. Later in life he traveled to Los Angeles. Once settled in, he created several popular online shorts for Channel 101. Some notable examples of his work (both animated and live action) include *House of Cosbys* and *Two Girls One Cup: The Show.*

Justin is afraid of his mortality and hopes the things he creates will make lots of people happy. Then maybe when modern civilization collapses into chaos, people will remember him and they'll help him survive the bloodshed and violence. Global economic collapse is looming. It's going to be horrible, and honestly, a swift death might be preferable than living in the hell that awaits mankind.

Justin also really hates writing about himself in the third person. I hate this. That's right. It's me. I've been writing this whole thing. Hi. The cat's out of the bag. It's just you and me now. There never was a third person. If you want to know anything about me, just ask. Sorry this wasn't more informative.

KYLE STARKS is an Eisner-nominated comic creator from Southern Indiana, where he resides with his beautiful wife and two amazing daughters. Stealy values him at 32 and a half Grepples or 17-and-a-half Smeggles depending on market value at the current time. Check out his creator-owned work: *Sexcastle* and *Kill Them All.*

CJ CANNON is a self-taught artist living in Nashville, Tennessee. When they're not working on comics, outside riding their bike, or drumming, they're almost always in the house drawing gross fanart and fandom smut for similarly gross people. CJ has: two cats, three hermit crabs, a hamster, an eldritch abomination, a pacman frog, and a leopard gecko.

MARC ELLERBY is a comics illustrator living in Essex, UK. He has worked on such titles as *Doctor Who*, *Regular Show*, and *The Amazing World of Gumball*. His own comics (which you should totally check out!) are *Chloe Noonan: Monster Hunter* and *Ellerbisms*. You can read some comics if you like at marcellerby.com.

KATY FARINA is a freelance comic artist and illustrator from Charlotte. Her work includes *Amazing World of Gumball* OGN volumes 1 and 2 and *Capture Creatures*. Outside of drawing comics, reading comics, and thinking about comics, she... uh, usually just goes to her local comic shop. She loves a good cup of coffee, and coffee loves her. Her greatest passion is to tell good stories that will inspire others!

CHRIS CRANK has worked on several recent Oni Press books like *The Sixth Gun*, *Brides of Helheim*, *Terrible Lizard*, and others. Maybe you've seen his letters in *Revival*, *Hack/Slash*, *God Hates Astronauts*, or *Dark Engine* from Image. Or perhaps you've read *Lady Killer* or *Sundowners* from Dark Horse. Heck, you might even be reading the award winning *Battlepug* at battlepug.com right now!

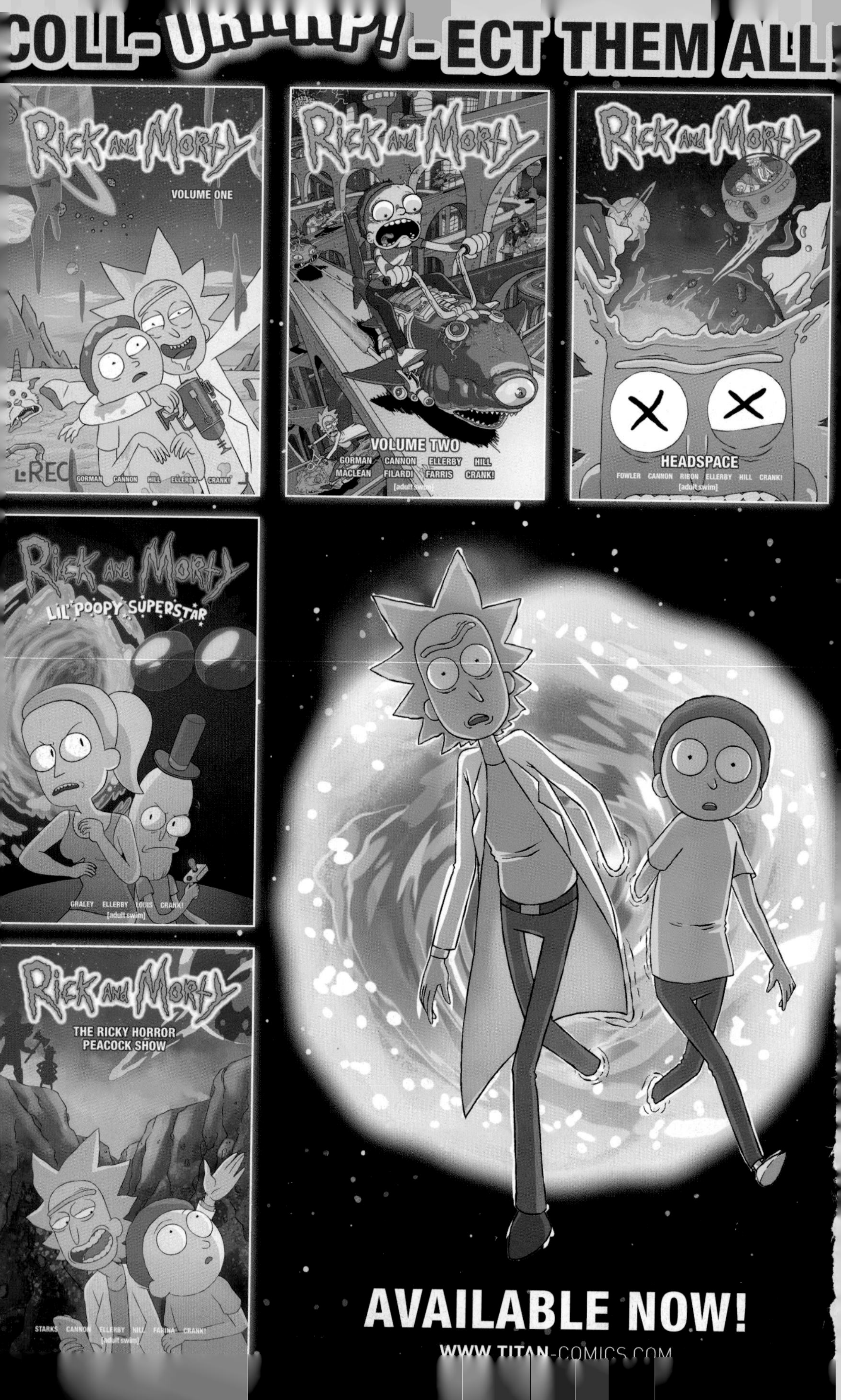

COLL-
-ECT THEM ALL!
Rick and Morty
VOLUME ONE
GORMAN CANNON HILL ELLERBY CRANK!
Rick and Morty
VOLUME TWO
GORMAN CANNON ELLERBY HILL
MACLEAN FILARDI FARRIS CRANK!
[adult swim]
Rick and Morty
HEADSPACE
FOWLER CANNON RIBON ELLERBY HILL CRANK!
[adult swim]
Rick and Morty
LIL' POOPY SUPERSTAR
GRALEY ELLERBY LOUIS CRANK!
[adult swim]
Rick and Morty
THE RICKY HORROR PEACOCK SHOW
STARKS CANNON ELLERBY HILL FARINA CRANK!
[adult swim]
AVAILABLE NOW!
WWW.TITAN-COMICS.COM